W9-BUA-893

Contents

WORD ANNOYANCES™

How to Fix the Most ANNOYING Things About Your Favorite Word Processor

Guy Hart-Davis

O'REILLY®

Beijing · Cambridge · Farnham · Köln · Paris · Sebastopol · Taipei · Tokyo

Word Annoyances™
How to Fix the Most Annoying Things About Your Favorite Word Processor

by Guy Hart-Davis

Illustrations © 2004 and 2005 Hal Mayforth c/o theispot.com.

Published by O'Reilly Media, Inc., 1005 Gravenstein Highway North,
Sebastopol, CA 95472.

O'Reilly books may be purchased for educational, business, or sales promotional use.
Online editions are also available for most titles (*safari.oreilly.com*). For more information, contact our corporate/institutional sales department: 800-998-9938
or *corporate@oreilly.com*.

Print History:		**Editor:**	Brett Johnson
June 2005:	First Edition.	**Production Editor:**	Sanders Kleinfeld
		Art Director:	Michele Wetherbee
		Cover Design:	Ellie Volckhausen
		Interior Designer:	Patti Capaldi

RepKover™ This book uses RepKover™, a durable and flexible lay-flat binding.

0-596-00954-2
[C]

Introduction

Word is arguably the best word processor on the planet, and it's certainly the most widely used. That gives it the chance to be the most annoying word processor on the planet—and Word grabs that chance with both hands.

In a straw poll of typical Word users, you'll usually find that its AutoCorrect and AutoFormat As You Type features annoy 10 out of 10 people. (The AutoFormat As You Type feature is the one that decides unilaterally that you're creating a numbered list when you aren't, or automatically slips in a hyperlink precisely where you don't need one—ah, it annoys you too!) AutoText also scores highly, but not as highly as the squiggly red and green underlines with which Word endeavors to disrupt your concentration.

Unheralded crashes provoke universal fury, and even relatively harmless toolbars come in for savage abuse. But worst of all is the realization that dawns on most Word users: Word is trying to help you, and its help is making things worse. Life would be so much less annoying if only you could tell Word how to do things your way…

Now you can.

Do You Need This Book?

Does Word annoy you? Then buy this book. It's all about making Word less annoying. I've been using Word for 16 years now and have run into most of its annoyances. Other people have been good enough to share their Word annoyances with me, too. The result is hundreds of concentrated annoyances with solutions that will calm your colleagues, impress your friends, and confound your enemies.

This book focuses on Word for Windows, because that's what most of you are using. Many of the annoyances carry through to the Mac as well, although you'll need to make minor adjustments to the solutions, such as looking for options in the Preferences dialog box rather than in the Options dialog box. Chapter 10 discusses Mac-specific annoyances that don't plague Windows users.

What's Covered in This Book?

Here's a taste of what the 10 chapters in this book have to offer you:

Chapter 1, *Installation, Repair, and Configuration*

Prevent Word from demanding the installation CD, or install multiple versions of Word on the same PC. Deal with crashes and slow running. Sort out your toolbars and menus, and create a Work menu for frequently used documents. Dispose of the Office Assistant, either temporarily or forever.

Chapter 2, *Creating and Saving Documents*

Exploit the power of templates to minimize the annoyances of creating and saving documents at home or at work. Use Microsoft Office Application Recovery to mitigate a crash, and get the AutoRecover feature under control. Learn why master documents tend to corrupt—and how to recover as much as possible when your master document does corrupt.

Chapter 3, *Text Entry and Editing*

Deal with common annoyances in Word's views; Outline view is usually the prime offender, but the other views get in on the act. Bring "Smart Cut and Paste" under control, turn off "Click and Type," and assert your dominance over AutoCorrect and AutoText. Escape unwanted copyright symbols, harness the power of Find and Replace to change your documents automatically, hack out columns of tabs or spaces, and keep the same text updated in different parts of the same document.

Chapter 4, *Formatting and Layout*

Get the mysterious "Normal template" under control and change its settings. Tame direct formatting and get a grip on styles. Hammer out annoyances with list numbering, graphics, hyperlinks, and tabs. Create different headers on different pages, and divide a printed page into multiple separate pages.

Chapter 5, *Forms, Revising, Proofing, and Finalizing*

Prevent users from accessing certain parts of a document—and force them to fill in the rest with suitable data. Deflate comment balloons, turn off revision marks for formatting, and view the revision marks for only some reviewers. Check spelling, share custom dictionaries with your colleagues, create an exclusion dictionary of words you mustn't use, and upgrade the Thesaurus.

Chapter 6, *Printing, Faxing, and Scanning*

Does Word prompt you to save a document you've printed but haven't changed? Or does Word 2003 simply crash when you try to print? Learn to deal with printing annoyances, add faxing capabilities to Word, and scan hardcopy text and graphics into your documents.

Chapter 7, *Tables, Columns, and Text Boxes*

Should you draw tables or simply insert them? Learn how to make a table appear at the start of a page—and how to get a table away from the start of a document when it's stuck there. Force Word 2003 to let you use the Cell Height and Width dialog box, and fix header rows so that they won't walk from one page to another. Mix different numbers of columns in the same document, and create a series of linked text boxes throughout a document.

Chapter 8, *Automate Away Annoyances with Macros*

The annoyances discussed in other chapters have fixes or workarounds in the Word user interface—but for annoyances that don't, macros written in Visual Basic for Applications (VBA) offer a solution. Learn to record macros, edit them, and write them from scratch, with examples of specific VBA-quashable annoyances and generic approaches that you can turn on your own annoyances.

Chapter 9, *OLE, Mail Merge, and Office Applications*

Annoying as Word can be on its own, it can be even worse in combination with the other Office applications. Learn how to minimize annoyances with object linking and embedding (OLE); discover how to use mail merge effectively and how to convince Word you've stopped using mail merge; and see how to outwit key annoyances when using Word in conjunction with Excel, PowerPoint, and Access.

Chapter 10, *Mac Word Annoyances*

Deal with crashes and performance annoyances on the Mac; find out why you should panic when Word incessantly repaginates a document; and learn how to outfox Word's "Unable to save" message, restore page setup to your preferred size, and turn off auto-capitalization in tables.

That was just a taste of the contents. Though broken up into categories to make this look like a book, the annoyances are all over the map. Browse the table of contents, investigate the index, or simply dip into the book at random and see which annoyance you find.

"You Haven't Covered My Pet Annoyance"

We feel your pain! If you'd like to share yours—and any solutions, for that matter—feel free to reach out. Send your emails to *annoyances@oreilly.com*. Also, visit our Annoyances web site, *http://annoyances.oreilly.com*, for more tips and tricks, as well as information on upcoming books.

Conventions Used in This Book

The following typographic conventions are used in this book:

Italic

Used for new terms where they are defined, URLs, filenames, file extensions, directories, pathnames, and program names.

Constant width

Used for commands, statements, properties, keywords, variables, objects, methods, and other code items.

Constant width bold

Indicates commands or other text that you should type literally (rather than substituting text appropriate to your computer's configuration or the particular situation).

Constant width italic

Indicates commands or other text that you should replace with values suitable to your computer's configuration or the particular situation.

Menus and navigation

This book uses arrow symbols to indicate menu instructions. For example, "choose File → Open" means that you should open the File menu and choose the Open item from the menu. But when you need to click a tab, check or uncheck an option box, or click a button in a dialog box, this book tells you that clearly.

Pathnames

Pathnames show the location of a file or application in the Windows or Mac OS X filesystem. Windows folders are separated by a backward slash—for example, *C:\Temp\Documents*. Mac OS X folders are separated by forward slashes—for example, *~/Library/Preferences*. In Mac OS X, a tilde (~) represents your *Home* folder.

O'Reilly Would Like to Hear from You

Please address comments and questions concerning this book to the publisher:

O'Reilly Media, Inc.
1005 Gravenstein Highway North
Sebastopol, CA 95472
(800) 998-9938 (in the United States or Canada)
(707) 829-0515 (international or local)
(707) 829-0104 (fax)

We have a web page for this book, where we list errata, examples, and any additional information. You can access this page via:

http://annoyances.oreilly.com

To comment on or ask technical questions about this book, send email to:

bookquestions@oreilly.com

For more information about our books, conferences, Resource Centers, and the O'Reilly Network, see our web site at:

http://www.oreilly.com

About the Author

Guy Hart-Davis has been using Microsoft Word for more than 15 years, during which time he has seen its capabilities increase steadily and its annoyances increase exponentially. His other books include *Word 2000 Developer's Handbook* (Sybex) and *How to Do Everything with Your iPod and iPod mini* (McGraw-Hill).

Acknowledgments

Many wonderful people helped me during the writing of this book. My thanks go especially to the many Word users who wrote in with specific annoyances, almost all of which are covered in this book. (The exceptions were the ones for which there's no fix or workaround.)

At O'Reilly, my thanks go to Robert Luhn, Brett Johnson, Andrew Savikas, and the rest of the team who worked on the book.

Installation, Repair, and Configuration

Installation should be a snap, whether you're installing Word on its own or as part of Office. You slide in the CD, make a few simple decisions, type in the product key, and let the installation roll. The first time you run one of the applications in Office XP (also known as Office 2002) or Office 2003, you have to activate Office. But after that, you're on your way.

This process gives you a default installation of Office. If you're installing Office from scratch, you get all the Office applications installed with the default configurations. If you're upgrading an existing version of Office, the installation removes any existing versions of the applications and picks up your existing configurations for the new versions of the applications.

But one size seldom fits all—not comfortably, anyway. Word may bug you for the installation CD when you try to access particular features. You may want to run two or more different versions of Word on the same PC, rather than allowing the upgrade to remove your existing version. You may choose not to activate Word (or Office) immediately on your PC. You may find that Word runs wretchedly slowly or that you need to reinstall it. Whether you installed Word from scratch or upgraded it, you'll probably want to configure some of its basic options. This chapter shows you how to deal with all these annoyances—and plenty more.

INSTALLATION

Stop Word from Demanding the Installation CD

The Annoyance: Word keeps demanding the installation CD so that it can install missing components.

The Fix: By the time you find Word doing this, the horse has already bolted, and it's hard to close the stable door. If you're reading this Annoyance while mulling over whether to install all of Word (or Office) or just those parts of it that you immediately need, mull no longer: unless your computer is critically short of hard disk space, install all the components.

If the version of Word (or Office) you're installing gives you the choice, leave the installation cache on the computer rather than deleting it. That way, Word (or Office) will have the necessary files to either repair itself if components get corrupted or install additional features (if there are any you haven't installed).

Install Multiple Versions of Word on the Same PC

The Annoyance: I need to run two or more versions of Word on the same PC so that I can troubleshoot my clients' Word problems. However, Word just wants to overwrite earlier versions of itself.

The Fix: Word and the other Office applications usually overwrite previous installations of Office on the general principle that you couldn't possibly want them not to. If you're upgrading to a new version of Office, this behavior makes sense, as it prevents you from leaving the old version of Office hanging around. But it's not good news if you want to be able to test your files with the new version of Office before you commit to it.

When you run Office 2003 Setup, the Type of Installation screen (see Figure 1-1) offers you the choice between the Recommended Install (an upgrade) and another type of install. Office XP Setup provides similar choices with different

USE VIRTUAL MACHINES FOR DEVELOPMENT OR SUPPORT

If you provide support for Word (or other applications) to clients, or if you develop software, consider using virtual machines for your testing and development. A virtual-machine application lets you run a software-based PC within Windows or another operating system. Any changes you make and any crashes that occur are confined to the virtual machine, rather than affecting your productivity applications.

The most widely used virtual-machine applications for Windows are Microsoft's Virtual PC (*http://www.micro-soft.com/windows/virtualpc/default.mspx*) and VMware's VMware Workstation (*http://www.vmware.com/products/desktop/ws_features.html*). You can download a time-limited evaluation version of each application.

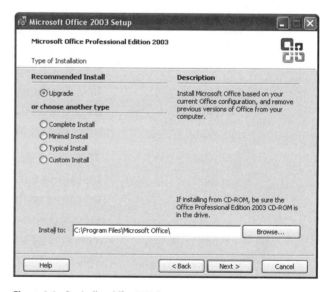

Figure 1-1. Don't allow Office 2003 Setup to press-gang you into upgrading if you actually want to perform a parallel installation.

PROBLEMS RUNNING TWO OR MORE VERSIONS OF WORD ON THE SAME PC

Once you've installed two or three versions of Word on the same PC, you'll soon see why Microsoft doesn't recommend that you do so.

Only one version of Word can be associated with any given file type at a time. If no other version of Word is running, either the associated version or the last version you ran will open when you double-click a document of that file type. If another version of Word is running, the document opens in the running version rather than in the associated version. Usually, the last version you installed grabs the association. To change the association manually, open a Windows Explorer window (e.g., by choosing Start → My Computer), choose Tools → Folder Options, and work on the File Types tab.

Each time you start a version of Word other than the last version you ran, you'll see the Windows Installer dialog box configuring Word. Let the Windows Installer proceed—it's generally harmless and will usually finish in a few seconds. However, sometimes you may run into problems, such as a font registration error (see Figure 1-2). Click the Retry button to retry the registration. If that fails, click the Ignore button. If Word won't run correctly after the Installer finishes, choose Start → Control Panel → Add or Remove Programs, click the appropriate version of Office, click the Change button, and follow the procedure for repairing Office. If you didn't keep the installation cache on your computer, you may need to supply the Office CD.

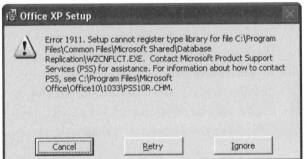 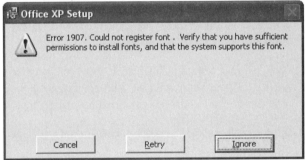

Figure 1-2. Running multiple versions of Word on the same installation of Windows may result in errors.

wording and arrangement. The screens list different applications for the different editions of Office—Professional, Professional Enterprise, Small Business, or Standard—but the principles are the same.

Choose the appropriate type of install—for example, a Complete Install. On the Previous Version of Office screen or the Remove Previous Versions of Office Applications screen, select the "Remove only the following applications" option and uncheck the boxes for applications you want to keep. Outlook 2003 refuses to share a PC with earlier versions of Outlook, so you'll need to sacrifice Outlook 2000 or Outlook XP.

Keep Shortcuts for Both Word 2000 and Word XP on the Same Computer

The Annoyance: I've installed Word 2000 and Word XP on the same computer, but there's only one set of shortcuts on the Start menu.

The Fix: When you install Office XP on a computer that already has Office 2000 installed, Office XP tends to grab the Office 2000 shortcuts on the Start menu. You need to re-create the shortcuts for the Office 2000 applications you choose to keep. Here's the easiest way to re-create them:

> Office 2003 puts its Start menu short-cuts in a *Microsoft Office* folder rather than directly on the All Programs menu, so it doesn't overwrite the Office XP or Office 2000 shortcuts.

1. Choose Start → Run, type `%programfiles%` in the Run box, and press Enter or click the OK button. (`%programfiles%` is an environment variable that contains the path to your *Program Files* folder.)

2. If the Program Files window shows a blue background with the message "These Files Are Hidden," click the "Show the contents of this folder" link.

3. Open the folder containing Office. Usually, this is called *Microsoft Office*, but it will have a different name if you or whoever installed Office customized the installation.

4. Open the folder containing Office 2000. The default name for this folder is *Office*.

5. Right-click each Office 2000 application (for example, *WINWORD.EXE*) and choose Send to → Desktop (Create Shortcut) to create a shortcut on the Desktop.

6. Close the window, rename the new shortcuts as needed (for example, from "Shortcut to WINWORD.EXE" to "Word 2000"), and then drag the shortcuts to where you want them—for example, to the Start menu.

Install Word on Both OSes in a Dual-Boot Configuration

The Annoyance: My PC dual-boots Windows XP and Windows 2000 Professional. I want to use the same copy of Word from each OS, rather than installing it twice.

The Fix: You can do this, but there are a few restrictions. First, each OS should be installed on a separate partition. If the OSes share a partition, you may find that Windows exhibits what Microsoft terms "irregular" behavior. Second, the partitions must normally use the same format—either NTFS (which is best) or FAT32. If one partition is NTFS and the other is FAT32, you'll probably need to install Office separately on each partition.

WHAT'S A PARTITION?

A *partition* is a logical division of a physical drive. You typically decide the partition structure of a drive when installing an operating system, but if you're running Windows XP or Windows 2000, you can also create new partitions (or delete existing partitions) by using the Disk Management tool. (To run Disk Management, choose Start → Run, type `diskmgmt.msc`, and press Enter.)

Disk Management can't resize existing partitions without deleting them first. To resize an existing partition, use either a third-party tool, such as Symantec's Partition-Magic (*http://www.symantec.com*) or V Communications' Partition Commander (*http://www.v-com.com*), or an alternative solution such as the Knoppix distribution of Linux, which comes on a bootable CD. (See Kyle Rankin's *Knoppix Hacks*, also published by O'Reilly, for details on partitioning with Knoppix.)

Install All Necessary Graphics Filters

The Annoyance: JPEG must be the most widely used picture format on the planet, given that almost every digital camera produces JPEGs of one sort or other. But Word won't let me put a single JPEG in my documents. It doesn't even seem to like GIFs. Every other word processor I've used can handle GIFs and JPEGs! Did I just get out of the wrong side of the bed this morning?

The Fix: It sounds like the graphics filters you need aren't installed or are corrupted. Choose Start → Control Panel → Add or Remove Programs, click the Office item, and click the Change button. In the Office Setup Wizard, choose the Add or Remove Features option. In Office 2003, check the "Choose advanced customization of applications" box. Expand the Office Shared Features category and the Converters and Filters category underneath it. Click the Graphics Filters item and choose "Run all from My Computer" from the drop-down menu. (Alternatively, expand the Graphics Filters category and choose the individual graphics filters you need.)

Make the Most of the Word Product-Activation Grace Period

The Annoyance: Every time I start Word, up pops the Activation Wizard, bugging me to activate Office. I don't want to activate it until I know whether I'm going to upgrade my computer or get a new one.

The Fix: There's no fix for this one. If you want to use Word (or Office) beyond the trial period on a PC, you must activate it. Activation is intended to cut down on piracy by preventing you from installing Office on more than one computer at a time. (You can move Word from one PC to another and then reactivate it, which is useful when you get a new PC.)

You may disagree with the principle of having to activate software you've bought, but Office 2003's and Office XP's activation grace period is pretty generous; it lets you launch the Office programs up to 50 times altogether before forcing you to activate them. If you scrupulously avoid closing the programs, you can stretch those 50 uses to several months. Every now and then, one of the programs will crash or hang; that'll cost you a restart, as will the times when you have to restart Windows XP or Windows 2000.

Here are two more things you might want to know about activation:

- You can't reset the pre-activation counter by reinstalling Office on the same computer. But if you use a different PC, or a different virtual machine, it works.

- If product activation fails with a connection error, check that HTTP port 80 and HTTPS port 443 are open on your firewall. The easiest way to check is to open a browser and try to access *http://www.microsoft.com:80* and *https://www.microsoft.com:443*, one after the other. If either connection fails, your firewall is blocking that port and needs to be configured to allow traffic to pass. If you don't administer your firewall, consult the administrator.

> If you set up your PC to dual-boot different versions of Windows, you can install the same copy of Office on each version of Windows without product-activation problems occurring.

Install Word for Only One User

The Annoyance: I'm the only user of my computer who needs to use Word, but the Office installation routine has set up each of the applications for all the users of the computer. How can I prevent the other users from using Word?

The Fix: What you're asking for here is the kind of thing that administrators of Windows-based networks can do easily by using group policies. But I'm guessing that you're asking about a standalone installation, in which case there's no option to install Word (or, more generally, Office) for only one or some of the machine's users. Instead, the installation routine automatically makes Word (or Office) available to all users.

The best fix for this problem is to get another computer for the other users. The next best fix is to set up your computer as a dual-boot machine: one operating system with Office (or Word) for you, the other operating system without it.

If neither of these simple fixes appeals to you, follow this involved series of steps to approximate the effect you want. You'll need a copy of Tweak UI (*http://www.microsoft.com/ windowsxp/downloads/powertoys/xppowertoys.mspx*), as well as access to the other user accounts on your PC:

1. If you haven't already applied a password to your user account and made it private, do so. Choose Start → Run, type `control userpasswords`, and press Enter to open the User Accounts window. Click your account, click Create a Password, type the password twice, and click the Create Password button. When Windows XP asks if you want to make your files and folders private, click the Yes, Make Private button.

2. Install Word (or Office) in a private folder within your user profile, rather than in the *Program Files* folder (the default and recommended location). That way, other users won't be able to access it directly through Windows Explorer. Even when you do this, however, the installation routine creates Start menu shortcuts and other associations that let the other users of your computer start the Office applications. You'll have to deal with these as well.

3. Still in your user account, open a Windows Explorer window to the *Documents and Settings\All Users\Start Menu\ Programs* folder—the folder that contains items that appear on each user's Start menu. Choose Start → Run, type `%userprofile%\Start Menu\Programs`, and press Enter to open another Windows Explorer window to your own *Programs* folder. Drag the *Microsoft Office* folder from the all-users' *Programs* folder to your *Programs* folder. Go up one level in each window to the *Start Menu* folder, and drag the New Office Document shortcut and the Open Office Document shortcut from the all-users' folder to your folder. This removes the Office-related items from the Start menu.

4. Log on to the first of the other user accounts and do the following:

    a. Run Tweak UI and use the Templates feature (see Figure 1-3) to delete all the Office-related items from the New submenu on the context menu for a Windows Explorer window (or the Desktop).

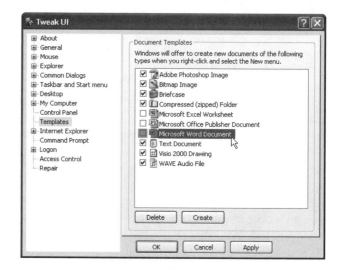

Figure 1-3. Use Tweak UI to remove Office items from the New submenu of the Windows Explorer shortcut menu to prevent other users from running Word.

    b. Choose Start → My Computer to open a Windows Explorer window; then choose Tools → Folder Options and click the File Types tab. Click the File Types column heading to sort the Registered File Types list alphabetically. Scroll down to the items starting with "Microsoft Office" (for Office 2003) or "Microsoft" (for Office XP or Office 2000). Delete all the Office-related items that you can dispense with, and change those you must keep so that they are associated with other applications. For example, you might associate the *.doc* extension with WordPad or another word processor. Scan down the list for Office icons in the Extensions column—for example, "Outlook" items are listed separately, and the Rich Text Format file type is usually associated with Word—and delete or change them as necessary.

5. Repeat Step 4 for each of the other user accounts that you want to restrict.

> **Warning**
> If a user starts one of the Office applications, the Windows Installer installs that application and its helper applications in the *Program Files* folder and creates a Start menu item for that application if there isn't one already.

RECOVERY AND BACKUP

Move Word to Another Computer

The Annoyance: So I activated Word—and now I need to move it to another computer.

The Fix: As you'd guess, if your installation of Word is part of Office rather than a standalone installation, you must move all the Office applications to the other computer. Provided you do that, and remove Office from the original computer, transferring the program files is easy enough: a standard installation on the new computer and a standard removal from the original computer.

> If you're using Windows XP and need to transfer all your files and settings from one computer to another (rather than transferring just your Word or Office settings), you can use the Files and Settings Transfer Wizard instead of the Save My Settings Wizard. Choose Start → All Programs → Accessories → System Tools → Files and Settings Transfer Wizard, and then follow the prompts.

Transferring your Word settings and files takes more work. This is usually the best way to proceed:

1. First, close all the Office applications on the first computer and use the Save My Settings Wizard to save your Word settings to a file. You'll find the Save My Settings Wizard on the All Programs → Microsoft Office 2003 → Microsoft Office Tools menu for Office 2003 and on the All Programs → Microsoft Office Tools menu for Office XP. Save the settings on a network drive that both computers can access, on a removable drive (such as a USB memory key or an iPod), or to your hard disk. Then burn the settings to CD or DVD.

> Microsoft used to provide a Save My Settings Wizard for Office 2000 that you could download from the Microsoft web site. At the time of this writing, the download is no longer available.

2. Next, copy the Word-related files from your original computer to your transfer location:

   - Copy the templates from your workgroup templates folder. If you're not sure where this folder is, open Word, choose Tools → Options, click the File Locations tab, and check the readout. If you can't see the full path for the item, double-click it and then examine the "Look in" drop-down box in the Modify Location dialog box.

   - Copy the *.ACL* file containing your unformatted Auto-Correct entries. Choose Start → Run, type `%userprofile%\Application Data\Microsoft\Office`, and press Enter. Copy the *MSOnnnn.ACL* file whose number (represented by *nnnn*) matches the code for the language you're using. For U.S. English, the code is 1033, so the corresponding configuration file is named *MSO1033.ACL*. Leave the Windows Explorer window open for the moment.

> If you're not sure which AutoCorrect file you're using, add an AutoCorrect entry in Word and then check the files to see which was modified at the appropriate date and time.

- In the Windows Explorer window, go up one level to the *%userprofile%\Application Data\Microsoft* folder, and then double-click the *Proof* folder. Copy your custom dictionaries to your transfer location. If you've saved other custom dictionaries in different folders, copy them too. (If you're not sure where they are, open Word, choose Tools → Options, click the Spelling & Grammar tab, click the Custom Dictionaries button, select each dictionary file in the Custom Dictionaries dialog box, and check the "Full path" readout.)

> These instructions concentrate on Word. In practice, if you're transferring all the Office applications, you will probably want to transfer key files from the other applications as well.

3. Next, install Office on the destination computer. Run the Save My Settings Wizard on the destination computer to apply the saved settings.

4. Move the templates, AutoCorrect file, and dictionary files from the transfer location to the corresponding locations on the destination computer. Word will discover the templates, AutoCorrect file, and *Custom.dic* when you run it, but you will need to add the other dictionaries manually. To add a dictionary, choose Tools → Options, click the Spelling & Grammar tab, click the Custom Dictionaries button, and then click the Add button.

5. On the original computer, choose Start → Control Panel → Add or Remove Programs, click the Office entry, and click the Remove button.

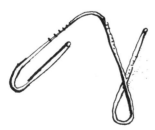

Reinstall Word

The Annoyance: Word has gotten so flaky it's barely worth using. Sometimes it starts okay but then hangs; sometimes it gives me errors about there being no space on my hard disk or being unable to save a file; and sometimes it produces registration errors on startup. I've tried using Help → Detect and Repair, but it hasn't fixed the problem.

The Fix: What you need to do is back up all critical Word files and then reinstall Word from the Office CD or from the installation cache on your hard disk.

See the bulleted list in the previous Annoyance ("Move Word to Another Computer") for details on the items that you should back up. To reinstall Word, choose Start → Control Panel → Add or Remove Programs, click the Office item, and click the Change button. In the Office Setup Wizard, follow the procedure for reinstalling Office. In Office 2003, choose the Reinstall or Repair option; in Office XP or Office 2000, choose the Repair Office option. You may need to provide your Office CD.

STARTUP AND SHUTDOWN

Word 2000 Closes on Startup

The Annoyance: When I try to start Word 2000, it just closes, without even an error message. Excel and PowerPoint do the same.

The Fix: This usually happens only with an Office 2000 installation that has either Service Release 1 (SR-1) or Service Release 1a (SR-1a) installed. The problem is that the installation CD key is faulty. You can tell because the CD key will start with the characters GC6J3. You need to get a valid CD key from your Office reseller or from Microsoft, and then delete the relevant key from the Windows Registry (see *http://support.microsoft.com/?kbid=255503* for details). After doing so, start Word and enter the valid CD key when prompted for it.

Word Hangs on Startup

The Annoyance: When I try to start Word, it hangs.

The Fix: *Normal.dot*, the global template, may be corrupted. Proceed as follows:

1. If Word is still running, close it. Right-click an open space in the taskbar or the notification area (the area with the clock at the right or bottom end of the taskbar) and choose Task Manager. Click the Applications tab, click the Word entry (its entry in the Status column should say "Not Responding," as shown in Figure 1-4), and then click the End Task button. In the End Program dialog box, click the End Now button.

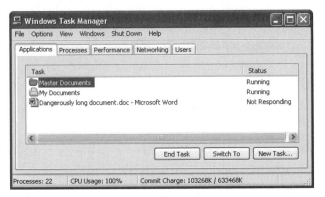

Figure 1-4. Use the Windows Task Manager to check whether an application has stopped responding. If it has, select it and click the End Task button to close it.

2. Choose Start → Run, type `winword /a`, and press Enter. Using the /a switch starts Word without loading any add-ins and without loading *Normal.dot*. If Word hangs again, use the Task Manager to close it. Then choose Start → Control Panel → Add or Remove Programs, click the Microsoft Office item, click the Change button, and follow the procedure for repairing Office. Skip the rest of this list.

   If Word starts, the problem is most likely with *Normal.dot* or any add-ins (templates or other files that add features to Word) set to load automatically when you start Word. Proceed to Step 3.

3. Choose Tools → Options, click the File Locations tab, and check the "User templates" readout. Open this folder in Windows Explorer. Rename the *Normal.dot* file with another name. Choose Tools → Templates and Add-Ins, uncheck the boxes for all the items in the "Global templates and add-ins" list, and then click the OK button. This prevents Word from loading the global templates and add-ins on a normal startup.

4. Close Word (choose File → Exit), restart it normally (for example, from the Start menu), and then close it again. Word automatically creates a new *Normal.dot* in the default folder.

5. Open Word again, choose Tools → Templates and Add-Ins, and click the Organizer button. In the Organizer dialog box, click the Close File button on the side that says Document1 (Document), click the resulting Open File button, select the renamed *Normal.dot*, and click Open.

6. If Word is able to access the renamed *Normal.dot* without hanging, use the controls on the four tabs of the Organizer dialog box to copy the styles, AutoText entries, custom toolbars, and macro project items (macros, user forms, and classes) to the new *Normal.dot*.

7. Click the Close button to close the Organizer dialog box, and then Shift-click the File menu and choose Save All to save the changes to the new *Normal.dot*.

8. If Word was using global templates or add-ins, choose Tools → Templates and Add-Ins, check the box for the first template or add-in, click the OK button, and then restart Word. See if the instability returns. If so, stop using that template or add-in. If not, load another add-in and restart Word again. Continue until you have added all of the add-ins one by one and identified (and removed) any that cause problems.

Word Takes Forever to Start

The Annoyance: Word takes many seconds, or even a couple of minutes, to start—even on my 4 GHz Pentium.

The Fix: First, does your computer have enough memory? (See "Check That Your Computer Has Enough Memory," later in this chapter.) If not, that may be your problem; if so, continue with this fix.

If Word is running at the moment, make sure you're not loading an absurd number of global templates and add-ins. Choose Tools → Templates and Add-Ins to display the Templates and Add-ins dialog box (see Figure 1-5). In the "Global templates and add-ins" area, uncheck the boxes for any global templates or add-ins you want to unload. Alternatively, select a global template or add-in and click the Remove button to remove it from the list. Make sure you click each template or add-in in turn and look at the "Full path" readout at the bottom of the Templates tab. If the template or add-in is in your Word *Startup* folder, you must remove it manually so that Word doesn't load it automatically when you restart the program. Choose Start → Run, type `%userprofile%\ Application Data\Microsoft\Word\Startup`, and press Enter to open a Windows Explorer window to your Word *Startup* folder. Move each template or add-in that you don't want Word to load automatically to another folder.

Word's Two Types of Add-Ins

Word uses two main types of add-ins: *global templates*, which are templates either stored in the Word *Startup* folder (which makes Word load them automatically) or manually loaded using the Templates and Add-ins dialog box, and *COM add-ins*, which are either dynamic link library files (DLLs) or ActiveX executable (EXE) files.

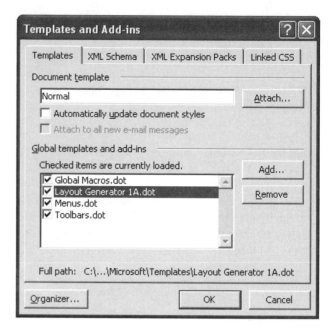

Figure 1-5. Loading too many global templates and add-ins can make Word take much longer to start.

Next, check which COM add-ins are installed (if any). You'll need to add the COM Add-Ins command to a menu first:

1. Choose Tools → Customize to open the Customize dialog box, then click the Commands tab.

2. Click Tools in the Categories listbox.

3. Click the COM Add-Ins command in the righthand listbox and drag it to the menu in which you want it to appear (e.g., Tools).

(The next time you exit Word, save your Normal template if Word prompts you to do so.)

Now select the COM Add-Ins command from the menu in which you placed it. Use the control in the COM Add-Ins dialog box (see Figure 1-6) to unload any add-ins that you don't want to load or to remove any that you no longer need at all.

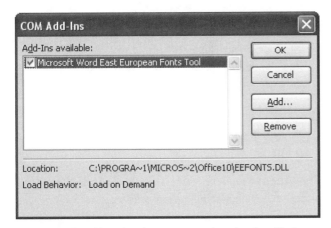

Figure 1-6. COM add-ins also take up memory and can slow down Word. Unload or remove any add-ins that you don't need.

If your global templates and add-ins aren't the culprit, your *Normal.dot* file might be corrupt. Try launching Word without *Normal.dot* or other add-ins: select Start → Run, type `winword /a`, and press Enter.

If Word *still* starts slowly, you may need to re-register it. Choose Start → Run again, type `winword /r`, press Enter, and wait while the Windows Installer configures Office. When it finishes, start Word normally.

Word 2003 Runs Slowly

The Annoyance: I've upgraded from Word 2000 to Word 2003, but Word 2003 runs so slowly that I wish I hadn't bothered.

The Fix: Word 2003 is much more demanding than Word 2000 and typically runs more slowly. Choose Tools → Options and try the following suggestions for improving performance:

- On the Spelling & Grammar tab, uncheck the "Check grammar as you type" box. If you can do without on-the-fly spellchecking, uncheck the "Check spelling as you type" box as well.

- On the View tab, uncheck whichever of the following you can dispense with: the Highlight box, the ScreenTips box, the Smart Tags box, and the Animated Text box. You may want to leave the ScreenTips box checked if you use revision marks in your documents.

- On the General tab, uncheck the "Provide feedback with animation" box.

- On the Save tab, uncheck the "Embed smart tags" box. If you save your documents diligently, uncheck the "Save AutoRecover info every" box as well.

- On the Edit tab, make sure the "Mark formatting inconsistencies" and "Auto-Keyboard switching" boxes are unchecked. Depending on your editing preferences, also consider switching off the "Use smart cursoring," "Use smart paragraph selection," "When selecting, automatically select entire word," "Keep track of formatting," "Show Paste Options button," "Smart cut and paste," and "Enable click and type" options. If you're not clear what these options do, see Chapter 3.

Word may also be suffering from a surfeit of fonts. If the Font drop-down list or Font dialog box includes fonts you never use, consider removing some. Choose Start → Control Panel → Appearance and Themes → Fonts to open the *Fonts* folder, select the fonts you don't need, and drag them to another folder for temporary storage. (You can delete the surplus fonts if you prefer, but it's usually better to keep them in case you need them later.)

> **Warning**
> Don't remove any of the following fonts that Windows requires for its interface: Arial, Microsoft Sans Serif, Tahoma, Marlett, Times New Roman, Courier New, Symbol, and Wingdings. Windows protects Marlett and doesn't display it in the *Fonts* folder.

Check That Your Computer Has Enough Memory

The Annoyance: I've had four computers on which Word crashes for lack of memory, but Microsoft doesn't publish the memory requirements for Word.

The Fix: Microsoft gives general memory requirements for Office (and for the individual applications if you buy them separately). For example, Office 2003 says "128 MB of RAM or above recommended," and Office XP gives a requirement for each supported OS (128 MB for Windows XP, 64 MB for Windows 2000 Professional, 32 MB for Windows Me or Windows NT, or 24 MB for Windows 98), plus 8 MB for each application running simultaneously.

These miserly recommendations will give wretched performance, because they're barely enough for the operating system itself to work well—and Word needs plenty of RAM on top of that. A typical Word 2003 session with a couple of documents open often takes 50 MB of RAM and 25 MB of virtual memory. Word XP is a bit less greedy for RAM than Word 2003, and Word 2000 much less so. But if you want Word to run without problems, make sure your PC has more than enough RAM. If you're running Windows XP or Windows 2000, consider 256 MB the bare minimum for using Word.

To check on memory:

- If you're not sure how much memory your computer has, right-click My Computer and choose Properties (or press Windows Key+Break) to display the System Properties dialog box. Check the Computer readout on the General tab.

- To check how much memory is in use, right-click a blank space in the taskbar or notification area and choose Task Manager; then click the Performance tab and look at the Total readout and the Available readout in the Physical Memory area. These numbers are in kilobytes; divide by 1,024 to get the number of megabytes.

- To check how much memory Word is using, click the Processes tab, find *WINWORD.EXE* in the Image Name column, and look at the Mem Usage column. That's the

amount of RAM. To see the amount of virtual memory, choose View → Select Columns, check the Virtual Memory Size box, and click the OK button. You may need to resize the Windows Task Manager window to display the VM Size column.

Make Word Start Automatically When You Log On

The Annoyance: I need to use Word all the time in my work. It'd be handy to have Word start automatically when I log on.

The Fix: Click the Start menu and navigate to a Word icon, then drag it to the All Programs → Startup submenu. Next time you log on, Word will start.

> If your PC doesn't have a Startup submenu on the Start menu, choose Start → Run, type `%userprofile%\start menu\programs\startup`, and press Enter to open a Windows Explorer window to your *Startup* folder. Drag a Word shortcut to this folder.

Prevent Word from Creating a Blank Document at Startup

The Annoyance: When I start Word, the last thing I need is yet another blank document based on the Normal template—I'd rather have one based on my template. Actually, what I really want is for Word to open the document I need to work with.

The Fix: Word offers you a blank document based on the Normal template as a token of its continuing devotion, rather like your cat might lay out the occasional eviscerated rabbit for your early-morning dining delight. (Well, by now you should know better than to walk around barefoot without switching on the light, shouldn't you?)

Instead of continuing to dispose of the useless blank document by clicking the Close button (and wishing you could dispose of the rabbit with similar ease), you can prevent Word from creating the document, make it create a document based on a template of your choice, or have it open a document for you. To do so, use Word's startup switches (startup options) in the shortcut that you use to start Word.

Create a suitable shortcut for a startup switch

Depending on the version of Word and how it was set up, you may not be able to use the Word shortcut that appears on the Start menu—some of these shortcuts don't let you edit the command used to start Word. To check, right-click the Word shortcut and choose Properties, then look at the Shortcut tab. If the Target text box is grayed out, you need to create a new shortcut.

To do so, locate *WINWORD.EXE* (usually in a folder named some variation of "*Office*" in the *Program Files* folder, which you can access by choosing Start → Run, typing %programfiles%, and pressing Enter) and create a shortcut to it wherever you find most convenient. For example, right-click *WINWORD.EXE* within its parent folder and choose "Create shortcuts here," rename the shortcut from "*Shortcut to WINWORD.EXE*" to a snappier name, and then drag the shortcut to your Start menu, if that's where you want it.

Right-click the new shortcut, choose Properties, and then click the Shortcut tab. The next sections discuss the switches you can use. Enter the switches on the Target line of the Shortcut tab after the final double quotation marks. For example:

```
"D:\Program Files\Office 2003\OFFICE11\
WINWORD.EXE" /n
```

Prevent Word from creating a blank document

If all you want to do is to prevent Word from creating a blank document at startup, add the /n switch to the shortcut that starts Word (as shown above).

Open a document based on your preferred template

If you want to open a document based on a template other than the Normal template, use the /t switch and specify the template name:

```
"D:\Program Files\Office 2000\OFFICE11\
WINWORD.EXE" /tMagazine.dot
```

If the template name contains spaces, enclose it in double quotation marks. You may need to include the full path.

Open a document on the Most Recently Used list

To make Word always open one or more of the documents on its Most Recently Used list (the list that appears at the foot of the File menu), use the /m switch, the word file, and the file's position. For example, /mfile1 opens the document at the number one position on the list.

Open a specific document

Opening a recent document can be useful, but it'll often stick you with a document you don't need. What's usually more useful is to open one or more specific documents when you start Word. To do so, enter the full path and filename of each file after the program file, with a space between each name, and all in the same line:

```
"D:\Program Files\Office 2000\OFFICE11\
WINWORD.EXE" "c:\Docs\Book1.doc"
```

Control When the Task Pane Appears

The Annoyance: The Getting Started task pane that appears when I start Word gets me started all right—the wrong way. How do I get rid of it?

The Fix: Choose Tools → Options, click the View tab, uncheck the Startup Task Pane box in the Show area, and then click the OK button.

If you find that the task pane doesn't obey the Startup Task Pane setting in Word 2003, change the Registry setting that controls it:

1. Close Word and create a system restore point before tackling the Registry: choose Start → All Programs → Accessories → System Tools → System Restore, click the "Create a restore point" option, click the Next button, and follow through the prompts.

2. Choose Start → Run, type regedit, and press Enter to open the Registry Editor.

3. Navigate to this Registry key:

   ```
   HKEY_CURRENT_USER\Software\Microsoft\
   Office\11.0\Common\General
   ```

4. Right-click the *DoNotDismissFileNewTaskPane* key, choose Delete from the shortcut menu, and click the OK button to confirm the deletion. Choose File → Exit to close the Registry Editor.

5. Restart Word.

Word Takes Ages to Close a Document

The Annoyance: The longer I've been working on a document, the longer Word takes to close it. And if I use Save As to save the document under a different name, it takes even longer to close.

The Fix: Sorry, there's no fix for this problem, other than shortening your sessions with any particular document. What's happening is that Word is disposing of the temporary files that it has created while you've been working with the document. (See "Understand and Deal with Temporary Files" in Chapter 2 for an explanation of when and why Word creates these temporary files and what they contain.) Word is also clearing out of its Undo buffer the data for the undoable actions in this document. (It leaves the data for any other documents that are open.)

Word Asks Whether to Save Changes to Normal.dot

The Annoyance: When I close Word, it asks me whether I want to save changes to *Normal.dot*. What is *Normal.dot*, and why is it doing this to me? I haven't done anything to it.

The Fix: You probably *have* done something to *Normal.dot*, but only inadvertently. *Normal.dot*, also called "the Normal template," is the default template on which Word bases documents unless you tell it to use another template. In addition to typical template items such as styles, page margins, and default font and paragraph settings, *Normal.dot* contains your formatted AutoCorrect entries and your AutoText entries. It's also a convenient place to store VBA items such as macros and user forms.

If you've created a formatted AutoCorrect entry or an AutoText entry, or if you've changed your default font, page layout, or paragraph settings, you've changed *Normal.dot*. Similarly, if you've created or installed a VBA item, you may have changed *Normal.dot*. If Word prompts you to save it (see Figure 1-7), click the Yes button.

Figure 1-7. You can prevent Word from prompting you to save Normal.dot.

If you're not aware of having made any such changes, it's possible that your computer has a macro virus that has made a change against your will. If so, you won't want to save changes to *Normal.dot*. Check your computer for viruses immediately.

If you want Word to save any changes to *Normal.dot* automatically without prompting you, choose Tools → Options, click the Save tab, and uncheck the "Prompt to save Normal template" box.

Word Says Normal.dot "Is in Use by Another Application or User"

The Annoyance: When I accept Word's offer to save *Normal.dot*, it says "This file is in use by another application or user." What's this all about? I'm alone here, and Word is the only application I'm running.

The Fix: It's okay: Word is the other application, and you're the other user. This message usually means that you've got two separate instances of Word open (as opposed to having two documents open in separate windows in the same Word session). The instance you started first has a lock on *Normal.dot*, so the second instance (the one you're trying to close) can't save changes to *Normal.dot*.

Click OK in the warning dialog box (see Figure 1-8). Word then displays the Save As dialog box so that you can save *Normal.dot* under a different name (or in a different folder) to preserve the changes you've made to it. You'll then need to merge these changes back into your original *Normal.dot*.

Figure 1-8. If Word claims Normal.dot is in use when you try to save changes, you probably have two instances of Word open.

Typically, this is worth the effort only if you've been creating VBA code in *Normal.dot*. If you've simply created an AutoText entry or performed a small customization, it's usually easier to do it again in your original *Normal.dot*.

If you don't think you have two or more instances of Word open, click on each of your document windows in turn and pull down the Window menu to see what Word windows it lists. Any windows that are in another session of Word will not appear on the Window menu.

> **t i p**
>
> If you really don't have two or more instances of Word open, a crash may have left a locking file for *Normal.dot* that makes Word think another instance is running. Quit Word and restart Windows to clear out the locking file automatically.

MENUS

Display Full Menus

The Annoyance: I just installed Word 2000/XP/2003, and the menus have shrunk in the wash. Why do I have to click the button with the two little arrows to get the rest of the menu?

The Fix: To make Word display the full menu immediately just this once, double-click the menu name. To make Word always display the full menus, use one of the following options.

- In Word 2003 or Word XP, choose ███, click the Options tab, and check the "A███ menus" box.

- In Word 2000, choose Tools → Customize, c███ Options tab, and uncheck the "Menus show recently██ commands first" box.

Prevent Menu Items from Changing Position

The Annoyance: Every time I open a menu, the wretched items have shifted position! How do I turn off St. Vitus's Dance?

The Fix: Choose Tools → Customize, and then click the Options tab. In Word 2003 or Word XP, check the "Always show full menus" box. In Word 2000, uncheck the "Menus show recently used commands first" box.

Microsoft calls this feature "personalized" menus, but most people call it a menace. Word starts you off with its default set of menu items—those that the Microsoft focus groups used the most. As you use menu items, Word keeps score and migrates your most frequently used menu items to the top of each menu so that you can find them more easily.

The other Office applications do this as well, and you quell this behavior in all of them using this technique. Your choice for personalized menus applies in all the Office applications, not just the one in which you're applying the setting, so you can't use full menus in Word but use personalized menus in Excel and PowerPoint (not that you would normally want to).

Cut Menus Down to Size

The Annoyance: Half the commands on the menus are useless to me. I'd like to get rid of them to clear out the clutter.

...ut which commands you
...wn to size. There's a quick
...a menu that you can use
...nder, but if you plan to
...ould use a more formal

...nu command is to press
... Word turns the mouse
...lick the menu containing
...menu opens. Click your

victim, and it'll disappear.

The more formal method of removing a menu command is to use the Customize dialog box:

1. Open a document based on the template you want to change.

2. Choose Tools → Customize and click the Commands tab. Make sure that the "Save in" drop-down list shows the document or template you want to affect. If you want the change to affect all documents, choose *Normal.dot*.

3. Click the menu that contains the command, drag the command into the document area, and drop it.

4. Click the Close button.

5. Shift-click the File menu and choose Save All. If Word prompts you to save changes to *Normal.dot*, click the Yes button.

> **t i p**
>
> You can easily replace any item you remove from a menu or a toolbar. Start by choosing Tools → Customize, clicking the Commands tab, and selecting the document or template in the "Save in" drop-down list. To replace a single item, drag the command to the appropriate menu or toolbar. To reset a menu, right-click it and choose Reset from the shortcut menu. To reset a toolbar, select it on the Toolbars tab and click the Reset button.

Create a Work Menu

The Annoyance: There are a handful of documents that I need to be able to open easily. Sometimes they appear on the Most Recently Used list on the File menu, but I work with many other documents, so they're not always there.

The Fix: Microsoft provides a Work menu (see Figure 1-9) that you can add to the menu bar so that you can keep up to nine documents readily available.

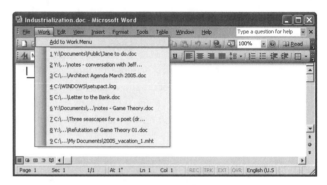

Figure 1-9. Add the Work menu to the menu bar (or to a convenient toolbar) for quick access to the documents you use most often.

To add the Work menu to the menu bar, choose Tools → Customize, click the Commands tab, and make sure that the "Save in" drop-down list shows the document or template you want to affect. (Usually, *Normal.dot* is the best choice.) Select the Built-in Menus item, and drag the Work menu to the menu bar or a toolbar you always keep open. Shift-click the File menu and choose Save All. If Word prompts you to save changes to *Normal.dot*, click the Yes button.

To add the current document to the Work menu, choose Work → Add to Work Menu. To remove a document, press Ctrl+Alt+-, click the Work menu, and then click the document you want to remove.

TOOLBARS

Sort Out the Standard Toolbar and Formatting Toolbar

The Annoyance: The Standard toolbar and Formatting toolbar have decided to share a row and to each hide half their buttons.

The Fix: Choose Tools → Customize, click the Options tab, check the "Show Standard and Formatting toolbars on two rows" box, and click the Close button. In Word 2000, this option is implemented the other way around: the checkbox is called "Standard and Formatting toolbars share one row," and you need to *uncheck* the box.

Put a Close Document Button on the Standard Toolbar

The Annoyance: If you open a document, you'll more than likely want to close it sometime, but there's no Close button on the Standard toolbar.

The Fix: You can put a Close button on the Standard toolbar easily enough, and you can put a Close All button on it as well:

1. Choose Tools → Customize. In the Customize dialog box, click the Commands tab if it's not already displayed.

2. Make sure that *Normal.dot* is selected in the "Save in" drop-down list.

3. With the File item selected in the Categories listbox, scroll down to the Close item in the Commands list. Drag it to the Standard toolbar and drop it there (see Figure 1-10).

4. If you choose, drag the Close All item to the Standard toolbar as well. If you do, you'll find that its icon is identical to that of the Close button, which can be confusing. To change one of the buttons, click it on the Standard toolbar and click the Modify Selection button in the Customize dialog box. Then take one of the following actions:

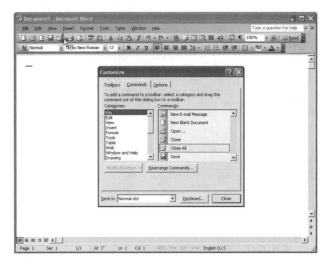

Figure 1-10. Use the Customize dialog box to add a Close button—and, if you like, a Close All button—to the Standard toolbar to make closing your documents easier.

- Click the Text Only (Always) item to display only text for the button instead of the icon.

- Click the Image and Text item to display both the icon and the text. This produces the most intelligible button, but it occupies more space than you may want to give it.

- Click the Edit Button Image item and use the Button Editor (see Figure 1-11) to change the image. You can edit one pixel at a time, or wipe the slate so that you can start from scratch.

- Click the Change Button Image item and choose one of the ready-made buttons on the panel.

5. Click the Close button to close the Customize dialog box.

6. Shift-click the File menu, and then click Save All to save the changes to *Normal.dot*.

> If you don't want to add a Close button to the Standard toolbar (or another toolbar), you can close a document by clicking the close button (the X button) in the upper-right corner of its window.

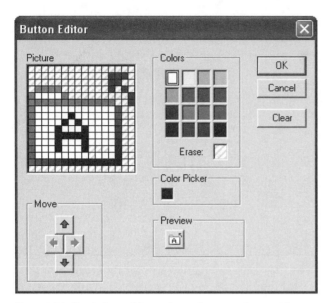

Figure 1-11. Use the Button Editor to change the icon on a button, either subtly or completely.

Consolidate Your Toolbars into a Custom Toolbar

The Annoyance: I use buttons on about 10 different toolbars, and between them they're turning the document window into a document porthole.

The Fix: Word has plenty of toolbars, as you say, and you can save valuable screen space by consolidating the buttons you use onto a single toolbar—either an existing toolbar or (usually better) a custom toolbar. Here's how to create a custom toolbar:

1. Display all the toolbars that you normally use.

2. Choose Tools → Customize and click the Toolbars tab.

3. Click the New button, type a name for the new toolbar, verify that the "Make Toolbar Available to" drop-down list shows the appropriate document or template (again, *Normal.dot* is usually the best bet here), and click the OK button.

4. Click the Close button to close the Customize dialog box.

5. Hold down Ctrl+Alt and drag each desired button from the other toolbars to the new custom toolbar. To rearrange the buttons on the new toolbar, hold down the Alt key and drag a button. To create a separator line between buttons, drag the righthand button a short distance to the right (or drag the lower button down a short distance if the toolbar is vertical rather than horizontal).

Reset Menus or Toolbars That Someone Else Has Customized

The Annoyance: A new temp borrowed my desk last week while I was out of town, and she messed up my menus and toolbars in the name of progress.

The Fix: You can reset the menus and toolbars to their default settings in moments. Choose Tools → Customize and click the Toolbars tab. Click the toolbar or menu you want to reset (to reset all menus on the menu bar, select the Menu Bar item) and click the Reset button. In the Reset Toolbar dialog box, make sure that Word has selected the right template or document, and then click the OK button.

After you close the Customize dialog box, Shift-click the File menu and choose Save All. If Word prompts you to save changes to the Normal template, click the Yes button.

Get Rid of Proprietary Toolbars

The Annoyance: Since I installed Adobe Acrobat, Word always displays an Acrobat toolbar when I start it. I can hide the toolbar, but it always comes back.

The Fix: This toolbar, which is called PDFMaker, is part of the *PDFMaker.dot* template that Acrobat automatically installs on the assumption that you want to be able to create PDF documents (documents in Adobe's Portable Document Format) at any moment from Word. If you do want to create PDFs, the toolbar is handy; otherwise, it's an annoyance.

To remove this template, you must first unload the *PDFMaker. dot* add-in. Choose Tools → Templates and Add-Ins, click the *PDFMaker.dot* add-in, and note its location in the "Full path" readout. If it's in the *Startup* subfolder of your *Office* folder, exit Word, open a Windows Explorer window to that folder, and move *PDFMaker.dot* to a different folder. Otherwise, select *PDFMaker.dot* and click the Remove button. When (*if*) you need to create a PDF, reload the *PDFMaker.dot* add-in. Choose Tools → Templates and Add-Ins, and either check the box for *PDFMaker.dot* or click the Add button, navigate to and select the template, and click OK. Then click the OK button to close the Templates and Add-ins dialog box.

Other applications may install their own menus or toolbars. These are usually part of a global template that you can unload if you so choose.

Choose One or Multiple Word Buttons on the Taskbar

The Annoyance: Having multiple Word windows and multiple Word taskbar buttons bugs me to distraction. Why can't Word behave the same way as Excel and keep all the documents in the same window?

The Fix: There's good news on this front (unless you're using Word 2000): Word 2003 and Word XP let you choose whether to keep each open Word document in its own window (with its own taskbar button) or keep all open Word documents in a single window (with a single taskbar button for the active document). Figure 1-12 shows an example.

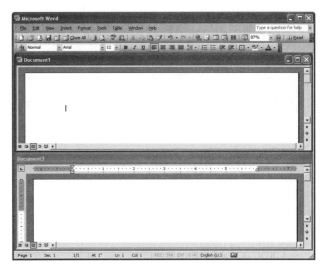

Figure 1-12. Word 2003 and Word XP can display all open documents in a single Word window or each open document in its own window; Word 2000 can manage only multiple windows. Word users can argue for hours about which is better, but you can switch between the two options in seconds.

To make the switch, choose Tools → Options and click the View tab if it's not already displayed. Uncheck the "Windows in Taskbar" box if you want to show all open documents in a single Word window that has one taskbar button. If you check this box (the default setting), you see a separate window for each open document, each of which has its own taskbar button.

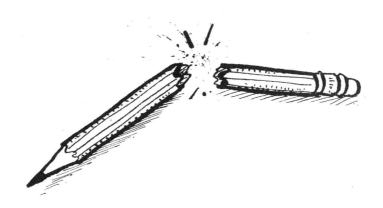

Creating and Saving Documents

You can't get much done in Word without creating and saving documents—and once you've used Word even a little, you'll know it's a good idea to save a document immediately after creating it to ensure that you don't lose work if Word, Windows, or your computer crashes.

Creating a new document is simple in a basic word processor, but Word, being more complex, offers templates that can both help and hinder you. Templates can save you a lot of time, but they can also cause problems—for example, they sometimes become corrupted, and you might even find that your new "blank" document always contains unwanted text that you must dispose of before you can work in your document.

Saving could be simple too—if Word didn't provide a whole tab's worth of save options to confuse the issue. Some of these options are pretty much guaranteed to cause annoyance, while others can help you work faster and recover as much of your work as possible if Word crashes. This chapter helps you distinguish friend from foe and shows you how to rout the foes and harness the friends.

Last but nothing like least, you may make the often-fatal mistake of using Word's master document feature for that huge, all-important project you're working on…. Read on to learn how to minimize master document annoyances, hassles, and grief.

TEMPLATES

Get Rid of Text in the Default Document

The Annoyance: When I start Word, I get a document that already contains text—a letter I wrote last month. I have to select the text and delete it before I can start working on my new document. The same thing happens when I click the New Blank Document button on the Standard toolbar—the document I get isn't blank at all.

The Fix: You've somehow saved your document into *Normal.dot*, the global template that's always open when Word is running. In theory, it's hard to get text into *Normal.dot* unintentionally, but it seems to happen surprisingly often.

Choose Tools → Options, click the File Locations tab, click the "User templates" item in the list, and check the Location readout. If the readout is abbreviated to fit into the space, click the Modify button, click the "Look in" drop-down list, and note the full path to the folder. Then close the dialog boxes.

Choose File → Open, navigate to the templates folder, choose "Document templates" in the "Files of type" drop-down list, and open *Normal.dot*. Delete the offending text, choose File → Save, and then choose File → Close.

Create a Template for Each Document Type You Use Frequently

The Annoyance: My work involves creating many documents in three basic types: letters, reports, and task lists. I seem to spend half my time performing the same actions over and over again.

The Fix: Create a template for each type of document you need to create. Choose File → New and click either "On my computer" (in Word 2003) or "General templates" (in Word XP) in the New Document task pane to display the Templates dialog box. In Word 2000, choose File → New to display the equivalent New dialog box.

Select the existing template on which you want to base the new template; for example, choose Blank Document if you want to start from scratch, or one of the letter templates if you need to create a letter. Select the Template option and click the OK button. Choose File → Save and assign the new template a descriptive name. Save it in the default location—your user templates folder—unless you have a good reason to put it elsewhere.

Lay out and format the document, entering any text that all documents based on this template will need. For example, in the template for a customer service letter, you might enter the entire document except for the customer's address, the details of the complaint, and the response or resolution.

Use styles to apply formatting consistently throughout the document. (Chapter 4 discusses styles.)

Create AutoText and AutoCorrect entries for boilerplate text that doesn't specifically belong in any template. To continue the example of the customer service letter, you might create AutoCorrect entries for phrases or sentences that the customer service representatives will often need to enter without changes. (Chapter 3 covers bending AutoCorrect and AutoText to your will.)

Save the changes to the template, and then close it.

To create a document based on a template, open the Templates or New dialog box as described above. Select the template, and then click the OK button.

> To create a template from an existing document, choose File → Save As, select Document Template in the "Save as type" drop-down list, specify the name, and click the Save button. (Word automatically changes to your user templates folder when you select the Document Template item.) Templates and documents are almost exactly the same, except for the file extension.

Create a Document Based on an Existing Document

The Annoyance: I often need to create new documents based on existing documents, but it's not worth creating templates. Copying the relevant parts from one document to another saves some time, but not that much.

The Fix: In any version of Word, open the document and use File → Save As to save it under a different name or in a different folder. Change the new document as necessary.

Word 2003 and Word XP provide another way to create a document based on an existing document. In Word 2003, choose File → New and click "From existing document" in the New Document task pane; in Word XP, choose File → New and click "Choose document" in the New Document task pane. In the New from Existing Document dialog box, select the document and click the Create New button.

Save a Preview for a Template

The Annoyance: Most of the templates in the Templates dialog box have preview pictures. I want to add previews to my custom templates so that users can get an idea of what they're used for.

The Fix: Open the template (choose File → Open, or right-click the template in a Windows Explorer window and choose Open from the shortcut menu). Choose File → Properties, click the Summary tab, check the "Save preview picture" box, and then click the OK button. Save the template and close it.

Use a Template Outside Your Default Templates Folder

The Annoyance: The Templates dialog box doesn't let you browse for templates that aren't located in the default folder.

The Fix: The problem is that Word doesn't know where your templates are unless they're in one of its two templates folders: the *user templates* folder and the *workgroup templates* folder. Each of these folders can have as many subfolders as necessary.

tip

The Templates dialog box is called the New dialog box in Word 2000, but it works the same way.

You can use Windows shortcuts to tell Word where your templates are:

- To add a template to the General tab of the Templates/New dialog box, put a shortcut to the template in your user templates folder or your workgroup templates folder.

- To add a folder of templates that will appear as a new tab in the Templates/New dialog box, put a shortcut to the folder in your user templates folder or your workgroup templates folder.

Warning

Depending on your security settings, Word may prevent you from running macros and VBA code in templates not stored in one of your templates folders.

By default, the user templates folder is set during installation to a folder within your user profile (for example, *%userprofile%\ Application Data\Microsoft\Templates*). The workgroup templates folder is not set during a conventional installation (although it can be set during a scripted installation)—if you don't have a workgroup templates folder assigned and you can store your templates in one folder (or its subfolders), you can make that folder your workgroup folder. Choose Tools → Options, click the File Locations tab, double-click the "Workgroup templates" item, select the folder in the Modify Location dialog box, and then click the OK button twice. Your templates will then appear in the Templates/New dialog box (see Figure 2-1).

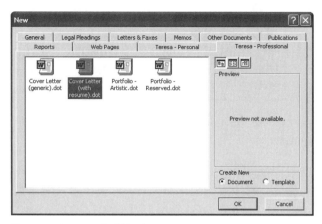

Figure 2-1. Designate the folder that contains your templates as your workgroup templates folder to make the templates appear in the Templates (or New) dialog box.

MANAGING YOUR TEMPLATE FOLDERS

There's a limited amount of space on the two rows of tabs in the Templates/New dialog box, so plan your template folders carefully. Here are a few guidelines:

- To avoid having multiple tabs with the same names, do not duplicate names between the user templates folder and the workgroup templates folder.

- Keep the number of template folders down so that they all fit into the dialog box.

- Keep the folder names short if you need to fit more tabs into the dialog box. If the names won't fit, the Templates/New dialog box includes a tab named More that shows the remaining folders. You can double-click a folder in this tab to access the templates it contains. (This extra step makes accessing your templates a little slower.)

Another option is to create a document directly from a template. Open a Windows Explorer window to the folder that contains the template, and then double-click the template. (The default action in Windows for a Word template is to create a new document based on it, not to open the template. To open the template, right-click it and choose Open.)

SAVING

Save Your Documents the Best Way

The Annoyance: I've deleted everything in this document except one paragraph, and the file is still far too large to send via email.

The Fix: This happens because Word's *fast-saving option* works by appending the latest changes to the end of the file instead of saving the entire file. So when you delete most of the document, Word adds the details of that deletion to the end of the document, but the material remains in the document file. This not only makes the file size even bigger than it was before, but it can be indiscreet or even dangerous when you share documents with other people—your documents may still contain material that you deleted long ago.

Unless you're working with huge files on a slow computer, fast saving won't usually save you enough time to compensate for its disadvantages.

Word performs a normal save, which is called a *full save*, every 15th fast save, or when you've made so many changes to the document that it makes more sense to rewrite the file than to append further changes. However, you shouldn't rely on this full save to ensure that your document contains only the data you think it does.

In a full-saved file, the actual order of characters stored in the file is the same as their order in the document; in a fast-saved file, the order is different. Corruption is more likely to occur in fast-saved files than in full-saved files. Fast saving works only on local drives, not on network drives.

To turn off fast saving, choose Tools → Options, click the Save tab, and uncheck the "Allow fast saves" box. While you're on the Save tab, modify some other save options:

- Check the "Always create backup copy" box to make Word keep a backup copy that consists of the previously saved version of the document. (See the "How Word Creates the Backup Copy" sidebar.)

- Specify whether you want Word to perform background saves by checking or unchecking the "Allow background saves" box. Allowing background saves enables you to resume work more quickly after issuing a Save command, because you can continue working while Word completes the save. However, it usually makes each save take longer. Unless your documents are huge and your computer slow, or your documents are saved on a server to which you have a slow connection, background saves are unlikely to save you much time. Word displays a pulsing disk icon in the status bar to indicate a background save.

Save All Open Documents at Once

The Annoyance: I've got a stack of documents open. Why must I save changes to them one by one? Where's the Save All command when you need it?

The Fix: It's hiding. Shift-click the File menu, and then click Save All. Don't press Alt+Shift+F to display the File menu: that doesn't work, and the key combination might be assigned to a command or a macro.

If you find Shift-clicking the File menu awkward, put the Save All command directly on a menu or toolbar. Choose Tools → Customize, click the Commands tab, and verify that the appropriate template is selected in the "Save in" drop-down list. With the File item selected in the Categories listbox, scroll down the Commands list to the Save All item, and then drag it to the menu or toolbar of your choice. Shift-click the File menu and choose Save All to make sure that the changes to the template get saved.

HOW WORD CREATES THE BACKUP COPY

Checking the "Always create backup copy" box on the Save tab of the Options dialog box ensures that you will always have a backup copy of the document you're working with. This backup is a copy of the next-to-last saved version of the document, so it's not necessarily the same as the current saved version of the file.

You can't make the backup copy exactly the same as the current version by saving the file twice in succession (for example, by pressing Ctrl+S twice), because Word will save the document only when it is "dirty"—that is, when it contains unsaved changes. After the first save, the document is clean until you change it. Still, by saving your documents frequently, you can keep the backup copies very close to the current versions. (See "Double-Save a Document" in Chapter 8 for a macro that works around this.)

When Word saves a document and fast saving is turned off, Word actually saves the current document to a temporary file in the same folder as the active document. When the save is complete, Word either deletes or renames the previously saved version of the file, freeing up the file's "real" name, and then renames the temporary file with the real name.

Word performs this apparently unnecessary shuffle to reduce the possibility of losing changes to the file while the save operation is happening. This loss is unlikely to occur but can be catastrophic if it does—the entire document may be corrupted.

If you check the "Always create backup copy" checkbox, Word renames the previously saved version of the file as the backup copy rather than deleting it. The temporary files can provide a safety net if your document gets badly mangled (see "Recover a Document After a Crash," later in this chapter).

Word's fast-saving feature appends the latest changes to the end of the file instead of writing a whole new file, so it doesn't work with the "Always create backup copy" option.

Close All Open Documents at Once

The Annoyance: Can I close all my open documents at the same time?

The Fix: Yep. Shift-click the File menu, and then click Close All. You'll be prompted to save any unsaved changes, as usual. Alternatively, if you find Shift-clicking awkward, you can choose Tools → Customize and put a Close All button on a toolbar or menu.

You can also close all documents by exiting Word and restarting it. However, what you'll more often want to do is close all the open documents except the one you're working on. To do so, you need a macro; see "Close All Documents Except the Current One" in Chapter 8.

Change Word's Default Folder for Saving Documents

The Annoyance: Word always wants me to save my documents in the *My Documents* folder. I suppose this folder makes sense for many users, but I have other ideas.

The Fix: You can change the default folder easily. Choose Tools → Options, click the File Locations tab (see Figure 2-2), select Documents in the "File types" list, and click the Modify button. In the Modify Location dialog box, select the folder you want to use, and click the OK button.

From the File Locations tab of the Options dialog box, you can also change the default folders for clip-art pictures, user templates, workgroup templates, AutoRecover files, tools, and startup files.

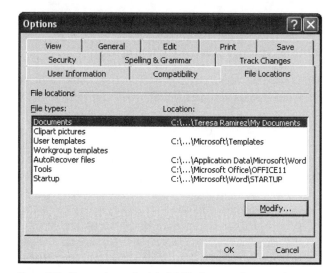

Figure 2-2. You can change the default folder for saving documents by using the File Locations tab of the Options dialog box.

Find a Document You've Lost

The Annoyance: I work on so many documents, I keep losing them.

The Fix: Short of reorganizing your filesystem, your best bet is to search for the lost documents.

Word 2003 and Word XP provide the Search task pane (see Figure 2-3) for either basic or advanced searches. Choose File → File Search in Word 2003 or File → Search in Word XP to display the Search task pane. Click the Advanced File Search link or the Basic File Search link to toggle from one mode to another.

Basic searching casts a wide net, searching for your search terms in filenames, keywords, and contents. It even looks for matches for different forms of the words you've specified in the file contents. For example, if you use "buy" as a search term, Word finds documents containing "bought" in their contents as well. You can narrow the search by including multiple words.

Advanced searching lets you not only specify which property you're searching for but also create complex searches. You can use "And" and "Or" operators to relate the conditions to each other.

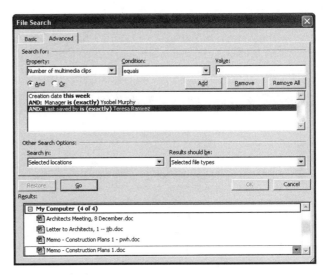

Figure 2-4. The File Search dialog box gives you more space for putting together complex searches and examining their results.

Figure 2-3. The Search task pane toggles between a Basic File Search and an Advanced File Search.

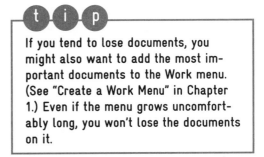

If you tend to lose documents, you might also want to add the most important documents to the Work menu. (See "Create a Work Menu" in Chapter 1.) Even if the menu grows uncomfortably long, you won't lose the documents on it.

For advanced searching, you may find it easier to use the File Search dialog box (in Word 2003 and Word XP) or the Find dialog box (in Word 2000). Choose File → Open, click the Tools button in the Open dialog box, and choose Search (for Word 2003 or Word XP) or Find (for Word 2000) from the drop-down menu. The File Search dialog box (see Figure 2-4) offers Basic and Advanced tabs that provide the same options as the Search task pane but give you more room to see what you're doing. The Find dialog box in Word 2000 provides a similar set of options but doesn't divide them into Basic and Advanced searches. The Find dialog box also lets you save searches you've performed, which is useful if you often need to find documents that match a certain set of criteria.

Keep Separate Versions of the Same Document

The Annoyance: My office has a complex round-robin procedure for creating and reviewing documents: agendas, minutes, reports, you name it. We usually save a new copy of each document after each stage of the review, with a suffix of the last reviewer's initials to distinguish between them. I'm wondering if we can use versions instead.

The Fix: Word's versions feature might help here. It lets you keep two or more versions in the same document, and you can switch back and forth between versions as necessary.

To save your edits as a version, choose File → Versions to display the Versions dialog box (see Figure 2-5) and click the Save Now button. Enter comments about the version in the Save Version dialog box, and click the OK button.

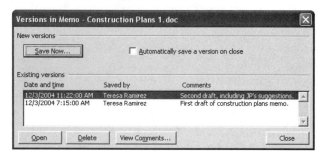

Figure 2-5. Select the "Automatically save a version on close" box if you want Word to create a new version of the document each time you finish working with it.

Once you've created multiple versions of a document, you can open one of the versions by choosing File → Versions, selecting the version you want, and clicking the Open button. You can delete a version from the Versions dialog box by selecting the version and clicking the Delete button.

DISADVANTAGES OF VERSIONS

Versions have several disadvantages:

- **Only one person can work with a versioned document at a time.**

- **A document with versions typically contains text that you can't see in any given version. When distributing a versioned document, you must double-check that it doesn't contain any content that is inappropriate for the recipients. Generally, this means deleting all but the relevant version of the document. Alternatively, you can open the desired version of the file and choose File → Save As to save it as a separate file.**

- **A document containing versions can quickly balloon to a large file size.**

Remove Personal Data from a Document

The Annoyance: Last month, a colleague blew the whistle on a few corners our boss had been cutting. She anonymously dropped HR a document, but it turned out that her name was hidden in it somewhere—so now she's no longer working here.

The Fix: In each document you save, Word stores your username (as entered on the User Information tab of the Options dialog box) and other identifying information. Word 2003 and Word XP let you easily remove personal data from a document; Word 2000 does not, but you can choose File → Properties and manually delete particular items of information.

To remove personal data from Word 2003/XP documents, choose Tools → Options, click the Security tab, and check the "Remove personal information from file properties on save" box. For security, you may also want to check the "Warn before printing, saving or sending a file that contains tracked changes or comments" box so that Word prevents you from saving or sending a file that contains text that may be hidden from you.

After choosing these options, you must save the document to make the options take effect.

Remove Office-Specific Tags from Web Pages

The Annoyance: When Word renders a document into HTML, it puts weird tags in it. How can I remove the excess tags?

The Fix: The tags you're objecting to are the Office-specific tags that Word uses to store information needed to re-create the document in its entirety. These tags store all kinds of information that's not displayed in the document, such as author and editing information; menu, toolbar, and keyboard customizations in the document; and even VBA code (macros, user forms, and classes). This extra information not only makes your web pages larger than necessary but also threatens your privacy.

The process of exporting an entire document to HTML so that it can be brought back into Word without any loss is called *round-tripping*. Word's "Web Page" and "Single File Web Page" formats save the data for round-tripping, while the "Web Page, Filtered" format does not. Use "Web Page, Filtered" for pages you want to put on your web site, but be warned that Word's HTML is verbose. If you know HTML, you may prefer to save a document in "Web Page, Filtered" format, open it in a text editor or HTML editor, and strip out unnecessary information manually before posting it to your web site.

To get rid of the Office-specific tags in Word 2003 or Word XP, choose File → Save as Web Page and then choose Web Page, Filtered in the "Save as type" drop-down list. Specify the filename, folder, and title, and click Save. When Word warns you that Office-specific tags will be removed (see Figure 2-6), click the Yes button.

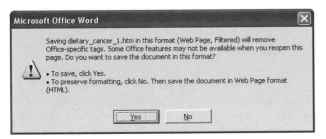

Figure 2-6. When saving a Word document as a web page, you can strip out the Office-specific tags by using the "Web Page, Filtered" format.

Word 2000 doesn't offer a built-in option for stripping out Office-specific tags. Your best bet is to use a third-party utility, such as the free HTMLTidy (*http://tidy.sourceforge.net*).

CRASHES AND CORRUPTION

Use Application Recovery to Mitigate a Crash

The Annoyance: Every now and then, Word hangs but doesn't crash. I can see my document, but I can't do anything to save my latest changes.

The Fix: Depending on the version of Word you're using, you may be able to do some damage control.

First, if what you can see of the document contains unsaved changes, take a picture of what's there and save it. With the focus on the Word window, press Alt+Print Screen. That copies a picture of the Word window to the Clipboard. Open Paint (Start → All Programs → Accessories → Paint) and press Ctrl+V to paste the picture. Press Ctrl+S and save the picture in a convenient folder. (If the Word window has gone white or is showing chunks of other applications, skip this step.)

Next, if you're using Word XP or Word 2003, launch Microsoft Office Application Recovery by choosing Start → All Programs → Microsoft Office 2003 → Microsoft Office Tools → Microsoft Office Application Recovery (for Word 2003), or Start → All Programs → Microsoft Office Tools → Microsoft Office Application Recovery (for Word XP). In the Microsoft Office Application Recovery window (see Figure 2-7), select the entry for Word and click the Recover Application button.

Figure 2-7. Microsoft Office Application Recovery can sometimes save data even after Word has hung.

Microsoft Office Application Recovery attempts to recover the data in the open document, and then displays a dialog box (see Figure 2-8) offering to send an error report to Microsoft.

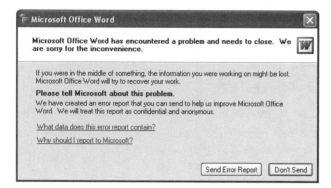

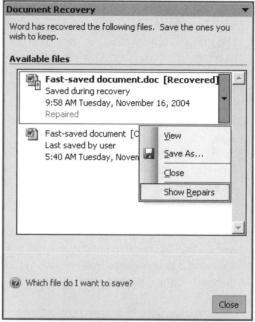

Figure 2-8. Choose whether to send an error report on the crash to Microsoft. If you've reported the error before, it's probably not worth doing so again.

The recovery then takes place, and Microsoft Office Application Recovery automatically restarts Word. Any recoverable documents appear in the Document Recovery pane with their types (Recovered or Original), details of when and how each was saved (for example, "Saved during recovery" or "Last saved by user"), and whether they have been repaired.

Click a document to open it, or right-click a document and choose a command from the shortcut menu (see Figure 2-9, top). Choose the Show Repairs command to display the Show Repairs dialog box (see Figure 2-9, bottom), which lists any errors that Word has repaired. Sort the errors by error description or by location, click the error you want to see, and click the Go To button. Check the document for damage, and then save it under another name.

RECOVERY IN WORD 2000

If you're using Word 2000, you don't have Microsoft Office Application Recovery. Instead, right-click a blank space in the taskbar or notification area, choose Task Manager from the shortcut menu, and then click the Applications tab. Click the Microsoft Word item, and then click the End Task button. Restart Word manually. If there's a viable AutoRecover file, Word opens it for you automatically; check it and save it under another name if it's usable. If there's no AutoRecover file or it's not usable, open the latest temporary document in the folder in which you were working, and then try to recover your document from it.

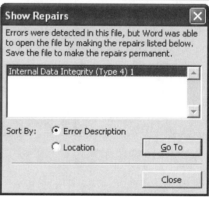

Figure 2-9. Document recovery usually enables you to recover much of the document that you were working on when Word crashed. The document may contain errors that Word has repaired.

Turn Off Error Reporting

The Annoyance: I've sent Microsoft an error report 50 times about the same error in Word, but I haven't received a response. I don't need to see these useless error-reporting prompts again.

The Fix: Turn off error reporting for Word. Press Windows Key+Break (or open the Start menu, right-click My Computer, and click Properties) to display the System Properties dialog box. Click the Advanced tab, and then click Error Reporting.

In the Error Reporting dialog box (see Figure 2-10), you can select the Disable Error Reporting option to turn off all error reporting. However, it's usually more useful to click the Choose Programs button, click the Add button at the bottom of the dialog box, and add each program for which you want to disable error reporting. Type the name of the executable file for Word—*winword.exe*—or click the Browse button and browse to it. Click the OK button to close each of the four open dialog boxes.

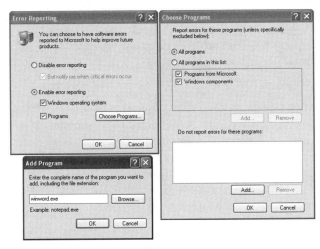

Figure 2-10. If Word keeps crashing with the same error, you can turn off error reporting.

Recover a Document After a Crash

The Annoyance: Word crashed again. Microsoft Office Application Recovery didn't do any good this time, and when I try to open the document, Word crashes yet again.

The Fix: This doesn't sound good, but all is not yet lost. Here's what you should do:

1. Open a Windows Explorer window to the folder that contains the document and make a couple of copies of the file. The easiest way to create a copy is to Ctrl-drag the document within the folder, but Copy and Paste works fine too. These copies are insurance against the possibility that your efforts to open the document will end up trashing it further. Leave the Windows Explorer window open.

2. Start Word again, choose File → Open, select the document, click the drop-down arrow on the Open button, and choose "Open and Repair." If all goes well, Word will fix whatever is ailing the document and open it. Choose File → Save As and save the document under another name so that the entire document is written afresh. With the document still open, choose File → Save As again, choose Rich Text Format in the "Save as type" drop-down list, and save the document as a rich text file. Close the document, and copy the new document and the rich-text document to a backup medium in case the problem returns.

3. If Word can't open the file but is set to create backup copies of documents (i.e., if the "Always create backup copy" box on the Save tab of the Options dialog box is checked), try to open the backup file. In the Windows Explorer window, switch to Details view (View → Details), and click the Name column heading to sort the files by name. Double-click the backup file, which will be named *Backup of <document's name>.wbk*. If it opens, save it under a different name. For good measure, save it in Rich Text Format as well, as described in the previous step.

4. If Word isn't set to create backup copies, look in the Windows Explorer window for a temporary file of the document. In Details view (View → Details), click the Type column heading twice to produce a reverse sort by file type. This will put the "Word Temporary File" type near the top of the list. Identify the latest temporary file of your document by its date and file size (its file size will be nearly the same as that of your document file). Right-click the file, click "Open with," and choose the Word item (for example, Microsoft Office Word). If the document opens, save it under a different name. Save it in Rich Text Format as well, as described in Step 2.

5. If you don't have a backup copy or a temporary file, try using WordPad to open the document that makes Word crash. In the Windows Explorer window, right-click the file, click "Open with," select WordPad, and click the OK button. WordPad understands only some of Word's formatting, so it has a better chance of not getting confused by errors in the document's formatting table. If WordPad

can open the document, save it under a different filename. You'll have lost the formatting that WordPad can't read, but you should have the text of the document, plus the basic font formatting.

6. If WordPad can't open the document and you're prepared to lose even the font formatting, use Word's "Recover text from any file" converter to recover the text. Choose File → Open, select "Recover text from any file" in the "Files of type" drop-down list, select the document, and click the Open button. Save the resulting document under another filename. You'll need to manually remove extraneous information and odd characters from the document, and you'll have to reformat headers, footers, footnotes, and endnotes, which will appear as normal text paragraphs in the document.

7. If Word's "Recover text from any file" converter can't open the file, open it with Notepad instead. This is the last resort and will cost you all the formatting in the document, but you should be able to recover the text. Depending on how the document is formatted, you will probably need to replace box-like characters with paragraph marks, but this tends to be far preferable to re-creating the document from scratch. In the worst case, the text may contain corruption that you will need to remove manually. Save the file under a new name from Notepad, and then open it in Word.

> If you have another word processor installed on your computer, try using it to open a damaged version of the document. Word processors such as Corel WordPerfect and OpenOffice.org include text converters that can read most Word features but are fairly tolerant of document corruption, bypassing it as features they can't interpret. Again, you're likely to lose much of the document's formatting, but you may be able to recover most of the text.

Control or Turn Off AutoRecover

The Annoyance: Every few minutes, Word seems to save something by itself; I see the readout flicker across the status bar. But I know it's not saving my document, because the document still contains unsaved changes.

The Fix: What you're seeing is Word's AutoRecover feature automatically saving a backup version of the document in case Word, Windows, or your computer crashes. When you restart Word after a crash, it automatically opens the latest AutoRecover documents so that you can choose which to recover (see the previous Annoyance, "Recover a Document After a Crash"). If you close a document normally, Word deletes its AutoRecover document.

If you've lost work in Word documents to crashes, chances are you now save the active document whenever you've made any changes to it that you want to keep. (Yes, I too obsessively press Ctrl+S at the end of each burst of typing.) In this case, AutoRecover offers little benefit. To turn it off, choose Tools → Options, click the Save tab, and uncheck the "Save AutoRecover info every" box.

If you tend to forget to save your documents, make sure the "Save AutoRecover info every" box is checked and set a suitable length of time in the Minutes drop-down list. The default is 10 minutes, which is fine if you're poking at a document. If you're typing 100 words per minute, shorten the interval and check "Allow background saves" so that you can keep working through most of the AutoRecover process. (Of course, you're better off saving your documents more frequently.)

Word saves AutoRecover documents using the name *AutoRecovery save of <document's name>.asd*. For example, the AutoRecover document for a file called *Benefits statement.doc* would be named *AutoRecovery save of Benefits statement.asd*. Word saves AutoRecover documents in the folder specified in the "AutoRecover files" line of the File Locations tab of the Options dialog box (Tools → Options). The default location for Word 2003 is your *%userprofile%\Application Data\Microsoft\Word* folder.

UNDERSTANDING TEMPORARY FILES

Temporary files are files that Word creates to store data temporarily as it works on the documents that you have created deliberately. Word uses several different types of temporary files for different purposes. You don't need to know all the details to use Word effectively, but understanding the basics of temporary files not only clears up various mysteries about how Word works but also can help you recover from assorted annoyances.

The temporary files you're most likely to notice are those that Word keeps in the same folder as the document itself. These contain versions of your document that you have saved earlier in the current editing session. When you close the document normally, Word deletes the document's temporary files. In a long editing session, the temporary files can stack up, and Word may take several seconds to delete them. This is why Word sometimes seems to take a surprisingly long time to close a document that you've already saved.

The temporary files you're next most likely to notice are the owner files that Word uses to lock the documents you (or other users) open. When someone opens a document, Word creates an owner file, giving it a name consisting of the document's name with the first two characters replaced by ~$. For example, for a document named *Second Thesis.doc*, Word creates the owner file *~$cond Thesis.doc*. (Very short document names receive a different treatment.) When you try to open a document, Word checks for the existence of an owner file, which would mean that someone else currently has the document open. Word deletes the owner file when the document is closed. Owner files won't trouble you when Word is running properly, but if Word crashes, these files may be left undeleted. If this happens, you may need to delete them manually to restore normal behavior.

Word creates several other kinds of temporary files, including a temporary file that it creates at startup to enable you to use OLE (Automation) objects in your documents. You're unlikely to need to work with these other temporary files, except to delete them en masse after Word has crashed.

Open Files Saved in Another Format

The Annoyance: Back when the TRS-80 was pretty hot, I had a much smaller computer from a maker that's long since disappeared. I've still got a handful of floppies with documents I created back then—in whatever format that computer used. I'd like to open the documents in Word for a quick trip down Memory Lane—I mean, to write my memoirs.

The Fix: Sure, go right ahead. Word will try to identify the converter needed. If there's an issue with the encoding, Word displays the File Conversion dialog box (Figure 2-11 shows an example) so that you can choose the correct encoding for the document.

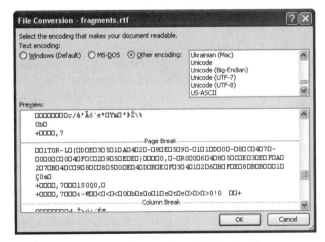

Figure 2-11. When opening a file saved in another format, you may sometimes need to choose the correct encoding.

Depending on the format that the old computer used for saving text, you may get pure text, text with some formatting codes, or text in what appears to be an advanced state of decomposition.

Even if the text is adulterated, you can clean it up easily enough in Word by using a sequence of find-and-replace operations. The easiest way to do this is to record a macro as you perform the necessary replaces and then run it on each of the documents in turn. You might also consider inserting all the documents into a single document so that you can clean them up all at once.

If you have documents created by a custom word processor in a format that Word can't read, and you still have access to the word processor, try saving the documents in a format that Word *can* read. Most word processors offer common formats such as Text Only and Rich Text Format (which includes standard formatting such as bold, italic, fonts, and alignment).

Batch-Convert Many Files Between Formats

The Annoyance: My company switched from WordPerfect to Word, which is okay. Nothing could be simpler than opening all those old WordPerfect documents and converting them to Word documents...except that there are about 10,000 of them, and I'm going to be here all weekend doing it!

The Fix: Relax. This is the kind of operation you can easily automate with a macro—but you don't need to, because Microsoft provides the Batch Conversion Wizard for you.

First, see if the Batch Conversion Wizard is installed on your computer. Choose File → New → On My Computer (in Word 2003) or File → New → General Templates (in Word XP) to display the Templates dialog box. In Word 2000, choose File → New to display the New dialog box. Click the Other Documents tab and see if the Batch Conversion Wizard is listed.

If the Batch Conversion Wizard isn't installed, install it. Choose Start → Control Panel → Add or Remove Programs, select the Office item, and then click the Change button. Select the Add or Remove Features option, and choose the advanced customization option. At the advanced customization screen, expand the Microsoft Word item and the Wizards and Templates item under it. Click the More Wizards item and select "Run all from my computer" from the shortcut menu. Finish the installation, return to the Templates (or New) dialog box, and click the Other Documents tab.

Select the Batch Conversion Wizard item and click the OK button. The wizard creates a new template and displays a dialog box (see Figure 2-12). Follow the procedure for specifying whether you want to convert to Word or from Word, designating the source folder and destination folder, selecting the files, and setting the conversion running.

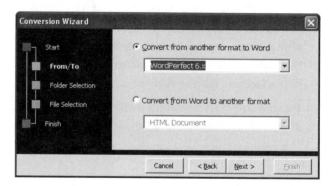

Figure 2-12. The Batch Conversion Wizard enables you to convert a batch of files to or from Word in a single operation.

Make Local Copies of Documents on Network or Removable Drives

The Annoyance: My company has several offices, and the way the servers are set up, it's hard to tell which document is on a local server and which is on a remote server. Opening a document on a remote server not only takes ages, but sometimes the connection fails when I'm trying to save changes—so I lose my work.

The Fix: If you don't know how fast a connection you'll have with the server that's providing the file, the easiest fix is to use Windows Explorer to copy the file to your hard disk. When you've finished working with it, copy it back to the server.

This two-step process is tedious but effective, and it works with all versions of Word.

Word XP and Word 2003 include an option intended to help you avoid losing data when working with remote files. Choose Tools → Options, click the Save tab, check the "Make local copy of files stored on network or removable drives" box, and click the OK button.

In theory, that should take care of the problem, but Word is more complicated than that. First, Word interprets "removable drive" to mean a drive with a total capacity of 3 MB or less—in other words, a floppy drive. Zip or other removable disks, memory cards, and CDs don't qualify. Second, if the drive *does* have a capacity of 3 MB or less, Word copies the file to your *Temp* folder anyway, regardless of whether the "Make local copy of files stored on network or removable drives" box is checked or unchecked. In other words, the option really applies only to network drives—which, luckily, is probably what you're most interested in anyway.

> Word automatically makes a copy of any file you open from a floppy because a floppy disk has such a low capacity that it will quickly become full if Word stores temporary files on it. Floppy disks also read and write data far more slowly than hard disks, so storing a copy and keeping the temporary files on the hard disk is much more efficient.

Once you've checked the "Make local copy of files stored on network or removable drives" box, Word makes a local copy each time you open a file from a network drive. The temporary document is stored in a temp file with an auto-generated name with the *.tmp* extension (for example, *~WRC1744.tmp*) in your *%userprofile%\Local Settings\Temp* folder.

As you make changes to the document, Word uses the temporary file as its reference file instead of using the document on the network drive. When you save the document, Word saves the changes in the temporary file and then saves them to the network drive. (Word saves the changes in the temporary file first in case the network drive has become unavailable.) When you close the document, Word deletes the temporary file.

INSTALL THE WDLOCALCOPY ADD-IN

If you find that Word XP tends to uncheck the "Make local copy of files stored on network or removable drives" setting even though you've set it, install the *WdLocalCopy.dll* add-in, which ensures that this checkbox is selected whenever you run Word:

1. Browse to the Microsoft Knowledge Base (*http://support.microsoft.com*), search for Article 313397, and click the "Download WdLocalCopy.exe Now" link.

2. Extract the file to your Office folder—for example, *Program Files\Microsoft Office\Office10*.

3. Choose Start → Run, and type `Regsvr32` and the path to the *WdLocalCopy.dll* file—for example, `regsvr32 "c:\program files\microsoft office\office10\wdlocalcopy.dll"` (including the quotation marks if the path include spaces, as this example does). Then click the OK button. This installs the add-in so that it runs automatically each time you start Word.

Understand Document Locking

The Annoyance: I work in an office, and my colleagues frequently manage to keep open the documents I want to work on, leaving me stuck with the File in Use dialog box and the choice of Read Only, Notify, or Cancel.

The Fix: When someone opens a document, Word creates a locking file called an *owner file* to prevent anyone else from opening the document until the first person closes it; Word then deletes the owner file, removing the locking. (See the sidebar "Understanding Temporary Files," earlier in this chapter for more on Word's owner files.) If you want to work with (i.e., change) a locked document, there's no real solution other than tracking down whoever opened it and asking that person to close the file. The owner file contains that person's name, but the information is taken from the User Information tab of the Options dialog box, so it may not be correct.

At least the choice Word offers you when you try to open a locked file (Figure 2-13) is marginally better than the old "Abort, Retry, Fail?" error message, one of the banes of DOS users. You have three options:

- Clicking the Cancel button cancels the request to open the document.

- Clicking the Read Only button opens a read-only copy of the document. You can save this document under another name, in another folder, or both, but you'll need to merge any changes you make with the original document when your colleague has finished working with it. If you simply want to print the document, Read Only is a good choice.

- Clicking the Notify button opens a read-only copy of the document, which again you can save under a different name, in another folder, or both. The only difference is that if the original document becomes available while you're working with the read-only copy, Word displays the File Now Available dialog box (see Figure 2-14). Click the Read-Write button to open the file. If you haven't made any changes to the read-only copy of the document, you can now edit the original document as usual. If you *have* made changes to the read-only copy, Word displays the File Changed dialog box (see Figure 2-15), which offers you the options of discarding your changes or saving them in a different document so that you can open the original document. You can then integrate the changes manually or, even better, by using Tools → Compare and Merge Documents (Tools → Merge Documents in Word 2000). You can also click Cancel to cancel your request to open the file that was locked for editing.

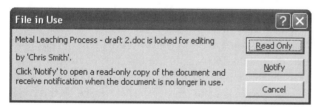

Figure 2-13. Only one person can work on a document at the same time. If you try to open a document that someone else already has open, Word displays the File in Use dialog box.

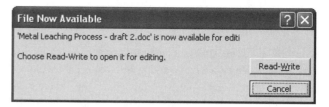

Figure 2-14. If the original document becomes available, you can open it and then decide whether to abandon any changes you've made to the copy you've been editing.

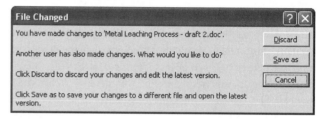

Figure 2-15. If you've changed the read-only copy of the file, click Save As in the File Changed dialog box to save your edits in a new file. You can then merge them into the original document.

Deal with Spurious "File in Use" Messages

The Annoyance: I get a "File in Use" error when I know that nobody else has the document open.

The Fix: This error means that the owner file (see the previous Annoyance, "Understand Document Locking") hasn't been deleted as it should have been—for example, because Word or Windows crashed, or because the PC suffered a power outage. If the error message says the file is in use by "another user" rather than giving the user's name, the owner file has probably been corrupted.

To deal with this error, delete the owner file. The crash or outage will probably have left stray temporary files as well, so it's a good idea to clean these up, too:

1. Close all applications, restart Windows, and log in again.

2. Choose Start → Search to open a Search Results window. If Search Companion displays the "What Do You Want to Search For?" list, click "All files and folders."

3. Type ~*.do? *.tmp ~*.wbk in the "All or part of the file name" text box.

4. Choose the appropriate location in the "Look in" drop-down list—for example, Local Hard Drives.

5. Click Search and give your computer a few minutes to work.

6. Select all the files, right-click anywhere in the selection, hold down the Shift key, and choose Delete from the shortcut menu to delete the files.

After deleting the owner file and any temporary files, try opening the document again. If Word still displays the "File in Use" dialog box, check your hard disks for errors, and then defragment them.

MASTER DOCUMENTS

Avoid Master Documents if Possible

The Annoyance: When documents become too big and unwieldy to email around, we turn to using master documents and subdocuments so that team members can work simultaneously on the various parts, which can then be exchanged easily. However, it's our experience that Word master documents and subdocuments are easily subject to corruption. We often find that we have to revert to an older version, or even just start over.

The Fix: You've hit the nail on the head. Master documents *are* unreliable, because they're so complex. Let's take a minute to see why.

A *master document* is a document that contains two or more *subdocuments*, or component documents. You can edit the master document as a whole or edit its subdocuments separately. The advantage of master documents is that several people can work on different subdocuments at the same time, instead of only one person being able to open the same copy of the document at a time.

These are the essentials of how a document is put together:

- Each Word document contains many objects, from characters, words, and paragraphs to tables, graphics, equations, and more esoteric objects. Each object has *properties* (attributes) that control its appearance and behavior.

- In a document, Word stores each object's properties separately from the object itself and uses *pointers* (references) to indicate which properties apply to which objects.

- Word stores the properties for a section invisibly in its section break. (The section break appears at the end of the section.) If the document has only one section, Word stores the properties in the *default section break*, which is the final paragraph mark in the document. (This is the paragraph mark that you'll see if you start a new document and press Ctrl+Shift+8. Normally, Word won't allow you to delete the default section break, because doing so removes the formatting from the document.)

- The properties in a single Word document are complex enough. In a master document, the complexity is greatly increased by having a default section break for each subdocument *and* a default section break for the master document. Word has to merge the properties for each subdocument into the master document. When this process breaks down, corruption results.

- The master document is just a container for the subdocuments. It doesn't actually contain the text of the subdocuments.

The easiest way to escape the annoyances (or worse) of master documents is to avoid them altogether. If you decide you must use master documents, the next Annoyance, "Enable Multiple People to Edit a Document at the Same Time," explains how to do so. See also the sidebar "Working Safely with Master Documents."

For an alternative to using master documents, see "Enable Several People to Edit a Document Simultaneously," later in this chapter. Chapter 5 discusses other alternatives: comments, revision marks, and comparing and merging documents.

Enable Multiple People to Edit a Document at the Same Time

The Annoyance: I understand that master documents can get corrupted, but we need to use them to get our manual finished on time. Where's the command to create a master document—or a subdocument, for that matter?

The Fix: So you've been warned, but you want to go ahead. Okay. The commands for creating and working with master documents and subdocuments lurk at the west end of the Outlining toolbar (see Figure 2-16). Click the Master Document View button if the other buttons aren't displayed.

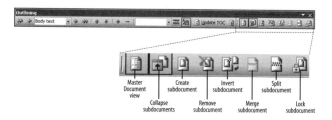

Figure 2-16. You'll find the commands for master documents on the Outlining toolbar.

You can create a master document either by dividing an existing document into subdocuments or by adding existing documents into a new master document.

To create a master document:

1. Set up a folder for your master document and subdocuments. If your colleagues will need to access the documents (which is the usual reason for using a master document), create the folder on a shared drive.

2. Open the existing document that will become the master document, or create a new document and save it in the folder you set up on the shared drive.

3. Choose View → Outline to switch to Outline view.

4. Create the outline of the document by typing headings or promoting existing paragraphs to headings (using the two leftmost buttons on the Outlining toolbar). Use the same level of heading for each subdocument. Usually, it's best to use Heading 1s for the headings that will make up the master document and Heading 2s as the subdocument headings. If your existing document doesn't use the built-in heading styles, format your outline styles so that they have the appropriate levels by using the "Outline level" drop-down list on the Indents and Spacing tab of the Paragraph dialog box. (See Chapter 4 for details on creating styles.)

5. To create a subdocument from part of the existing document, collapse Outline view so that you can easily select the relevant part, select that part, and click the Create Subdocument button on the Outlining toolbar. Word creates the subdocument. When you save the master document, Word automatically saves the subdocument under a name based on the heading that introduces the subdocument.

>
>
> You can create multiple subdocuments at the same time by selecting more than one heading of the same level and then clicking the Create Subdocument button on the Outlining toolbar. For example, if you select three Heading 2 sections, Word creates three subdocuments.

6. To insert an existing document as a subdocument, position the insertion point in the appropriate place, click the Insert Subdocument button on the Outlining toolbar, select the document, and click the Open button.

So far, so good. You can also merge two subdocuments (select them and click the Merge Subdocument button on the Outlining toolbar), split a subdocument into two (place the insertion point, and then click the Split Subdocument button on the Outlining toolbar), or remove a subdocument (click in it, and then click the Remove Subdocument button on the Outlining toolbar). Removing a subdocument leaves its content in the master document. To prevent anyone from changing a subdocument, select it and click the Lock Document button on the Outlining toolbar.

WORKING SAFELY WITH MASTER DOCUMENTS

There's no failsafe way to work with master documents, because any master document can—some Word experts say *will*—become corrupted eventually. So your goal becomes prolonging the time before corruption occurs so that you can finish your project with the document still working. Follow these suggestions:

- Keep the number of subdocuments to a minimum. Aim to have no more than 15 or 20 subdocuments at most. The more subdocuments, the greater the chance of the master document getting corrupted.

- Make sure your computer has plenty of RAM and that enough of that RAM is available to Word. (How much is enough? It depends on the version of Word and the complexity and length of the document. Figure at least 128 MB free to be safe. More is better.)

- On the Save tab of the Options dialog box (Tools → Options), make sure that the "Allow fast saves" box is unchecked and the "Always create backup copy" box is checked.

- Save your work frequently as usual, but also save a new copy of the master document frequently, under a different name. Keep the old copies for when disaster strikes.

- Store your master document and all its subdocuments in the same folder. Back up this folder frequently, and keep the backups in case you need to recover text from an older version of the master document.

- If you notice Word exhibiting any strange behavior, save your work and exit Word immediately. Strange behavior may include displaying phantom insertion points skittering about the screen as Word tries to work out what appears where and how it should be formatted; the Word titlebar not displaying the correct name of the active document; the screen not refreshing fully; or Word paralyzing your computer by consuming all available processor cycles. (To find out if Word is the culprit, right-click in the notification area and choose Task Manager, click the Processes tab, and click the CPU column heading once or twice, as needed, to produce a descending sort by the percentage of CPU time used.)

Enable Several People to Edit a Document Simultaneously

The Annoyance: Master documents sound like overkill. What I need is something like master documents, but on a more humble scale. I need to edit a document on our intranet with two of my colleagues who work in remote offices.

The Fix: You can do this, provided your network administrator lets you use the Application Sharing features of either Windows Messenger or NetMeeting. The administrator might prevent you from doing so because Application Sharing poses security threats beyond those normally posed by Windows Messenger and NetMeeting. The quickest way to find out is to try running Windows Messenger (choose Start → All Programs → Windows Messenger) or NetMeeting (double-click an existing shortcut, or choose Start → Run, type conf, and then press Enter).

Establish a connection via Windows Messenger (double-click a contact) or NetMeeting (choose Call → New Call). Then:

- In NetMeeting, choose Tools → Sharing to display the Sharing dialog box (see Figure 2-17).

- In Messenger, click the Start Application Sharing link in the "I Want To" list in the Conversation window. If the other person accepts the invitation, Messenger displays the Sharing Session toolbar (see Figure 2-18). Click the App Sharing button to display the Sharing dialog box.

Select the Microsoft Word item and click the Share button. Your Word window will appear to the other people in the meeting. Click the Allow Control button if you want them to be able to request control of the document (usually a good idea for collaborative editing). Check the "Automatically accept requests for control" box if you want your collaborators

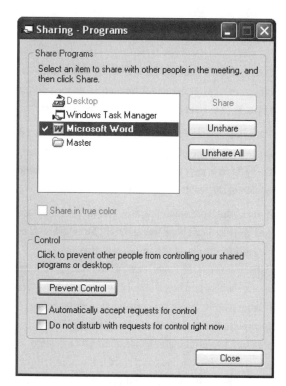

Figure 2-17. You can share Word (or another application) via NetMeeting.

Figure 2-18. Windows Messenger uses the Sharing Session toolbar to control application sharing.

to be able to take control of the application automatically, rather than your having to approve each request for control.

Make sure that the Word window isn't obscured by the Sharing window, the NetMeeting window, the Messenger window, or the Sharing Session toolbar. These windows will appear as blank patches to the people you're sharing with, unless you've chosen to share your entire desktop (which you shouldn't do: it's a severe security threat to your computer).

Once you've shared the Word window (see Figure 2-19), you and your collaborators can work together. Only one person can have control of Word at any given moment. To request control, the person double-clicks in the application. If you chose not to automatically accept requests for control, you'll be prompted to grant control each time.

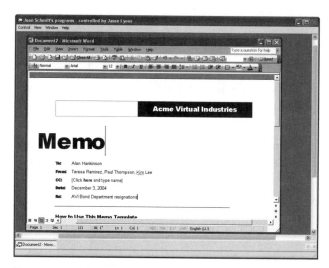

Figure 2-19. Working on a shared application tends to be uncomfortably slow, but two or more people can make changes to the same document in turn.

To stop sharing, choose Tools → Sharing (from NetMeeting), or click the Application Sharing button on the Sharing Session toolbar (from Windows Messenger), select the shared application, and click the Unshare button.

Recover a Corrupted Master Document

The Annoyance: My master document has become corrupted. I can still see most of the text, but the formatting looks as though a truck hit it. And there are groups of weird characters—things like þÿÿ (Is Word trying to learn Finnish?), Euro symbols, and empty-box characters.

The Fix: Word doesn't save AutoRecover information for master documents, so if Humpy Dumpty falls, restoring him to a semblance of togetherness tends to be a job for all the king's horses and all the king's men. Assemble a bucketful of patience, allow yourself plenty of time, and work calmly and methodically—easier said than done if you're looking at the wreck of several weeks of work.

When you're faced with a corrupted master document, *don't immediately save it.* Consider your options. There are three main strategies for recovering a corrupted master document, discussed in detail in the following sections:

- Revert to Word's backup document.

- Revert to your last uncorrupted backup.

- Repair the corrupted version. This is the most difficult option. It involves a considerable amount of detailed work and is usually only worth the effort if neither of the previous two strategies is viable—for example, because the master document contains many changes that the backup does not, or because you have neither a Word backup copy nor a manual backup of the master document.

Revert to Word's backup document of the master document

If you've been saving your master document frequently, reverting to Word's backup document is the easiest recovery path. This backup document will exist if you checked the "Always create backup copy" box on the Save tab of the Options dialog box (Tools → Options) in Word. The backup document (which will have a name such as *Backup of My Master Document.wbk* and will be located in the same folder as the master document) contains the document as it was the next-to-last time you saved it.

If the corrupted master document is still open and contains unsaved changes, the backup document is two generations back: it's not the document created the last time you saved the master document, but the document created at the save before that. Here's how to revert to Word's backup document:

1. Open a Windows Explorer window to the folder containing the master document. Verify that the backup document exists, that its date and time correspond to the next-to-last time you saved the master document, and that its size is approximately the same as that of the master document.

2. Close the master document without saving changes and exit Word.

3. Restart Word and open the backup document. The document is likely about to corrupt (just as the master document did), so remove the subdocuments, choose File → Save As, and save it to a "normal" Word document using a different filename.

4. Choose File → Save As again and save the document as a Web Page document, again using another filename. Using the Web Page format ensures that you have the text and formatting written out to a text-based format.

5. Close the web page and reopen the "normal" Word document you created. Check it carefully for corruption or loss.

Revert to a manual backup of the master document

If you've been making backups frequently, and the corrupted master document (and the Word backup document) contains only a few changes that the uncorrupted backup doesn't, this is a quick and effective strategy. Follow the steps in the previous list to check that the backup exists and that it's recent enough for your needs. Remove the subdocuments and save the backup document to a "normal" Word document, and then save it again as a Web Page document. Open the "normal" Word document and check it carefully.

Recover a corrupted master document manually

No good on the previous two approaches? Fear not! All hope is not lost—yet.

To recover as much of a corrupted master document as possible, follow these steps:

1. If the corrupted document is open, choose File → Save As, choose Web Page in the "Save as type" drop-down list, specify a different filename, and click the Save button. Exit Word (choose File → Exit).

2. Close any other applications you're running, and then check your computer for viruses with an up-to-date anti-virus application in case the problem has been caused by a macro virus.

3. Open a Windows Explorer window to your user templates folder. (If you don't know where this is, open Word, choose Tools → Options, click the File Locations tab, and look at the "User templates" readout. If you can't see the full path, double-click it and then examine the "Look in" drop-down list in the Modify Location dialog box.) Rename *Normal.dot* to another name of your choosing (in case corruption in *Normal.dot* has caused the problem with the master document), and then rename the template used for the master document—you'll create a new version of this too, in case the original caused the problem.

4. Restart Word and then exit it. This causes Word to create a new *Normal.dot*.

5. Restart Word again. Choose File → New → On My Computer (in Word 2003) or File → New → General Templates (in Word XP) to display the Templates dialog box. In Word 2000, choose File → New to display the New dialog box. Select the Blank Document item on the General tab, select the Template option, and then click the OK button to create a new template based on *Normal.dot*.

6. Choose File → Page Setup to display the Page Setup dialog box, and choose settings for the margins, paper size and orientation, and layout (for example, headers and footers) for your recovery document. Click the OK button.

7. Choose File → Save to display the Save As dialog box, and save the new template under a name of your choice.

8. With the new template still open, choose Tools → Macro → Macros to display the Macros dialog box. Click the Organizer button, and then click the Styles tab. One of the "Styles available in" drop-down lists will list the new template, while the other will show *Normal.dot*.

9. Click the Close File button on the side that lists *Normal. dot*, click the resulting Open File button, and use the Open dialog box to "open" the longest of the subdocuments. The document doesn't actually open, but its styles appear in the Organizer dialog box.

10. Select all the styles in the chapter except the styles named "Heading" ("Heading 1," "Heading 2," and so on). The easiest way to do this is to click the first style, scroll down to the bottom of the list, and Shift-click the last style; then hold down Ctrl while you click each of the "Heading" styles. Click the Copy button to copy the styles to your new template. If Word prompts you to decide whether to overwrite existing styles in the new template, click the Yes To All button. Click the Close button to close the Organizer dialog box.

11. Choose Format → Bullets and Numbering to display the Bullets and Numbering dialog box. On each tab, click each of the list types in turn; if the Reset button is available for that list template, click it and then click the Yes button in the confirmation dialog box. When you've finished, click the Close button.

12. Choose File → Save to save the template, and File → Exit to exit Word. Restarting forces Word to write the details of the list templates to the Registry (that's where it stores them).

13. Restart Word. Choose File → New → On My Computer (in Word 2003) or File → New → General Templates (in Word XP) to display the Templates dialog box. In Word 2000, choose File → New to display the New dialog box. Click your new template, then click the OK button to create a new document based on that template. Choose File → Save to display the Save As dialog box, and save the document in a new folder on a drive that has plenty of space.

14. Choose File → Open and open the first subdocument for the master document. Click the Show/Hide ¶ button on the Standard toolbar to display the formatting marks in the document.

15. Press Ctrl+H to display the Replace dialog box, type ^b in the "Find what" box, and leave the "Replace with" box blank. Click the Replace All button. This action removes all the section breaks from the document.

16. Press Ctrl+A to select the entire document, press Ctrl+Q to reapply styles (removing any customizations made to the styles), and press Ctrl+Spacebar to remove any direct character formatting.

17. With the whole document still selected, hold down the Shift key and press ← once to deselect the last paragraph mark in the document. (This is the "default section break" that contains the master table of the document's formatting.) Copy the text (press Ctrl+C), switch to your new document, and paste it in (press Ctrl+V). Save the new document (press Ctrl+S).

18. Repeat steps 14–17 for all the other subdocuments that were in the master document.

19. Insert any necessary section breaks manually. Don't replace the section breaks that were used only for the master document.

20. Use Outline view (see "Expand and Collapse Outline View Quickly" in Chapter 3) to check that the heading levels of your document are suitable.

21. Save the document and keep a truly paranoid number of backups.

Text Entry and Editing

Almost every document needs some text—and Word offers many features for helping you create it quickly and accurately without wearing out your fingertips. This chapter explores how to eliminate annoyances you may encounter when entering and editing text.

Does Word irritate you by displaying your document in the wrong view, or automatically selecting more text than you want it to? This chapter will show you how to use Word's views effectively and how to hone Word's automatic-selection and smart-cut-and-paste features so they select what *you* want, not what Microsoft's focus group thinks you want. With the decks cleared, you'll be ready to turn AutoCorrect and its sister feature AutoFormat As You Type from hyperactive menaces into your potent but dutiful servants, use Find and Replace to effortlessly remove most of the annoyances your colleagues build into their documents, and choose among eight different means of navigating through your documents.

But that's not all. This chapter also covers a bumper pack of assorted editing annoyances, as well as a few tips for mastering fields. For example, you'll learn how to stop Word from searching the Web for help, how to get rid of that pesky Office Assistant for good, and how to enter the same text easily in multiple parts of a document—and keep it updated automatically.

VIEWS

Expand and Collapse Outline View Quickly

The Annoyance: Outline view in Word 2003 and Word XP is annoying. I use it to move large sections of text easily, but by default, Word opens in Outline view with everything expanded, including the text. In Word 2000, there was an Outline toolbar with icons that made it easy to expand and contract the outline quickly. In Word 2003 and Word XP, you have to go through several mouse clicks to accomplish the same thing.

The Fix: You can tackle these Outline view annoyances in several ways.

The worst annoyance is Word's habit of opening the outline fully expanded. To make Word open the outline expanded only to a specified level, create two short macros to replace the ViewOutlineMaster and ViewOutline commands that the Word interface uses when switching to Outline view. See "Make Outline View Open Expanded to a Specified Level" in Chapter 8 for instructions.

If you can't summon the energy to create the macros, you may find using keyboard shortcuts to quickly expand or collapse the outline satisfactory:

Alt+Shift+1 through Alt+Shift+9

Collapse or expand to the specified heading level (1 through 9).

Alt+Shift++

Expand the selected item by one heading level.

Alt+Shift+-

Collapse the selected item by one heading level.

Alt+Shift+A

Toggle the display of all heading levels.

The other annoyance is that Word 2003 and Word XP use the Show Level drop-down list on the Outlining toolbar instead of the individual level buttons that Word 2000 and earlier

versions used. The drop-down list saves some space on the toolbar, but it makes changing levels with the mouse a click slower and demands greater accuracy.

To fix this annoyance, select Tools → Customize, click the Commands tab, and verify that *Normal.dot* is selected in the "Save in" drop-down list. Click All Commands in the Categories listbox, scroll way down, and then drag as many of the ShowHeading1 through ShowHeading9 buttons to the Outlining toolbar (see Figure 3-1) as you want to be able to access instantly. Drag the Show Level drop-down list off the toolbar and drop it in the document area to get rid of it.

Figure 3-1. If you find the Show Level drop-down list on the Outlining toolbar in Word 2003 and Word XP a menace, you can easily supplement or replace it with individual Show Level buttons.

Click the Close button, Shift-click the File menu, click Save All, and click the Yes button when Word prompts you to save changes to *Normal.dot*.

Switch Quickly Among Views

The Annoyance: So I'm working in my document, and I need to use several views. I choose View → Outline...choose View → Normal...choose View → Print Layout...choose again.... It seems like I'm addicted to the View menu. I'd like to get off it.

The Fix: Easy enough. If you still have the horizontal scrollbar displayed, click the appropriate button at its left end to change views (see Figure 3-2). You can also press Ctrl+Alt+O for Outline view, Ctrl+Alt+N for Normal view, Ctrl+Alt+P for Print Layout view, or Ctrl+Alt+I for Print Preview.

Figure 3-2. The horizontal scrollbar provides buttons for changing views quickly. If you prefer to hide the horizontal scrollbar, you can use keyboard shortcuts instead to change the view.

Learn to Live with the Wavy Underline

The Annoyance: In Word 97, in Outline mode (View → Outline), every collapsed heading has a wavy underline that starts about 0.5 inches to the left of the first word and extends approximately 1.5 inches (for short headings) to 4 inches (for longer ones) to the right. How can I get rid of the underlining? It's ugly and appears to serve no purpose.

The Fix: Sorry—no fix on this one. There is a purpose, though: the underlining is to indicate that there are paragraphs collapsed under the heading. Treat it as a visual aid to help you avoid deleting precious pages when you intend to delete only a heading.

Turn Off Formatting Display in Outline View

The Annoyance: I use Outline view all the time for taking notes in classes and meetings. The problem is that the formatting constantly changes when I tab in or out—if I tab in, I have to press Ctrl+I immediately to turn off italics. I just want the formatting to stay the same, but I can't find any way to make that happen.

The Fix: When you're tabbing in and out, you're changing the heading level, right? So what's happening is that Word is applying the different built-in heading styles. In the default *Normal.dot* template, the Heading 2, Heading 5, and Heading 8 styles use italic, so when you hit one of those levels, you'll get italics.

The easiest fix is to ignore the problem. Click the Show Formatting button on the Outlining toolbar to turn off the display of formatting. All your text will now appear in your default font, without any italics (unless your default font is italic).

If you don't want to lose all the font formatting in Outline view, change the Heading styles from italic to regular font. (See "Modify an Existing Style" in the Annoyance "Get Started with Styles" in Chapter 4 for details.) Bear in mind, though, that this change carries through in all views.

Change the Font Used for Outline View

The Annoyance: I've learned to click the Show Formatting button on the Outlining toolbar to turn off the display of formatting in Outline view, but I'd like to use a different font for working in this view.

The Fix: You just need to change the default font for the template attached to the document. Choose Format → Font, select the desired font details, click the Default button, and click the Yes button in the confirmation dialog box.

Be warned that this change will also affect other views if your styles use the default font. If you want to use this particular font only when using Outline view, create a new template with this font as the default. Attach the new template to the document when you want to work in Outline view, and reattach the document's previous template when you switch to a different view. (This solution is practical only for protracted sessions in Outline view. If you want to flip back and forth between Outline view and other views, it won't do you much good.)

If, when you switch views, the current selection disappears from the screen, press the left arrow key and then the right arrow key to bring it back into view.

Print from Outline View

The Annoyance: I want to print documents in Outline format, but I can't.

The Fix: You can, you know. If you're looking for an "Outline" option in the Print dialog box, don't worry—it's simpler than that. Switch to Outline view, expand or collapse the outline so that it shows only the levels you want to print, and then choose File → Print as usual.

Stop Print Layout View from Shortening Pages

The Annoyance: I'm using Print Layout view in Word 2003, and the page dimensions have gotten all weird. It's like someone lopped three-quarters of an inch off the top and bottom of the page.

The Fix: Word hides unoccupied whitespace to help you see the rest of your document more clearly. To restore all the whitespace, choose Tools → Options, click the View tab, and check the "White space between pages (Print view only)" box.

Edit in Print Preview

The Annoyance: Why can't I edit in Print Preview, so that I can see the effects of my edits?

The Fix: You can. Just click the Magnifier button on the Print Preview toolbar, and you're in business.

If you like editing in Print Preview, you'll probably want to make Print Preview automatically open in editing mode. You can do this, but only by using a macro. See "Make Print Preview Open in Editing Mode" in Chapter 8 for instructions.

SELECTING TEXT AND OBJECTS

Hone Word's Automatic Selection

The Annoyance: When I'm selecting with the mouse, Word suddenly grabs more text than I'm trying to get. Arrgh!

The Fix: It sounds like you're running afoul of Word's smart-selection features. Choose Tools → Options, click the Edit tab (see Figure 3-3), and see whether the "When selecting, automatically select entire word" and "Use smart paragraph selection" boxes are checked. If so, try unchecking them, and see if you prefer the resulting selection behavior.

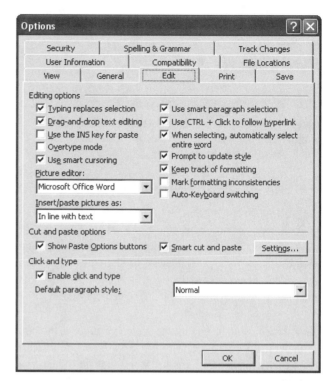

Figure 3-3. Many of the options on the Edit tab of the Options dialog box annoy nearly as many people as they help.

If you check the first box ("When selecting, automatically..."), when you drag from the beginning of a selection to another word, the selection is automatically extended to encompass both words—even if you deliberately dragged from the middle of the first word. As you extend the selection from two words to three, Word selects a word at a time, rather than partial words.

If you check the "Use smart paragraph selection" box and carefully try to select an entire paragraph *minus* the paragraph mark, Word will grab the paragraph mark anyway. As usual, Word is trying to be helpful, but many people find this kind of help annoying. (If you want to see your paragraph marks, click the Show/Hide ¶ button on the Standard toolbar or choose Tools → Options, click the View tab, and check the "Paragraph marks" box.)

Word 2000 offers neither smart paragraph selection nor most of the smart-cut-and-paste settings.

Control Smart-Cut-and-Paste Settings

The Annoyance: I used Word 2 for ages and got pretty darn good at selecting exactly what I needed to cut and paste. But now I've "upgraded" to Word XP, and it's driving me nuts. I cut just what I want to cut, and it knocks out a couple of extra spaces. I paste the text back in, and it jiggers the spaces around it. Tell me this is progress!

The Fix: You seem to disagree with the "smart cut and paste" feature's judgment. Choose Tools → Options and click the Edit tab. You can then either simply uncheck the "Smart cut and paste" box to turn off the feature altogether, or click the Settings button and use the options in the Settings dialog box (see Figure 3-4) to produce more acceptable behavior.

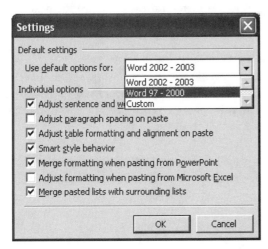

Figure 3-4. The Settings dialog box lets you set smart-cut-and-paste behavior to correspond to a particular version of Word, or choose custom settings that suit you.

Select Indented Text Accurately

The Annoyance: I often have problems when selecting text in a List style (e.g., a paragraph in a bulleted or numbered list). If I want to select the last element in the list so I can move it elsewhere in the document, Word not only selects the line I want, but also the first few characters of the line below the list (to the level at which the list is indented). I have to move the mouse back a few characters to deselect them, or, when using the keyboard like I usually do, use the left arrow

to go back a few characters. And if I go back *one* too many characters, even though the complete list line is selected, Word leaves an empty line in the List style, so I have to undo the cut and try again or take an extra step to delete the blank line Word left behind.

The Fix: The "Use smart paragraph selection" feature (on the Edit tab of the Options dialog box) might actually help you with this one. The problem you're having with a blank line in the List style being left behind is because you've accidentally deselected the paragraph marker at the end of the list item you cut. Experiment with it and see.

To avoid extra characters being selected, try some of these selection techniques:

Keyboard

Extend Selection mode is a feature for extending the selection without pressing Shift or dragging with the mouse. To turn Extend Selection mode on, double-click the EXT indicator on the status bar or press F8. Click at the point where you want to extend the selection, or use the arrow keys to extend the selection. Press Esc or double-click the EXT indicator again to turn off Extend Selection mode.

> While Extend Selection mode is on, you can press F8 a second time to select the current word, a third time to select the current paragraph, and a fourth time to select the whole document. Selecting a word or paragraph tends to be the most useful function of Extend Selection mode. To select a whole document more quickly than by using Extend Selection mode, press Ctrl+A or Ctrl-click in the left margin. To select a whole paragraph, double-click in the left margin next to the paragraph.

Mouse

Drag in the left margin (where the mouse pointer changes to an arrow pointing north-northeast) rather than dragging through the text itself.

Keyboard and mouse

Click to place the insertion point at the beginning of the text you want to select, scroll to the desired end point, hold down Shift, and click to select from the insertion point to where you click.

Turn Off "Click and Type"

The Annoyance: When I double-click in an empty line in a Word document, Word inserts a bunch of tab characters and paragraph marks. Did I ask for that? This happens quite often when I'm clicking on the document to bring it to the front so that I can work with it again.

The Fix: As an aside, there's much to be said for pressing Alt+Tab to "coolswitch" from application to application (or from one Word window to another). But the specific problem here is that Word's "Click and Type" feature is switched on. This feature lets you click in a hitherto-unused area of a document and start typing in it. Click and Type adds any blank paragraphs and tabs needed to bring the insertion point to where you click.

To switch it off, choose Tools → Options, click the Edit tab, and uncheck the "Enable click and type" box.

> If you like to use Click and Type, use the "Default paragraph style" drop-down list on the Edit tab of the Options dialog box to set the paragraph style Word should use for the paragraphs it creates. The default style is Normal.

AUTOCORRECT AND AUTOTEXT

Enter Any Amount of Text Quickly in a Document

The Annoyance: I'm sick of typing the same thing over and over. Can't Word do it for me?

The Fix: You bet: in any number of ways, depending on what you're trying to achieve:

Enter a short text item automatically

Create an AutoCorrect entry for the text. See the "Use AutoCorrect Most Effectively" sidebar for details. Alternatively, create an AutoText entry (see the next Annoyance, "Use AutoText, or Don't—It's Your Choice").

Enter a large amount of text in a document

Create a template for the document type (see "Templates" in Chapter 2). Put all the standard text in the template, and it will appear in each new document you create based on that template.

Reuse a section of text once from another document

Copy the text from the source document and paste it into the destination document.

Reuse the entire contents of a document

In Word 2003, choose File → New and click "From existing document" in the New Document task pane; in Word XP, choose File → New and click "Choose document" in the New Document task pane. In the New from Existing Document dialog box, select the document and click the Create New button. In Word 2000, open the existing document, choose File → Save As, and save it under a different name. You can also use the Insert → File command to insert an existing document in the current document.

Reuse the entire contents of several documents

Create a new document, and then use the Insert → File command to insert each of the existing documents in turn.

Use AutoText, or Don't—It's Your Choice

The Annoyance: Back in the good old days of Word 2 (and the horrors of Windows 3.11 for Workgroups—no, I don't miss 'em), I used to use glossaries all the time for storing chunks of text so I could lump them quickly into my documents. Then Word 6 introduced AutoCorrect and killed glossaries stone dead—for me, anyway. But all the subsequent versions of Word still have glossaries, except that they're now called AutoText. What's the point? I can see that entries like "Page X of Y" are good for inserting fields in a header or footer. But nobody in their right mind is going to wade through three levels of menu to save typing "Dear Sir or Madam"—or are they?

The Fix: You've got a point. Most of the canned AutoText entries are practically useless. And given that AutoCorrect entries can be triggered automatically by the right sequence of letters, AutoText seems like a step backward.

AutoText has a couple of advantages over AutoCorrect, though. First, you can move AutoText entries from one template to another, while your unformatted AutoCorrect entries are stuck in a file deep within your user profile and your formatted AutoCorrect entries are locked inside *Normal.dot*. Second, because AutoText isn't triggered simply by your typing, you can use real words as the short versions of your AutoText entries. Consequently, they can be much easier to remember than AutoCorrect entries.

Transfer Your AutoText Entries Between Templates

The Annoyance: AutoText is great! I've created several hundred AutoText entries for boilerplate items that go into my documents—and I've got a bunch more to create. But Word seems to start slowly, and when I look at *Normal.dot*, I see it's several megabytes.

The Fix: Well, you've hit the downside of AutoText: by default, every AutoText entry you create goes into *Normal.dot*, so you can eventually clog it up so much that Word becomes lethargic.

What you need to do is transfer as many AutoText entries as possible into other templates and then load them only when you need them. For example, if some of the AutoText entries are for projects related to a particular template, transfer them to that template. That way, they'll be available when you're working in that template, but not at other times. For AutoText entries that you want to have available for a variety of projects, use a global template other than *Normal.dot*.

To transfer AutoText entries from one template to another, choose Tools → Macro → Macros, click the Organizer button, and click the AutoText tab (see Figure 3-5). Make sure that "Normal.dot (global template)" is selected in one of the "AutoText available in" drop-down lists, then click the Close File button on the other side of the dialog box. Click the resulting Open File button, and open the destination template. In the "In Normal" list, select the AutoText entries you want to copy to the other template, and then click the Copy button. Close the Organizer dialog box and save your changes to the destination template.

Remove Mystery Lines from Your Documents

The Annoyance: Word suddenly inserted a decorative line as I was typing in a document. I've tried dragging across it, but I can't select it—so I can't get rid of it.

The Fix: This is the AutoFormat As You Type feature being helpful again by automatically applying a border when you type a string of text that matches one of its entries.

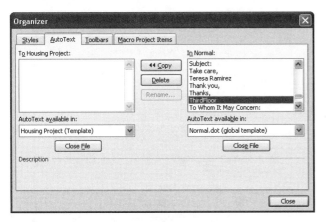

Figure 3-5. Use the AutoText tab of the Organizer dialog box to copy AutoText items from Normal.dot to another template.

If you haven't done anything since Word inserted the line, press Ctrl+Z to undo the line.

If Word 2003 or XP is displaying a Smart Tag button, click it and choose Undo Border Line to get rid of the line (see Figure 3-6). Click the button again and choose Stop Automatically Creating Border Lines to suppress this behavior in the future.

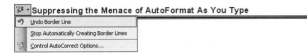

Figure 3-6. The AutoFormat As You Type feature can automatically insert lines that you can't select manually to delete.

If Word isn't displaying a Smart Tag button, delete the line by selecting the paragraph marker before it and pressing Delete. Alternatively, select the paragraph containing the line and press Ctrl+Q to reset its formatting to the style's default formatting. You can also choose Format → Borders and Shading, click the None button, and then click the OK button, but the other methods tend to be faster.

To prevent Word from applying these borders, choose Tools → AutoCorrect Options (or Tools → AutoCorrect in Word 2000), click the AutoFormat As You Type tab, and uncheck the "Border lines" box ("Borders" in Word 2000) in the "Apply as you type" area. Click the OK button.

Here's how to use this feature to decorate your documents quickly.

1. Start a new paragraph.

2. Type three or more hyphens (for a thin line), underscores (for a thick line), asterisks (for a dotted line), tildes (for a zigzag line), equals signs (for a double line), or hash marks (for two thin lines with a thick line between them).

3. Press Enter.

Turn Off "AutoFormat As You Type" Options

The Annoyance: Word keeps changing the text I type. The smart quotes are actually helpful, but I just got a bulleted list out of nowhere—and exactly where I didn't want it.

The Fix: Choose Tools → AutoCorrect Options (or Tools → AutoCorrect in Word 2000), click the AutoFormat As You Type tab, and uncheck most of the options. Figure 3-7 shows the options for Word 2003 and Word XP; Word 2000 has one or two fewer options.

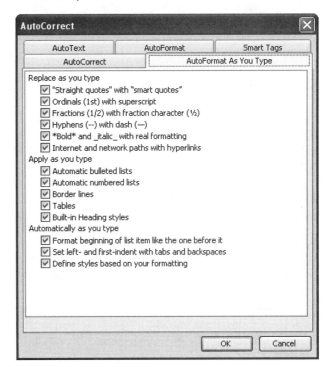

Figure 3-7. AutoFormat As You Type provides a dozen or so options for having Word apply formatting automatically to your documents when you type particular combinations of characters. Turn off all the options except those that suit you.

Most of the options are straightforward, but it helps to know the following:

- Automatic bulleted lists are triggered by paragraphs starting with an asterisk, hyphen, or greater-than sign followed by a space or tab.

- Automatic numbered lists are triggered by paragraphs starting with a number or a letter followed by a period and either a space or a tab.

- Automatic border lines are triggered by three or more hyphens, underscores, asterisks, tildes, equals signs, or hash marks. (See the previous Annoyance for more details.)

- Tables are triggered by combinations of hyphens and plus signs, where the plus signs mark the column borders. For example, if you type +--+--+--+--+, Word creates a four-column table. You can vary the column widths by using different numbers of hyphens. (For example, typing +-------+--+------+ produces a three-column table with a narrower column in the middle.) However, most people find it far easier to create tables with the Table → Insert → Table command or the Tables & Borders toolbar.

Save Work and Time with AutoFormat

The Annoyance: Oy! I've just received another "report" from our loquacious new rep: 40 pages of "news" formatted with no styles beyond Normal. Yes, you've guessed it: I have to make this presentable.

The Fix: You might as well try AutoFormat on it. It can't do any harm, and it might do some good.

Open the document and choose Format → AutoFormat to display the AutoFormat dialog box (see Figure 3-8). The first time you try this, click the Options button to display the AutoFormat tab of the AutoCorrect dialog box, and uncheck the boxes for any types of styles you don't want AutoFormat to apply and any items you don't want it to replace (for example, fractions with fraction characters).

Figure 3-8. If you receive an unformatted or skimpily formatted document, AutoFormat may be able to help.

Click the OK button to return to the AutoFormat dialog box. Choose between the "AutoFormat now" option and the "AutoFormat and review each change" option. The latter option tends to produce a bewildering array of revision marks that takes ages to work through. It's usually best to choose "AutoFormat now" and simply undo the entire AutoFormat if you don't like the results, but you may prefer to vet the changes individually. Whichever option you choose, use the "Please select a document type to help improve the formatting process" setting to tell Word which type of document your victim is: general document, letter, or email. This setting helps Word identify items such as an address block in a letter or unnecessary returns in an email.

Click the OK button and see what AutoFormat produces. If you selected the "AutoFormat and review each change" option, Word displays another AutoFormat dialog box that lets you choose to accept all the changes, reject all the changes, plow through the changes one by one, or visit the Style Gallery to apply a different look to the document.

Stop Word from Adjusting Your Capitalization

The Annoyance: Word keeps capitalizing words even though I'm trying to type them as lowercase. This makes it hard to create lists, write poetry, or use acronyms. I much prefer to make the choices myself rather than have Word make them for me.

The Fix: And make the choices yourself you can; you just need to reclaim a little autonomy from AutoCorrect. More immediately, you can press Ctrl+Z or choose Edit → Undo to undo any unwanted change that AutoCorrect has applied.

To change Word's behavior, choose Tools → AutoCorrect Options (or Tools → AutoCorrect in Word 2000) and uncheck the "Capitalize first letter of sentences" box and the "Capitalize first letter of table cells" box (in Word 2003 and Word XP, but not in Word 2000).

If necessary, uncheck the "Capitalize names of days" box as well; most people find this automatic correction unobjectionable, but your poems may disagree.

Scan down the list of "Replace text as you type" entries and delete any acronyms (or other entries) that you don't want to use.

Escape Unwanted Copyright Symbols

The Annoyance: Every time I type (c) in my document, Word changes it to a copyright symbol. (a), (b), and (d) are fine.

The Fix: This is a built-in AutoCorrect entry intended to help you insert the copyright symbol easily. Similarly, (r) produces a registration symbol, ®, and (tm) produces a trademark symbol, ™.

To prevent Word from doing this, choose Tools → AutoCorrect Options (or Tools → AutoCorrect in Word 2000). On the AutoCorrect tab, click the (c) entry to load it in the Replace box and the copyright symbol in the With box, and then click the Delete button. If you'd still like to be able to enter the copyright symbol via AutoCorrect, type your preferred entry in the Replace box (the copyright symbol will stay loaded in the With box) and click the Add button. Click the OK button to close the AutoCorrect dialog box.

Transfer Your AutoCorrect Entries to Another Computer

The Annoyance: I've built a great AutoCorrect list—but now I've got a new computer that doesn't have it. How can I transfer the entries?

The Fix: There are several possible fixes here. Word stores your AutoCorrect entries in two locations:

- Unformatted AutoCorrect entries are stored in a text file with an *.ACL* extension in the *Application Data\Microsoft\Office* folder in your user profile. (To open a Windows Explorer window to the folder, choose Start → Run, type `%userprofile%\Application Data\Microsoft\Office`, and then press Enter.) The file is named *MSOnnnn.ACL*, where *nnnn* matches the code for the language you're using. For U.S. English, the code is 1033, so the file is named *MSO1033.ACL*.

- Formatted AutoCorrect entries are stored in *Normal.dot*, which is in your user templates folder. (If you're not sure where your user templates folder is, choose Tools → Options, click the File Locations tab, and check the "User templates" readout.)

Once you know that, you can simply copy the *.ACL* file and *Normal.dot* to the appropriate folders on your new computer. That works fine, but there are three alternatives:

- Use the AutoCorrect Backup macro in *Support.dot*, a template included with a full installation of Office. (This template should be in the *Macros* folder in the Office folder—for example, *C:\Program Files\Microsoft Office\Office11\Macros*. If you can't find it, choose Start → Search and search for it. Double-click *Support.dot* to open a new document based on it, click the AutoCorrect Backup button, and follow the instructions for creating a backup copy of your AutoCorrect entries. On your new computer, open a new document based on *Support.dot*, click the AutoCorrect Backup button, click the Restore button, and then follow the procedure for restoring your AutoCorrect entries. This method is simple, but sadly it isn't foolproof: some complex AutoCorrect entries can cause the macros to fail.

- Use the Save My Settings Wizard (see "Move Word to Another Computer" in Chapter 1) to save your Word settings and key files to a shared location and then restore them on your new computer.

- Use the Files and Settings Transfer Wizard (Start → All Programs → Accessories → System Tools → Files and Settings Transfer Wizard) to transfer *all* (or most) of your Windows application settings from one installation of Windows to another.

Another possibility is to create a macro that extracts the AutoCorrect entries you want to keep. See "Export Your Auto-Correct Entries" in Chapter 8 for one approach to this problem.

Insert Symbols and Special Characters

The Annoyance: Insert → Symbol, change character set, scroll, scroll, scroll...click, click. Boring! There's got to be an easier way of inserting special characters than dredging through the Symbol dialog box.

The Fix: There is—three ways or four, depending on how you count:

- AutoCorrect includes entries for standalone symbols such as ©, ®, ™, and the ellipsis (...). You can add further entries manually if needed. Choose Insert → Symbol, select the symbol, click the AutoCorrect button, type the entry in the Replace box, and then click the OK button.

For Word to recognize your AutoCorrect entries, each entry must appear in the text with either a space or a punctuation character before and after it. In other words, while you can create an AutoCorrect entry that turns, say, "(y)" into "¥", you can't create an entry that turns "xxa" into "å" in the middle of a word. Instead, create an AutoCorrect entry for the entire word that you want to correct, so that AutoCorrect corrects the word when you type it without its accent. For example, you might create an entry that changed "laerdalsoyri" to "Lærdalsøyri."

- Word's AutoFormat As You Type feature replaces frequently typed symbols, such as em dashes, en dashes, and common fractions. To create an em dash, type two hyphens together without spaces between two words, and press the spacebar after the second word. To create an en dash, type the first word, a space, a hyphen, another space, and the second word, and then press the spacebar. To type a common fraction, type the numerator, a forward slash, and then the denominator, and press the spacebar. For example, **1/2** produces ½, and **3/4** produces ¾.

- Word includes built-in keyboard shortcuts for the most widely used symbols, which it deems "special characters." To learn these shortcuts, choose Insert → Symbol, click the Special Characters tab, and check the readout for the desired special character. To change a shortcut, or create a new shortcut, click the Shortcut Key button and work in the Customize Keyboard dialog box.

- The Symbol dialog box in Word 2003 and Word XP keeps a "Recently used symbols" list that enables you to easily insert one of the last 16 symbols you've used.

Insert a "Hard Space"

The Annoyance: My recently departed, late-lamented, and highly dedicated word processor let you insert a "hard space" that kept the words around it together, so if you wrote "Jose[hard space]Public," "Jose" and "Public" wouldn't be split at the end of a line if that was where the phrase happened to fall. Word doesn't offer hard spaces, even though it's a basic feature.

The Fix: Word *does* offer this feature, but it calls them "nonbreaking" spaces. To type a nonbreaking space, press Ctrl+Shift+Spacebar. If the key combination slips your mind, choose Insert → Symbol, click the Special Characters tab, and look for the "Nonbreaking Space" item.

> Word also offers nonbreaking hyphens, which you can insert by pressing Ctrl+_ (that's Ctrl and the underscore key).

Nonbreaking spaces appear as normal spaces unless you display all punctuation marks (click the Show/Hide ¶ button on the Standard toolbar) or display spaces (choose Tools → Options, click the View tab, and check the Spaces box). Spaces then appear as dots, and nonbreaking spaces appear as degree symbols (see Figure 3-9).

FIND AND REPLACE

Find and Replace Quickly

The Annoyance: I seem to spend half my time with the Find and Replace dialog box open. I find the first instance of the search term; close the dialog box, check the term, and make any edits needed; open the dialog box again and find the next instance; lather, rinse, and repeat. I guess I just feel it could be easier.

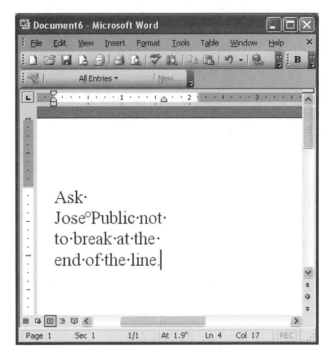

Figure 3-9. Use nonbreaking or "hard" spaces to keep words together. Non-breaking spaces appear as degree symbols when you have spaces displayed.

The Fix: And it can. First, the Find and Replace dialog box is modeless, so you can edit your document without closing the dialog box. All you need to do is get the dialog box out of the way so that you can perform the edits. That saves time, because you don't have to invoke the dialog box again to find the next instance.

> A *modeless* dialog box is one that you can leave open on screen while you continue to work in the application. Most dialog boxes are *modal*, which means that you have to dismiss them before you can do any more work in the application.

Second, when you perform a search, Word sets the browse object (see "Navigate with Browse Objects," later in this chapter) to Find and uses that search term. What that means is that you can find the next instance of the term by clicking the Next button (see Figure 3-10) below the vertical scrollbar or find the previous instance of the term by clicking the Previous button. Even easier and faster, you can press Ctrl+PageDown to find the next instance and Ctrl+PageUp to find the previous instance.

Figure 3-10. When you search, Word changes the Previous and Next buttons to Previous Find/GoTo and Next Find/GoTo.

Replace Styles and Formatting

The Annoyance: We have a standard template for our manuals that has a style for every occasion and a few dozen styles for the stockpot. So far, so good. But now we've acquired one of our competitors and need to "translate" all their documents from their three templates to our template. And yes, you've guessed it: I get to do the "translation."

The Fix: If you know VBA, you can write a quick macro to make this change. But if you don't know VBA, you can make the changes easily enough by using Find and Replace to replace each style from their templates with the corresponding style from your template. If you record a macro of yourself performing the replacements, you can then run it on other documents.

To replace one style with another style:

1. Make a two-column list of the styles you want to change and what you want to change them to. You can do this on paper, or in a Word table if you find that easier.

2. Open a document based on one of the other company's templates.

3. Choose Tools → Templates and Add-Ins, click the Attach button, select your company's standard manual template, and click the Open button. Check the "Automatically update document styles" box, and then click the OK button.

4. Choose Edit → Replace (or press Ctrl+H) to display the Replace tab of the Find and Replace dialog box.

5. If the "Find what" box contains text, press Delete to delete it.

6. Click the More button if the dialog box doesn't include the Search Options section.

7. If there are any formatting details under the "Find what" box, click the No Formatting button to remove them.

8. Click the Format button and choose Style from the shortcut menu to display the Find Style dialog box (see Figure 3-11). Click the first of the styles you want to replace, and then click the OK button.

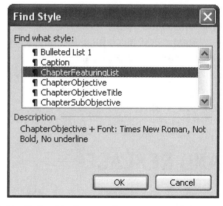

Figure 3-11. Find and Replace provides an easy way of changing one set of styles to another throughout a document.

9. Press Tab to select the "Replace with" box. If the box contains text, press Delete. If there are formatting details under it, click the No Formatting button to remove them.

10. Click the Format button and choose Style from the shortcut menu to display the Replace Style dialog box. Choose the corresponding replacement style, and then click the OK button.

11. Click the Replace All button to replace all instances of the style under the "Find what" box with the style under the "Replace with" box.

12. Select the next search style and the next replacement style, and repeat the replacement. Do this for all the remaining styles you wish to replace.

Replace Dumb Quotes with Smart Quotes

The Annoyance: Our reps are supposed to send me their reports as Word documents attached to email messages, but of course what most of them do is just type the reports directly in email. Some of the reports are so short, I'm sure they're at the beach (or bar, or both) on their BlackBerries. Anyway, I can copy the text from the emails into Word, but I need to smarten up the straight quotes in the emails. And boy, do they use a lot of those quotes!

The Fix: Provided that you've got the "'Straight quotes' with 'smart quotes'" box on the AutoFormat As You Type tab of the AutoCorrect dialog box (Tools → AutoCorrect) selected, you can change all these quotes quickly using Replace. Copy all the text into your document, choose Edit → Replace (or press Ctrl+H), and run two replace operations. In the first, replace " with ". In the second, replace ' with '. Word will automatically put in the smart quotes for you.

Replace with a Subscript

The Annoyance: Word can't search and replace a sub- or superscripted character *within* a word—for example, replacing "SO2" with "SO$_2$"; instead, it just subscripts the whole word. This is a major annoyance if you're editing a technical paper where the offending term crops up dozens of times.

The Fix: You're right, you can't do this directly with Find and Replace, because if you specify formatting for the "Replace with" text, it applies to the whole of that text. But what you can do is replace with the contents of the Clipboard. To do so, enter the text you want in your document, select it, and press Ctrl+C to copy it. Press Ctrl+H to display the Find and Replace dialog box, type the search text into the "Find what" box, and type ^c in the "Replace with" box. Word then replaces the found items with the contents of the Clipboard.

Another trick that's sometimes useful is to use two replace operations: one to isolate the text you want to affect, and the second to apply the change. This technique also works for replacing "SO2" with "SO$_2$". In the first replace operation, replace "SO2" with "SO" concatenated to a text string that will distinguish the "2" from instances of "2" that don't need to be changed—for example, "SOzx2zx." In the second replace operation, replace "zx2zx" with a subscript "2."

You can also use a macro to perform this type of replacement. See "Perform Find and Replace with Complex Formatting" in Chapter 8.

Perform a Two-Step Replace

The Annoyance: Okay, picture this: I've got a 500-page document with several thousand references to our product, the Bovine Super Defibrillator. Only sometimes it's just called the Super Defibrillator. I need to change all the instances to "Bovine Super Defibrillator." But if I do a Replace All, all the instances that already have "Bovine" change to "Bovine Bovine Super Defibrillator," which I don't want. And if I *don't* do a Replace All, I need to accept or reject the replacements one at a time.

The Fix: It's okay. Do the Replace All. Then do a Replace All of "Bovine Bovine" with "Bovine." Problem solved.

Find Any Character, Digit, or Letter

The Annoyance: Find and Replace isn't flexible enough! I need to check references to a bunch of different product codes, CP408 through CQ917. As you can imagine, searching for "C" with "Match case" on finds me every capital C in the document. I want a better way!

The Fix: There are two ways you can do this. The easiest way is to search for c^$^#^#^#, which finds a C followed by any single letter and then three digits. To find special items, use the codes explained in Table 3-1. You can enter them by clicking the Special button in the Find and Replace dialog box (see Figure 3-12) when the "Use wildcards" box is unchecked, but once you find how useful they are, you'll find it quicker to type them.

Table 3-1. Special codes for Find and Replace

Code	Meaning
^p	A paragraph mark.
^t	A tab.
^?	Any single character (letter or number). For example, ^p^t^? finds any character preceded by a tab that appears after a paragraph mark.
^#	Any digit. For example, ^p^# finds a paragraph that starts with a number.
^$	Any single letter (not a digit).
^^	A caret (the single caret is used to identify other codes).
^%	A section character (§).
^v	A paragraph character (¶—not a paragraph mark).
^n	A column break.
^+	An em dash (—).
^=	An en dash (–).
^e	An endnote mark.
^d	A field.
^f	A footnote mark.
^g	A graphic.
^l	A manual line break.
^m	A manual page break.
^~	A nonbreaking hyphen.
^-	An optional hyphen.
^s	A nonbreaking space.
^b	A section break.
^w	Whitespace (one or more spaces, one or more tabs, or a combination of the two).

Figure 3-12. The Special pop-up menu in the Find and Replace dialog box provides an easy way to enter the codes for special items.

The other way is to use *regular expressions*, or combinations of text and wildcards. Check the "Use wildcards" box and enter C[P-Q] (in capitals, as it's case-sensitive) in the "Find what" box, then click the Find Next button. See "Change 'Firstname Lastname' to 'Lastname, Firstname'," later in this chapter, for details.

Strip Blank Paragraphs from a Document

The Annoyance: Two hard returns after each paragraph, three hard returns after each heading, and *four* hard returns before a heading...will someone please tell my colleagues, many happy returns, but the typewriter is dead? I know I'm wasting time by telling them about styles, but if only they'd cut down on thumping the Enter key so many times, I'd be a far happier camper.

The Fix: Relax, you can fix this easily enough. Choose Edit → Replace, type ^p^p in the "Find what" box and ^p in the "Replace with" box, and click the Replace All button. When Word tells you how many replacements it has made, click the OK button, and then click the Replace All button again. That should take care of the problem: the first pass reduces each set of four hard returns to two, each set of three hard returns to two, and each set of two hard returns to one. The second reduces each remaining set of two hard returns to one.

Change "Firstname Lastname" to "Lastname, Firstname"

The Annoyance: Beautiful. Just beautiful. The chairperson just handed me the list of our members' names and asked—well, *told*—me to change it from "Firstname Lastname Membershipnumber" to "Membershipnumber Tab Lastname, Firstname." My future flashed before me, and it's looking tedious enough to bore a well.

The Fix: Word can do this for you. Open the document and select the part of it that contains the names. (If the whole document is the names, you don't need to select anything.

Otherwise, select only the names, as the pattern matches any sequence of three words.) Choose Edit → Replace (or press Ctrl+H) to display the Replace tab of the Find and Replace dialog box. Clear any formatting from the "Find what" box and the "Replace with" box. Enter (<*>) (<*>) (<*>) in the "Find what" box, with a space between each closing parenthesis and the opening parenthesis following it. Enter \3^t\2, \1 in the "Replace with" box, including the space after the comma. Check the "Use wildcards" box and click the Replace All button. Word changes the position of the words.

How does this work? You've just used three wildcard characters to build a regular expression. Once you check the "Use wildcards" box in the Find and Replace dialog box, you can use the wildcard characters shown in Table 3-2 to search for items. See the next Annoyance for another example of using wildcards in regular expressions.

Table 3-2. Wildcard characters for searching in Word

WIldcard	Meaning	Example using the wildcard
?	Any one character	sh?p finds "ship" and "shop".
*	A string of characters (including spaces)	w*d finds strings of text that start with "w" and end with "d," such as "wad," "wood," "wicked," and part of "stra*wberry d*onut." This also finds "wd," because the string can have zero length.
<	The beginning of a word or group of characters	<wear finds "wear," "wearisome," and other words with "wear" at the beginning, but not "swear" or "sportswear."
>	The end of a word or group of characters	>ble finds "horrible," "terrible," and other words that end in "ble," but not words such as "bleary" or "ablest."
()	Group wildcard characters	(<*>) finds a word by specifying a group with the start of the word, the * wildcard to find a string of characters, and the end of the word.
[]	One or more of the characters specified	w[aeu]d finds "wad," "wed," and "weed," but not "wood," because "o" is not included in the bracketed selection of letters.
[a-f]	One of the characters in the specified range	[l-r]ower finds "lower," "mower," "power," and "rower," but not words such as "tower" or "cower," which are outside the range. You must specify the range in alphabetical order.
[!a-f]	Any character except those in the specified range	[!l-r]ower finds "bower," "cower," "dower," "tower," and "vower," but not words such as "lower" or "mower," which are inside the range. Again, you must specify the range in alphabetical order.
{n,}	*n* or more instances of the previous character or expression	ke{1,}p finds "keep," "kepi," and "kept."
{n,m}	From *n* to *m* instances of the previous character or expression, where *m* is 255 or less	5{1,3} finds "5," "55," and "555."
@	One or more instances of the previous character or expression	pe@p finds "pep" and "peep."
\wildcard	Find the specified wildcard	* finds the * character.

You're not going to remember these wildcards, are you? No matter. Check the "Use wildcards" box in the Find and Replace dialog box, and you can click the Special button to display a pop-up menu of the wildcards (see Figure 3-13).

Figure 3-13. Once you've checked the "Use wildcards" box, you can enter wildcards from the Special pop-up menu in the Find and Replace dialog box.

Remove Duplicate Entries from a List

The Annoyance: So far, so good—the membership list is now in the format "Membershipnumber Tab Lastname, Firstname," and I've sorted it into ascending order using Table → Sort. But I can already see a ton of duplicate entries that I'll need to knock out.

The Fix: Regular expressions to the rescue again! Choose Edit → Replace to display the Find and Replace dialog box. Next, clear any formatting and check the "Use wildcards" box. Enter (*^13)(\1)@ in the "Find what" box and \1 in the "Replace with" box. Click the Replace All button. The \1 identifies a recurrence of the previous expression—in this case, any sequence of characters followed by a carriage return (represented by the code ^13). The @ makes Word find one or more occurrences of the repeated item. So the expression (*^13)(\1)@ finds a paragraph that is repeated by itself one or more times, and the replacement \1 replaces what is found (the repeated paragraph or paragraphs) with the paragraph itself.

NAVIGATING THROUGH DOCUMENTS

Master Navigation Keyboard Shortcuts

The Annoyance: I'm sick and tired of navigating with the mouse—every time I move my hand over to it, it wastes a couple of seconds. But moving around with the arrow keys sucks even more.

The Fix: Use the keyboard shortcuts shown in Table 3-3 to navigate quickly around your documents. If you want to select text, hold down the Shift key while you press the keyboard shortcut.

Table 3-3. Keyboard shortcuts for navigating in documents

Keyboard shortcut	Moves (or, with Shift, selects)
Ctrl+ ←	One word to the left, or to the start of the current word
Ctrl+ →	One word to the right, or to the end of the current word
Ctrl+ ↑	To the beginning of the current paragraph (if the insertion point is in it) or the beginning of the previous paragraph
Ctrl+ ↓	To the beginning of the next paragraph
Ctrl+Home	To the beginning of the document, text box, or other story (for example, a header)
Ctrl+End	To the end of the document, text box, or other story

Word calls the separate components of a document—the main document, text boxes, and other such items—*stories*.

Navigate with Bookmarks

The Annoyance: I need a way to move quickly from one part of a document to another. Hasn't Word got one?

The Fix: Word offers several ways of moving quickly about a document: bookmarks, browse objects (discussed in "Navigate with Browse Objects," later in this chapter), and Go To (discussed in "Navigate with Go To," later still in this chapter).

A bookmark is a marker in a document. A bookmark can either mark a particular point (between characters or objects) or enclose one or more objects: a character, a word, a graphic, and so on. Bookmarks are hidden by default, but you can display them if you choose (see the next Annoyance).

Pretty much everything you do with bookmarks involves the Insert → Bookmark command:

- To insert a bookmark, place the insertion point at the appropriate point or select the objects you want to include in the bookmark. Then choose Insert → Bookmark to display the Bookmark dialog box (see Figure 3-14), type an appropriately formatted name for the bookmark, and click the Add button.

> Bookmark names must start with a letter (not a number); can contain letters, numbers, and underscores after that; and can be up to 40 characters long. Each bookmark name must be unique in the document.

- To go to a particular bookmark, choose Insert → Bookmark, click the bookmark, and then click the Go To button.

- To delete a bookmark, choose Insert → Bookmark, click the bookmark, and then click the Delete button.

Figure 3-14. Bookmarks provide a handy means of accessing specific parts of a document.

Make Bookmarks Visible

The Annoyance: I'm using bookmarks to navigate among the different parts of my documents. The trouble is, I keep deleting the bookmarks while I'm working, because I can't see where they are.

The Fix: Choose Tools → Options, click the View tab, check the Bookmarks box, and click the OK button. Bookmarks that have contents appear with brackets around them (see Figure 3-15). Bookmarks that are just points appear as heavy I-beams.

A bookmark can appear as a point in the text or as brackets around one or more objects:

Figure 3-15. Turn on bookmarks if you're in danger of deleting them accidentally.

Place the Insertion Point Outside a Bookmark

The Annoyance: Okay, explain this. I select a paragraph, choose Insert → Bookmark, and create a bookmark around the paragraph. I turn on the display of bookmarks so I can see where the bookmark starts and ends. I need to add a paragraph before the one containing the bookmark, so I put the insertion point at the beginning of that paragraph and press Enter... and Word puts the new paragraph inside the bookmark rather than moving the bookmark down a paragraph. Arrgh!

The Fix: If you look closely, you may see that Word displays the insertion point within the bookmark brackets around the paragraph, in a brave attempt to show you what's happening. Anyway, the problem is that you've set the bookmark's range to encompass the whole paragraph, and when you place the insertion point at the beginning of the paragraph, Word considers it to be within the bookmark. To add a paragraph, you must place the insertion point at the end of the previous paragraph so that it's outside the bookmark.

If you've put the bookmark at the start of the document, you can't place the insertion point before it. Type the paragraph, select the paragraph that's supposed to contain the bookmark, choose Insert → Bookmark, and create the bookmark again.

Navigate with Browse Objects

The Annoyance: Why isn't there a way to find the next table or heading?

The Fix: Click the Select Browse Object button at the bottom of the vertical scrollbar (see Figure 3-16), select the appropriate browse object, and then use the Find Next and Find Previous buttons (or press Ctrl+Page Down or Ctrl+Page Up). You can also use Go To (discussed next). "Browse object" seems like a forbidding term, but it simply means "the thing you've told Word to look for." The possible browse objects are Go To, Find, Edits, Heading, Graphic, Field, Table, Endnote, Footnote, Comment, Section, and Page. Page is the default until you activate another browse object.

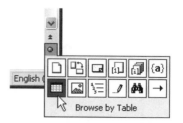

Figure 3-16. The Select Browse Object button and its panel provide quick navigation among 12 types of document objects.

Navigate with Go To

The Annoyance: I need to move quickly forward or back over a large number of pages in my documents.

The Fix: Choose Edit → Go To (or double-click an open space in the status bar—not one of the many readouts or items that clutter it). On the Go To tab of the Find and Replace dialog box (see Figure 3-17), click Page in the "Go to what" list, and either type the page number or enter a positive number (for example, +25) to move forward or a negative number (for example, –25) to move backward. Click the Go To button to make the jump.

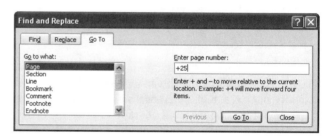

Figure 3-17. You can use the Go To tab to jump forward or back by a large number of pages.

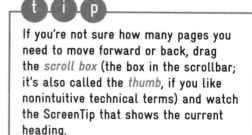

If you're not sure how many pages you need to move forward or back, drag the *scroll box* (the box in the scrollbar; it's also called the *thumb*, if you like nonintuitive technical terms) and watch the ScreenTip that shows the current heading.

Navigate with the Document Map

The Annoyance: When I'm working on my thesis, I often have to jump to different headings to enter text, check references, and so on. I switch to Outline view to find the heading I need, back to Normal view to work in the text, then back to Outline view to get back to where I was before. Is there an easier way?

The Fix: Choose View → Document Map to display the Document Map (see Figure 3-18), which works like a miniature version of Outline view at the left side of the window. Click a heading in the Document Map to jump to that page. You can expand or collapse the selected heading, or change the heading levels displayed, by right-clicking and choosing the appropriate command from the shortcut menu.

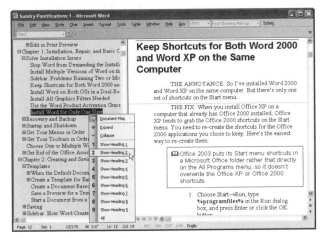

Figure 3-18. The Document Map provides a quick means of jumping from heading to heading in your document.

Customize the Document Map Style

The Annoyance: The Document Map is great—except that its font is far too small. I'm going to go blind peering at it. I've tried to customize it, but it doesn't even appear in the "All styles" category in the Styles and Formatting task pane. My friend who has Word 2000 tells me the style is called (logically enough) "Document Map." I've tried creating a new style with that name, but Word tells me the name is reserved for a built-in style.

The Fix: In Word 2000, you can simply choose Format → Style to display the Style dialog box, choose "All styles" in the List drop-down list, select Document Map in the Styles list, and click the Modify button to modify the style.

Word 2003 and Word XP hide the Document Map style and some other built-in styles from you. To force Word to display the Document Map style:

1. Choose Format → Styles and Formatting. In the Styles and Formatting task pane, choose Custom in the Show drop-down list to display the Format Settings dialog box.

2. In the "Styles to be visible" list, check the Document Map box, and then click the OK button.

3. Back in the Styles and Formatting task pane, click the Document Map style, click its drop-down arrow, and choose Modify from the pop-up menu to display the Modify Style dialog box.

Once you've opened the Modify Style dialog box, use its controls to modify the style. (See Chapter 4 for details on modifying styles.) Check the "Add to template" box to make sure your changes are saved to the template.

Scroll Automatically Through a Document

The Annoyance: I work on long—no, make that *looooooong*—documents and need to scroll through large chunks of text to get my bearings on what's where. I've tried using the Document Map, but it doesn't cut the mustard for me. And don't suggest Outline view, either: I need to see the headings and figures in the document as I go.

The Fix: Try AutoScroll. Choose Tools → Macro → Macros (or press Alt+F8), type `autoscroll` in the "Macro name" box, and press Enter or click the Run button. Word will display a "wait" cursor (the hourglass), but a shadowy double-headed vertical arrow will appear in the middle of the document window. Drag gently down (or up, if you want to scroll up) to start the scrolling. Drag further to scroll faster—you may find the adjustment delicate if your computer has a fast processor and dual overhead camshafts—or drag back the other way to slow, stop, or reverse the scrolling. Click or press Escape to turn off AutoScroll.

If you like AutoScroll, put its command on a toolbar or menu. Choose Tools → Customize, click the Commands tab, and verify that the correct template (for example, *Normal.dot*) or document is selected in the "Save in" drop-down list. Choose All Commands in the Categories list; then drag the AutoScroll item to the desired toolbar or menu. Close the Customize dialog box, Shift-click the File menu, choose Save All, and save changes to the document or template if Word prompts you to.

Return to Your Last Three Edits

The Annoyance: I'd like to be able to flip back to where I was last working.

The Fix: Press Shift+F5 one, two, or three times. A fourth press takes you back to the position from which you started.

> When you close a document, Word stores only the last editing location, not the last three; so when you reopen the document, you can use Shift+F5 only once to return to the last editing location. Because of the way that Word 2000 and later versions close files when you exit Word, Word may not save the last editing location in some files. However, if you close your files manually before exiting Word, it will always save the last editing location.

Work in Two Parts of a Document at Once

The Annoyance: I often need to work in two parts of a document at the same time. I'm getting whiplash from flipping back and forth.

The Fix: Split the window (choose Window → Split) or open a second window (choose Window → New Window). You may sometimes need to use both multiple windows *and* splitting when working with complex documents.

> You can use the Virtual Desktop Manager PowerToy (*http://www.microsoft. com/windowsxp/downloads/powertoys/ xppowertoys.mspx*) to run two or more virtual desktops.
>
> If you're generally underwhelmed by Word's navigation and editing features, check out WordToys (*http://www. wordtoys.com*). There's a free version that offers a wide variety of appealing enhancements, and a Professional version ($20) that provides even more.

SUNDRY EDITING ANNOYANCES

Copy Text Without Formatting

The Annoyance: When I copy text from Word and paste it into another application, all kinds of extraneous formatting tags go along for the ride. Then I have to reformat the text in the other application.

The Fix: There are two possible fixes here.

First, see if the application into which you're pasting the text has a Paste Special command. In the resulting dialog box, select the option called Text Only or Text Without Formatting, and then click the OK button.

If the application doesn't offer Paste Special, use Notepad to produce the same effect. Paste the text into Notepad, select it, copy it, and then paste it into the other application. This shuffle is ugly and clumsy, but it does remove the formatting, because Notepad doesn't support any formatting.

> **Warning**
> You might be tempted to use Word's own Paste Special command (Edit → Paste Special) to paste the material back into the same document (or into a different document) as unformatted text, select it again, copy it again, and then paste it into its destination application. The problem with this approach is that when you paste the text back into Word, it picks up the formatting of the paragraph into which you paste it, so it will still contain formatting when you copy it the second time and paste it into the destination application.

Hack Out Columns of Tabs or Spaces

The Annoyance: Our field office sends me database dumps that are aligned using spaces. I have to delete handfuls of spaces from the beginning of each line before I can use the text.

The Fix: You can fix this problem in two ways:

- If the spaces are in regular, rectangular blocks, Alt-drag to select columns of spaces (see Figure 3-19), and then delete them. (You can also select blocks of tabs—or any other characters—this way.)

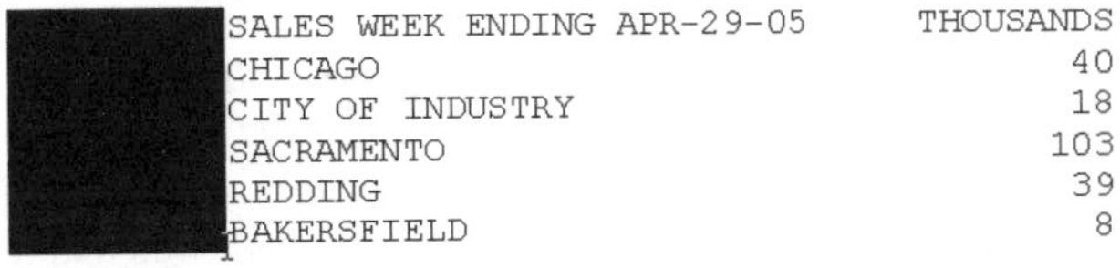

```
        SALES WEEK ENDING APR-29-05        THOUSANDS
        CHICAGO                                   40
        CITY OF INDUSTRY                          18
        SACRAMENTO                               103
        REDDING                                   39
        BAKERSFIELD                                8
```

Figure 3-19. Alt-drag to select columns of characters without selecting entire paragraphs.

- If the spaces aren't in regular blocks, use Find and Replace to select the whitespace. Choose Edit → Replace, enter ^p^w in the "Find what" box and ^p in the "Replace with" box, and then click the Replace All button. See "Find Any Character, Digit, or Letter," earlier in this chapter, for more details.

Eliminate the "Delete Block? No (Yes)" Message in the Status Bar

The Annoyance: When I try to delete a word I've selected, Word shows "Delete Block? No (Yes)" in the status bar instead of simply deleting it.

The Fix: Help for WordPerfect Users is turned on. To turn it off, choose Tools → Options, click the General tab, uncheck the "Help for WordPerfect users" box, and click the OK button.

Set Realistic Expectations for AutoSummarize

The Annoyance: I needed to produce a summary of my thesis quickly, so I used the Tools → AutoSummarize command—and got complete drivel. Correctly spelled drivel, mind you, but the text seemed to be chosen at random.

The Fix: Well, what did you expect? AutoSummarize has no idea what your document is about. It doesn't understand the contents. All it does is count the relative frequency of nouns, verbs, and so on and decide which are the most "important" based on frequency. Your chances of getting a usable summary for your thesis using AutoSummarize are negligible.

This suggests AutoSummarize is useless—but that's not entirely so. Say someone dumps a hundred-page report on you 10 minutes before the meeting at which you're supposed to elaborate on it—and the report is completely unformatted, so you can't skim through it and read the headings. You might try siccing AutoSummarize on the report and seeing what it produces. It doesn't take long, and you have nothing to lose.

Get an Instant Word Count

The Annoyance: I'm not paid by the word (though I'd love to be), but I use the Word Count feature to track my progress. The problem is, I'm getting bored with choosing Tools → Word Count to open the Word Count dialog box each time I want to check.

The Fix: All you need do is display the Word Count toolbar (see Figure 3-20): go to View → Toolbars or right-click any displayed toolbar and click the Word Count item. To force a recount, press Alt+C or click the Recount button.

Figure 3-20. Keep the Word Count toolbar open—or copy its controls to the menu bar or a toolbar—so that you can quickly see how many words your document contains.

> **tip**
>
> If you don't want to waste space by leaving the Word Count toolbar open, Ctrl+Alt-drag its controls to the menu bar (if there's space) or another toolbar that you keep open all the time. When you close the document or exit Word, save your changes to the template if Word prompts you to do so.

Correct a Way-Off Page Count

The Annoyance: When I open a long document, Word repaginates part of it, but the total number of pages is wrong.

The Fix: You might suspect that Word is just as lazy as your average donkey and that this partial repagination is its attempt to fob you off with a half-completed chore. But in fact, Word is probably more anxious to spend your precious processor cycles on spellchecking and grammar-checking your document to within an inch of its life. Repagination can wait until squiggly underlines of both colors have been applied.

If your need for repagination is transitory, press Ctrl+End to go to the end of the document, choose View → Print Layout to force repagination, and give Word a moment or two to comply. Press Shift+F5 to return to your last edit in the document. (Alternatively, if you have the Word Count toolbar displayed, click the Recount button. That too forces repagination.) If you need to force repagination on a regular basis, add the Repaginate command to a convenient keyboard shortcut (see the sidebar "Customize Your Keyboard Shortcuts") or menu, as described here:

1. Choose Tools → Customize to open the Customize dialog box, and then click the Commands tab.

2. Click Tools in the Categories list.

3. Drag the Repaginate command from the righthand list to the menu on which you want it to appear. For example, drag it to the Tools menu, wait for the menu to display, drag the command to the appropriate position, and then drop it.

The next time you exit Word, save your Normal template if Word prompts you to do so.

CUSTOMIZE YOUR KEYBOARD SHORTCUTS

To customize your keyboard shortcuts, select Tools → Customize, click the Commands tab, and then click the Keyboard button. In the "Save changes in" drop-down list in the Customize Keyboard dialog box, make sure the appropriate template or document is selected. For example, select Normal.dot if you want to affect your Normal template and all documents based on it.

To add a keyboard shortcut, click the appropriate category (for example, File) in the Categories listbox, and then select the command in the Commands list. Click in the "Press new keyboard shortcut" box, and then press the shortcut you want to use. Check the "Currently assigned to" readout to see if the shortcut is already assigned to a command; if so, decide whether to overwrite it or try another shortcut. Click the Assign button to assign the new shortcut.

To remove a keyboard shortcut, click the category and then select the command. Click the shortcut in the "Current keys" list, and then click the Remove button.

When you've finished customizing shortcuts, close the Customize Keyboard dialog box and the Customize dialog box. Shift-click the File menu, choose Save All, and save your changes to the document or template if Word prompts you to do so.

Remove Useless Smart Tags

The Annoyance: Some Smart Tags are useful—especially "paste to match existing text"—but Smart Tags for dates and names seems fairly useless to me. How likely is it that you will type a person's name and suddenly realize you need to email her?

The Fix: You tell me. But if you circulate a report, the recipients might want to be able to click a Smart Tag to grab the phone number or address of someone mentioned in it who has done something egregious.

Still, if you want to get rid of the Smart Tags you don't use, choose Tools → AutoCorrect Options and click the Smart Tags tab (see Figure 3-21). Uncheck the boxes in the Recognizers list for the items you don't want Word to use Smart Tags for, or uncheck the "Label text with smart tags" box if you want to stop using Smart Tags altogether. (Word 2000 doesn't offer Smart Tags, so you need worry about them only in Word 2003 and Word XP.)

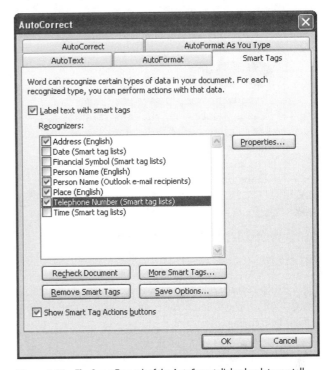

Figure 3-21. The Smart Tags tab of the AutoCorrect dialog box lets you tell Word which types of Smart Tags you want to create, or turn off Smart Tags completely.

To remove the Smart Tags from a document, click the Remove Smart Tags button. Word then reads you the riot act (see Figure 3-22) to make sure you really want to get rid of the Smart Tags. Click the Yes button to proceed.

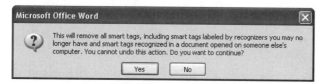

Figure 3-22. You can easily remove all Smart Tags from a document.

If you want Word to save your Smart Tags in a document, click the Save Options button on the Smart Tags tab of the AutoCorrect dialog box to display the Save dialog box, and then check the "Embed smart tags" box.

Stop Word from Searching the Web for Help

The Annoyance: Almost every Help search I do makes Word 2003 hit the Web for the response rather than reading a local help file.

The Fix: Word is usually searching both locally and on the Web. And not without reason: many of the best results for complex problems are in the Microsoft Knowledge Base (*http://support.microsoft.com*) rather than in the help files. But if you're looking for a quick answer to a straightforward question, or if you have a slow Internet connection, this can drive you up the wall.

To stop this annoyance, choose Help → Customer Feedback Options to display the Service Options dialog box and click the Online Content item in the Category list (see Figure 3-23). Clear the "Show content and links from Microsoft Office Online" box to prevent Office from accessing Microsoft Office Online at all. If you want to prevent Help from searching online but leave Microsoft Office Online available for other purposes, clear just the "Search online content when connected" box.

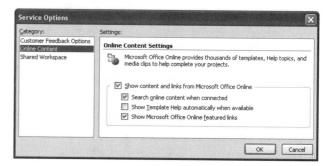

Figure 3-23. The Service Options dialog box is about the last place most people would look for the option that controls whether Word searches the Microsoft Office Online site for Help.

Get Rid of the Office Assistant

The Annoyance: The wretched animated paperclip keeps appearing—every time I try to get help from Office, and sometimes even when I'm just working. How can I get rid of it?

The Fix: Some people presumably love the Office Assistant characters—Clippit (the paperclip), Rocky the Dog, the Office Cat, the Genius, Mother Nature—but I've never met these people. Everyone who mentions the Office Assistant wants to get rid of it.

To prevent the Office Assistant from appearing, right-click the Office Assistant character that's currently bugging you and click Properties on the shortcut menu. On the Options tab of the Office Assistant dialog box (see Figure 3-24), uncheck the "Use the Office Assistant" box and click the OK button.

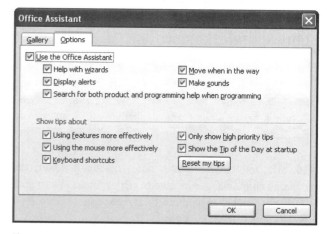

Figure 3-24. Even if you choose not to disable the Office Assistant fully, you can curb its interfering habits here.

The Options dialog box also lets you control what the Office Assistant does if you decide to use it. The top section of the tab gives you options for controlling whether the Office Assistant offers help with wizards, displays alerts when something is wrong, moves when it is in the way (a good idea if you're using the Assistant), makes sounds (usually a bad idea), and searches for both product and programming help when you're programming. The Show Tips About section lets you control which items, if any, the Office Assistant offers you tips about. For example, the "Using features more effectively" option controls whether the Office Assistant pops up suggestions about letter writing when you type one of its trigger phrases for letters.

What if you want the Office Assistant back? Simply choose Help → Show the Office Assistant, and the brute is back with you. Invoking the Office Assistant like this checks the "Use the Office Assistant" box on the Options tab of the Office Assistant dialog box, so you'll need to uncheck this checkbox when you want peace and quiet again.

Want the Office Assistant off your computer for all eternity (or until your next "upgrade" of Office)? Open the Control Panel and use the Add or Remove Programs feature to change your installation of Office. Expand the Office Tools item, click the symbol box next to Office Assistant, and then choose Not Available in the drop-down menu. Finish the installation routine, and the Office Assistant will be gone for good.

FIELDS

Make Fields Visible

The Annoyance: I keep tripping over the hidden fields in my documents. Isn't there a way of making them visible?

The Fix: Choose Tools → Options and click the View tab. In the "Field shading" drop-down list, choose "When selected" or "Always," as appropriate, and then click the OK button. Fields then appear with gray shading.

Use Cross-References to Keep Text Updated in Different Parts of the Document

The Annoyance: I need to enter the same text in several different parts of a document. Copy and paste works well enough, but I need to keep the text updated.

The Fix: The best solution is to keep the text updated in one part of the document and use cross-references to insert it in the other places. You can then update the cross-references automatically after you change the text. The easiest way to update all the fields in a document is to select the entire document (press Ctrl+A or choose Edit → Select All) and then press F9 or Alt+Shift+U.

You can make a cross-reference refer to a bookmark, a heading, a footnote or endnote, a figure or table, an equation, or a numbered item (such as a page number). For a text item in a paragraph, use a bookmark. Select the text, choose Insert → Bookmark, type the bookmark name, and click the Add button.

To insert the cross-reference, choose Insert → Reference → Cross-Reference. In the Cross-reference dialog box (see Figure 3-25), select "Bookmark" in the "Reference type" drop-down list, select "Bookmark text" in the "Insert reference to" drop-down list, choose the bookmark in the "For which bookmark" list, and click the Insert button.

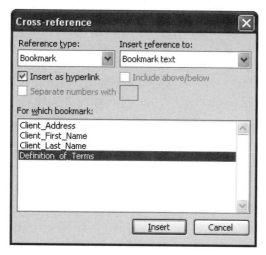

Figure 3-25. A cross-reference to a bookmark is the easiest way of keeping text updated in multiple parts of a document.

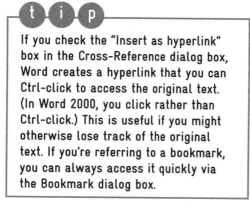

If you check the "Insert as hyperlink" box in the Cross-Reference dialog box, Word creates a hyperlink that you can Ctrl-click to access the original text. (In Word 2000, you click rather than Ctrl-click.) This is useful if you might otherwise lose track of the original text. If you're referring to a bookmark, you can always access it quickly via the Bookmark dialog box.

Insert a Date That Doesn't Change

The Annoyance: When I use a template that includes a date field (for example, on a letter), the date shown is always the date when I print the letter, even if I'm printing a fresh copy of a letter that was last changed five years ago.

The Fix: As is often the case, Word is trying to help, but you just don't appreciate its efforts.

If the date field you want to affect is in a document you just opened, and it's showing the correct date (for example, five years ago), click in the field and either lock it (press Ctrl+F11) or unlink it (press Ctrl+Shift+F11) so that it won't change. Then save your document.

To prevent the problem from occurring in new documents you create based on the template containing the field, open the template and choose Insert → Date and Time. In the Date and Time dialog box (see Figure 3-26), select the date format, uncheck the "Update automatically" box, and click the OK button. Choose File → Save to save the changes, and then choose File → Close to close the template.

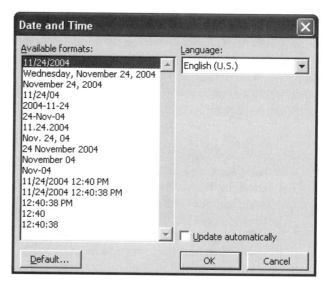

Figure 3-26. To prevent the date (and time) in a document from being updated when you save or print it, uncheck the "Update automatically" box in the Date and Time dialog box.

Formatting and Layout

As you saw in the previous chapter, getting text into a document and doing basic editing provides plenty of annoyances—but formatting and layout offer even more. Don't worry, though: this chapter shows you how to wrestle most of these annoyances into submission, and how to work around the rest.

Your first order of business is to sort out *Normal.dot*. If the default font, view, and margins aren't to your liking in *Normal.dot*, they won't be in any documents based on it either—which means all documents that you don't specifically base on another template.

Next up are direct formatting tips, numbering woes, and advice on using Word's styles. Formatting is easy to apply in moderation but can quickly become confusing, especially when Word starts switching the language on you without warning. Automatic numbered lists can be a great time-saver—when they work. Styles can save you even more time, provided that you know how to create them, apply them effectively, and deal with their quirks.

The second half of the chapter grapples with placing graphics where you want them (and making sure they don't get deleted by accident), controlling Word's enthusiasm for creating hyperlinks, using tabs correctly, and creating complex headers and footers.

NORMAL.DOT AND DEFAULT SETTINGS

Change the Default Font in Normal.dot

The Annoyance: The default font in all my documents is too small to read. I can zoom in, but I shouldn't need to. Anyway, I want to use Arial as the default font.

The Fix: It's easy to bend Word to your will. Start a new, blank document, choose Format → Font, select the font and size that suit you, click the Default button, and then click Yes in the confirmation dialog box to update the Normal template.

Change the Default Layout in Normal.dot

The Annoyance: Okay, so I've fixed the default font. That's an improvement—but there's a long way to go. What about getting Word to start with the view and the zoom I prefer?

The Fix: Your wish is my command—well, this time:

1. Open *Normal.dot*. To find *Normal.dot*, choose Tools → Options, click the File Locations tab, and check the "User templates" readout. (The default location is the *%userprofile%\Application Data\Microsoft\Templates* folder.) Open this folder in a Windows Explorer window, right-click *Normal.dot*, and choose Open from the shortcut menu.

2. Set the view and zoom you want.

3. Choose File → Save, and then choose File → Close.

4. Restart Word, and enjoy the difference.

Change the Default Margins

The Annoyance: The default left and right margins are 1.25". Why aren't they the standard 1" used on most business documents?

The Fix: Word uses 1.25" margins in case you want to write a letter. (Yes, this is apparently true.)

To change the default margins:

1. Open a document based on *Normal.dot*. You can do so by simply starting Word (assuming you're using a normal startup) and choosing File → New Blank Document, or by clicking the New Blank Document button on the Standard toolbar.

2. Choose File → Page Setup, and click the Margins tab if it's not displayed.

3. Set the margins you want.

4. If necessary, choose paper settings on the Paper tab or layout settings (such as the header or footer position) on the Layout tab. In Word 2000, the relevant tab is called Paper Size; there's also a Paper Source tab.

5. Click the Default button, and then click the Yes button in the confirmation dialog box (see Figure 4-1).

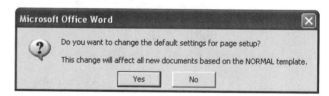

Figure 4-1. Change the default margins in the Normal template to affect the margins in all documents based on it.

DIRECT FORMATTING

Control Formatting When You Paste

The Annoyance: When I paste material from another part of the document or a different document, Word sometimes carries through the formatting and sometimes doesn't.

The Fix: Two separate things are happening here.

First, if the text that you paste includes a paragraph mark, it brings its style along with it. So, normally, when you paste one or more complete paragraphs, you get the styles that were applied to those paragraphs. You can override this behavior by choosing Edit → Paste Special, selecting the "Unformatted text" option, and clicking the OK button. This makes the paragraph you paste take on the style of the paragraph into which you paste it, which is what happens if you paste material that doesn't include a paragraph mark.

To make Word display paragraph marks, choose Tools → Options, click the View tab, and check the "Paragraph marks" box. To toggle the display of all formatting marks (including paragraph marks, spaces, and tabs), click the Show/Hide ¶ button on the Standard toolbar.

Second, the smart-cut-and-paste feature in Word 2003 and Word XP tries by default to apply the appropriate style when you paste a paragraph of text. Choose Tools → Options, click the Edit tab, check the "Smart cut and paste" box if it's unchecked, and click the Settings button to display the Settings dialog box. Uncheck the "Smart style behavior" box if you want to handle the styles manually. Uncheck the "Merge pasted lists with surrounding lists" box if you want to ensure that Word doesn't change the style of list items that you paste within another list.

If you leave these boxes checked, you can quickly change the formatting of text you've pasted in Word 2003 or Word XP by clicking the Paste Options Smart Tag and choosing the appropriate option from the pop-up menu (see Figure 4-2).

Company Integration Program

Figure 4-2. Use the Paste Options Smart Tag to adjust the formatting of text you've pasted in Word 2003 or Word XP.

Bring Spaced-out Pasted Text Down to Earth

The Annoyance: Here's a problem I run into all the time when I'm in either Word 2003 or Word 2004 for the Mac. Let's say I'm surfing the Web and find something really interesting. I select the text I want, copy it, open a Word document, and paste it in. Regardless of whether I use Paste Special or just plain Paste, the formatting is way off on every line—I get all sorts of weird tabs and spaces. This also happens with text from PDF files, Notepad, TextEdit, and occasionally older versions of Word. Why can't I just paste in the text without any formatting?

The Fix: Choosing Edit → Paste Special and selecting the "Unformatted text" option should give you plain text. If not, on Windows you can try bouncing the text through Notepad first: paste it into Notepad, copy it again, and then paste it into Word. That should get rid of any formatting nasties.

If the text still contains extra spaces and tabs, they're probably included in the PDF or web page for layout purposes. To remove them, either Alt-drag to select the column of unnecessary tabs or spaces (see "Hack Out Columns of Tabs or Spaces" in Chapter 3) or replace whitespace (^w; see "Find Any Character, Digit, or Letter" in Chapter 3) with a single space or tab, depending on the layout.

Copy Intricate Formatting Instantly

The Annoyance: After some intensive work in the Font dialog box, I've finally got this word formatted exactly right. Now I need to apply the same formatting to five other words in the document. Groan!

The Fix: Swallow that groan. You can fix this annoyance easily in any of three ways:

- Select the word you've formatted, double-click the Format Painter button on the Standard toolbar (it's the button with the paintbrush icon), and then drag over each of the words you want to format, in turn. Press Escape (or click the Format Painter button again) when you've finished.

- Copy the formatted word, paste it in over the first of the other words, select the pasted word, and retype the required word. Repeat as necessary. This method isn't as good as using the Format Painter button, but it's sometimes useful.

- Create a character style from the formatted word. Select the word, click in the Style listbox at the top of the Style drop-down list, and type the name for the new style. You can then apply the style to selected text from the Style drop-down list.

HOW WORD'S FORMATTING WORKS

Word offers enough formatting options to stop a Humvee in its tracks—and more than enough to waste plenty of your time. Here's what you need to know:

- A *style* is a collection of formatting for a regular paragraph, a list paragraph, a table cell, or one or more characters. For example, a Heading 1 style for top-level headings might use a different font than normal body text, a larger font size, different indentation, and extra space before and after it. Word 2003 and Word XP support four types of styles: paragraph styles, list styles, table styles, and character styles. Word 2000 and earlier versions have only paragraph styles and character styles. If you use a version of Word that supports list styles and table styles but need to work with people who use Word 2000 or earlier versions, it's best not to use list styles or table styles. Styles are the preferred way of applying almost all formatting in Word, because you can quickly find or change a style globally in your documents.

- *Direct formatting* is formatting that you apply directly to an object, such as a word or paragraph. For example, you might apply bold or italic formatting to a word or change the alignment or line spacing of a paragraph. When you use direct formatting, which you should do seldom rather than as a rule, use it in addition to applying a style (rather than instead of applying a style).

- *Page layout formatting* controls the overall layout of the page: the paper size and orientation (portrait or landscape), the page margins, the header and footer position, and so on.

- *Section formatting* controls the layout of a particular section (subdivision) of a document. The page layout of a document can vary from one section to another.

- A *theme* is a suite of canned elements (such as a background image, bullets, and icons) and styles (for headings, the Normal style, and hyperlinks) designed to give a document a particular look. The styles in a theme override those in the document's template. The main purpose of themes is to make web pages created using different templates share the same look, but you can also use themes in other documents if you choose.

Here's the best way to apply formatting:

1. Create a template that contains the styles you need.

2. Apply a paragraph style to each non-list and non-table paragraph, as your primary means of formatting. Apply a list style to each list paragraph and a table style to each table paragraph or cell. (If your documents need to be fully compatible with Word 2000 or earlier versions, use paragraph styles rather than list styles and table styles.)

3. Apply a character style when needed to pick out a particular element in a paragraph. For example, if a word must be bold and italic, you might apply a Bold Italic style that you have created (as described in "Get Started with Styles," later in this chapter).

4. Apply direct formatting only when absolutely necessary. If you need to apply the same direct formatting to multiple items in the same document, create a style for it.

Apply Sets of Formatting Instantly

The Annoyance: It's taking me hours to format all these paragraphs by hand.

The Fix: You need to use styles. See "Styles," later in this chapter, for details on how to save yourself many hours of effort.

Change Capitalized Text to Small Caps

The Annoyance: In every document my boss types, he formats THE HEADINGS IN ALL UPPERCASE instead of using a heading style. The Caps Lock key must be his best friend. I need to change all the headings to regular capitalization and small caps. I almost wish he were dictating instead.

The Fix: Sorry, there's no one-click fix for this one. In Word 2003 or Word XP, select the first offending heading, then hold down Ctrl as you select each of the other headings in turn. With all of them selected, choose Format → Change Case to display the Change Case dialog box (see Figure 4-3). Choose the Title Case option, and click the OK button. Then press Ctrl+Shift+K to apply small caps. (Alternatively, choose Format → Font, check the "Small caps" box, and then click the OK button.) Word 2000 sadly doesn't support multiple selections, so you'll need to treat the headings one at a time.

Selecting Title Case in Word's Change Case dialog box makes the first letter of each word uppercase and the remaining letters lowercase. This drives writers and editors up the wall, because words such as conjunctions and short prepositions should usually be lowercase in headings. You can create a macro that applies proper capitalization to most of the words in the headings, though; see "Apply Proper Capitalization" in Chapter 8.

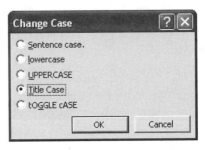

Figure 4-3. The Change Case dialog box is the quickest way to change uppercase text to Title Case.

Replace Spaced Indents with Real Indents

The Annoyance: One of my "traditional" colleagues just *loves* to put four spaces at the beginning of each paragraph. I think it might be a typewriter thing. Anyway, I need to replace those spaces with a first-line indent, but I can't figure out how to do so, as there are other instances of four or more spaces in the document.

The Fix: This sounds like a double-replace job. Replace ^p and four spaces with ^p and a distinctive string—for example, ^pfirstlineindent. Then replace firstlineindent (or whatever) with nothing but the paragraph formatting you need: delete the contents of the "Replace with box," choose Paragraph in the Format drop-down list, specify the indentation level, click OK, and click Replace All. Alternatively, once you've deleted the whitespace (by replacing ^p and four spaces with ^p), you can use a style to apply a first-line indent to all of the paragraphs. See the "Styles" section later in this chapter for more on using styles in Word.

Reveal Formatting and Codes

The Annoyance: Help! I'm a (maybe) recovering WordPerfect user, and I'm finding it hard to see which formatting is applied to a word. Why is there no Reveal Codes option?

The Fix: Because—in theory—you don't need Reveal Codes in Word. There are other ways of checking the formatting applied to an item:

- To check font formatting, choose Format → Font and check the settings in the Font dialog box (or look at the status of the controls on the Formatting toolbar).

- To check paragraph formatting, choose Format → Paragraph and check the settings in the Paragraph dialog box. (Again, you can look at some of the buttons on the Formatting toolbar for settings such as alignment.)

- To check tab formatting, look at the ruler or choose Format → Tabs and check the settings in the Tabs dialog box.

- To check the style, display the Style area at the left of the document window (choose Tools → Options, click the View tab, and set a suitable width—say, 1"—in the "Style area width" box). The Style area is available only in Normal view and Outline view.

> **If you work with the Style area displayed, you can double-click a style name in the Style area to open the Style dialog box with that style automatically selected.**

- To check the language, choose Tools → Language → Set Language and look at the setting in the Language dialog box.

- To check the page setup, choose File → Page Setup and look at the settings in the Page Setup dialog box.

In other words, the settings are all over the place, and you need to know where to turn to learn particular pieces of formatting information.

Word 2000, in response to 10 or so years of complaints (from Word users as well as WordPerfect users), introduced another option for getting formatting information: the "What's This?" feature. You choose Help → What's This? or press Shift+F1,

the mouse pointer displays an arrow with a question mark, and you click a paragraph to display details of its formatting (see Figure 4-4). Click further paragraphs as necessary, and then press Escape to restore the pointer to its normal self. This is better than the previous options, but not much.

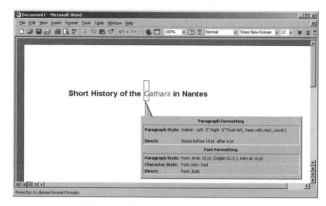

Figure 4-4. The "What's This?" formatting pop up is the precursor to Word 2003 and Word XP's Reveal Formatting task pane.

Word 2003 and Word XP improve matters a little with the Reveal Formatting task pane (see Figure 4-5), which you display by choosing Format → Reveal Formatting. This task pane provides a breakdown of the font, paragraph, and section formatting, plus any other relevant formatting—for example, table formatting if the selection is within a table. You can click one of the links to reach the relevant dialog box for more details.

If Word's Reveal Formatting task pane doesn't show you enough detail on which formatting is applied to which object, try CrossEyes ($49.99), by Levit and James (*http://www. levitjames.com/crosseyes/CrossEyes.html*). CrossEyes (see Figure 4-6) provides a pane at the bottom of the document that shows you all the details of the formatting.

Adjust the Conversion from WordPerfect

The Annoyance: My WordPerfect document got horribly mangled when I opened it in Word.

The Fix: You need to adjust the conversion parameters for WordPerfect. Choose Tools → Options, click the Compatibility tab (see Figure 4-7), and select the appropriate version of WordPerfect in the "Recommended options for" drop-down

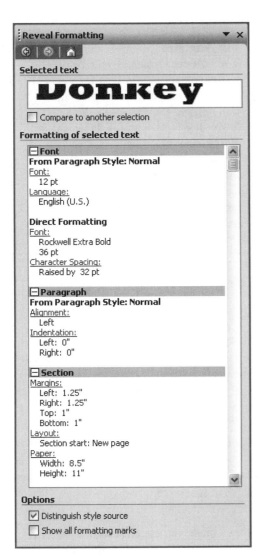

Figure 4-5. Word's Reveal Formatting pane is no substitute for WordPerfect's Reveal Codes feature, but it's the best that Word offers.

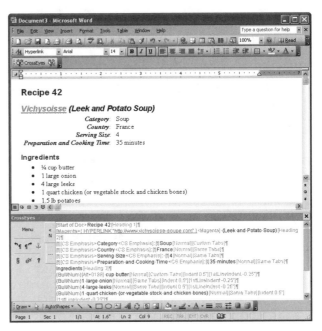

Figure 4-6. CrossEyes lets you see exactly which formatting is applied to which part of a document.

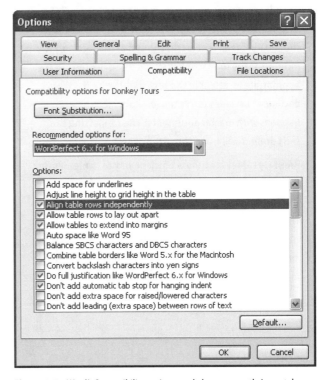

Figure 4-7. Word's Compatibility options can help you correctly import documents in other formats, but you may need to tweak the settings manually to get near-perfect results.

list—for example, "WordPerfect 6.x for Windows." The "Recommended options for" setting makes Word check the appropriate boxes in the Options list.

Try opening the WordPerfect document again with those settings in place. If you can identify particular problems, display the Options dialog box again and check or uncheck the appropriate boxes in the Options list manually. This will take some experimentation and may be worth doing only if you have a handful or more of WordPerfect documents that you need to convert. Otherwise, it may be easier simply to fix any mangled formatting.

WHY WORD AND WORDPERFECT DISAGREE ON FORMATTING

Word and most versions of WordPerfect are destined to disagree on formatting matters because they use different means of marking the formatting. WordPerfect considers a document to be a stream of characters flowing from the start of the document to the end of the document, and it embeds formatting codes at the appropriate places in that stream. For example, if a word in a WordPerfect document should be bold, there's a bold-on code, the text of the word, and then the bold-off code, all within the same text stream.

Word looks at formatting differently. In Word, each document is built of section, paragraph, and character units. The text of a Word document is saved more or less as plain text, with the formatting kept separate at the bottom of the file in a property table stored in the default section break. (If a document is divided up into sections, the property table for each section is stored in the section break that marks the end of the section.) The location of the formatting is stored using pointers to the appropriate locations in the text. This is why, if a Word document becomes corrupted (or simply too complex, as happens with master documents), the formatting can shift dramatically, or disappear altogether.

Property tables are a more efficient way of implementing formatting, but you can't simply look at the document stream and see which code is placed where. Word and WordPerfect include converters that do a good job of translating each method of formatting into the other method, but they may be unable to handle very complex formatting.

If Word's conversion of your WordPerfect document is still less than acceptable after you've tweaked the conversion options and you still have access to WordPerfect, open the document in WordPerfect and save it in Rich Text Format (RTF) or HTML format. Word will probably be able to read those formats more accurately, but you may lose advanced WordPerfect formatting and features in the conversion to RTF or HTML.

Embed Fonts in Documents You Send to Others

The Annoyance: I spent a while formatting our family newsletter so that it looked just perfect. But when our friends opened it on their computers, the fonts were all wrong: bland fonts were substituted for the ones I used. Worse, the font changes had messed up the layout.

The Fix: You've probably figured out what's wrong: your friends' computers don't have the fonts you used, so Word substituted other fonts. When the substitutes take up different amounts of space, the layout can change. The combined effects can be distressing.

There are two things you can do about this. First—yes, you've guessed it—you can simply stick to the fonts that everybody has, such as Arial, Times New Roman, and Tahoma. Documents that use only those fonts can look pretty bland, though. The second (and probably preferable) option is to embed the fonts you use in the document so that they'll be there for your friends to see. Here's how:

1. Choose Tools → Options and click the Save tab.

2. Check the "Embed TrueType fonts" box to embed the complete character sets of all the TrueType fonts you've used in the document.

3. Embedding the complete character sets bulks up the file size and is necessary only if you want your friends to be able to edit your document. It's usually best to also check the "Embed characters in use only" box to keep the bloating down a bit. If you use Word 2003 or Word XP, you may also want to check the "Do not embed common system fonts" box; your friends should have these fonts on their PCs.

4. Click the OK button.

5. Save the document. Check the file size before sending it via email; if you've used a lot of fonts and embedded the full character sets, it could be pretty hefty.

Make Word Display All Your Fonts

The Annoyance: I've installed a load of fonts, but Word's Font drop-down list and Font dialog box offer me only Device Font in three different sizes: 10cpi, 12cpi, and 17cpi. I figured out that "cpi" stands for "characters per inch," but that doesn't really help me. How can I introduce Word to my fonts?

The Fix: Word has somehow been set to print with a Generic/Text Only printer. You'll get similar effects (see Figure 4-8) if you've installed a very limited printer, such as a dot-matrix printer.

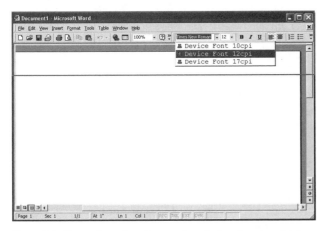

Figure 4-8. If most of your fonts disappear from the Font drop-down list, it usually means that you've got a Generic/Text Only printer installed.

Choose File → Print, click the Name drop-down list in the Print dialog box, select another printer, and click the Close button. Back in the document, check the Font drop-down list or the Font dialog box; your fonts should have flocked back, ready for use.

> Unless you, another user, or a macro has selected the Generic/Text Only printer or the limited printer in Word, chances are that it's set as your PC's default printer. To change the default printer, go to Start → Printers and Faxes, right-click the appropriate printer, and choose Set as Default Printer.

If the Name drop-down list in the Print dialog box doesn't contain any other printers, go to Start → Printers and Faxes and click the "Add a Printer" link in the Printer Tasks list. (If the Printers and Faxes item doesn't appear on the Start menu, go to Start → Control Panel → Printers and Other Hardware → Printers and Faxes.) Follow the Add Printer Wizard to add whichever printer should be installed.

If your fonts still don't show up, make sure they're in your *Fonts* folder. The easiest way to get there is to choose Start → Control Panel → Appearance and Themes → Fonts. If your fonts are missing, you'll need to reinstall them.

Turn Off Automatic Style Updating

The Annoyance: I applied bullets to two paragraphs I selected—but Word applied the bullets to every paragraph in the document.

The Fix: First, click the Undo button or press Ctrl+Z to remove the bullets. Then check out these two possibilities:

- Your paragraphs aren't really paragraphs, but rather continued paragraphs with "soft returns" (Shift+Enter) between them. To check, click the Show/Hide ¶ button on the Standard toolbar to show formatting marks, and see if the paragraphs end with a ↵ mark rather than a ¶ mark. If so, choose Edit → Replace, enter ^l in the "Find what" box and ^p in the "Replace with" box, and then click the Replace All button.

- Word has decided automatically to update the style—and either it's the style that you've applied to all the paragraphs in the document, or it's the style on which all the styles you've used are based (in a default document, heading styles and some other styles are based on the Normal style). If the paragraphs aren't soft returns, this is probably what's wrong. In Word 2003 or Word XP, choose Format → Style, click the paragraph's style in the Styles and Formatting task pane, click the drop-down arrow, and choose Modify to display the Modify Style dialog box. Uncheck the "Automatically update" box and click the OK button. In Word 2000, choose Format → Style to display the Style dialog box, click the style name in the Styles list, and click the Modify button. In the Modify Style dialog box, uncheck the "Automatically update" box, click the OK button, and then click the Apply button in the Style dialog box.

Stop Word from Changing the Language

The Annoyance: Word keeps changing the language, even if I tell it to ignore special characters. I set it to English Australia, and it changes to English US, English UK, or, worse, French!

The Fix: Turn off automatic language detection: choose Tools → Language → Set Language, then uncheck the "Detect language automatically" box in the Language dialog box.

Automatic language detection increases the amount of processing power that Word requires, so it's a good idea to turn off detection if you don't need it.

To adjust the languages that Word tries to detect automatically as you work, open the Microsoft Office Language Settings application (for example, for Office 2003, choose Start → All Programs → Microsoft Office → Microsoft Office Tools → Microsoft Office 2003 Language Settings) and use the options on the Enabled Languages tab. You'll need to restart all the Office applications before your changes take effect.

NUMBERING

Correct Automatic Numbering in Numbered Lists

The Annoyance: Automatic numbering of lists is wonderful until it goes wrong, and then it's a screaming nightmare. I'm working on a 300-page document that contains about 200 numbered lists explaining procedures. Each time I start a new list, the numbering gets all flaky. First off, Word assumes that I'm trying to continue the previous list, even if it's five pages back. So I right-click in the new list and choose Restart Numbering to tell Word to restart numbering for the list. It's okay for about the first three items, then it gets confused and starts again with number 1. If I right-click in the list and tell Word to continue numbering for this paragraph (which should be number 4), it continues the whole list from the previous list. I've seen this behavior in several versions of Word. I figured the problem would be fixed in Word 2003, but if anything, it's even worse than Word 2000.

The Fix: Bad news. If this starts happening, you're unlikely to find happiness in your near future. What's going wrong? The short answer is that Word's *list templates*, the templates on which lists are based, get uncomfortably wobbly once you've created more than a few lists in a document. There are a few ways that you can try to correct the numbering, but the best way to work around this weakness in Word is *not* to create list templates by clicking the Numbering button on the Formatting toolbar or using the Bullets and Numbering dialog box. Let's take a look at your options for correcting (or avoiding) the problem.

Restart each list manually

If you have the patience, you can restart each list manually by right-clicking its first item and choosing Restart Numbering from the shortcut menu. Word 2000 doesn't offer this command, so you must display the Bullets and Numbering dialog box, make sure the correct list template is selected, choose the "Restart numbering" option, and click the OK button.

Wait until the document is finished before you restart numbering, because otherwise the numbers may walk as you insert further lists.

> ## Warning
> Restarting a list manually places a restart marker in the first paragraph of the list. If you copy or move this paragraph, the restart marker goes with it. So if you restart a list, then copy the first paragraph and paste it later in the document to create a new list, the numbering on the first list changes from "restart" to "continue," continuing the numbering of the previous list. You'll have to insert a new restart marker at the beginning of that list to preserve the correct numbering.

Restarting lists manually is seldom a satisfactory solution, but if your goal is simply to get the document printed with steps numbered correctly, it may be enough.

Reset the list templates

If your list numbering has gone wobbly, try resetting the list templates. Choose Format → Bullets and Numbering to display the Bullets and Numbering dialog box. On each tab, click each of the list templates in turn; if the Reset button is available for that list template, click the button and click the Yes button in the confirmation dialog box. When you've finished, click the Close button.

This may fix the numbering problems for the time being. It's usually worth trying, as it takes only a moment or two.

Use a designated style to start each list

If you have the time to design (or redesign) a template to help avoid numbering problems, you can designate a style to start each list. The paragraph in this style is not part of the list, but indicates that the list starts after it. For example, you might create a style named Body List Intro to use for the body paragraph that leads into each list:

1. In Word 2003 or Word XP, choose Format → Styles and Formatting, and then click the New Style button. In Word 2000, choose Format → Style, and then click the New Style button.

2. Name the new Style "Body List Intro" (or your preferred name). Select the style you'll use for your numbered list in the "Style for following paragraph" drop-down list.

3. Check the "Add to template" box.

4. Click the Format button and choose Paragraph from the pop-up menu. On the Indents and Spacing tab, choose Level 1 in the "Outline level" drop-down list. Click the OK button to close the Paragraph dialog box.

5. Click the Format button again, and choose Numbering from the pop-up menu. Click the Outline Numbered tab, click the list template on which you want to base the list, and then click the Customize button.

6. In the Level list, make sure that 1 is selected, so that you're working with the top level of the list—that is, the introductory paragraph that will not have a number. Delete the contents of the "Number format" box (unless you want your introductory paragraphs to bear a number). Click the More button (unless the dialog box is already displaying a Less button), select Body List Intro in the "Link level to style" drop-down list, and select Nothing in the "Follow number with" drop-down list.

7. In the Level list, click 2, and edit the format in the "Number format" box—for example, change it to "1." instead of ".1." (with the leading period). Select the appropriate numbered list style in the "Link level to style" drop-down list. Check the "Restart numbering after" box, and choose Level 1 in the drop-down list. Then click the OK button twice to close the Customize Outline Numbered List dialog box and the New Style dialog box.

When you need to create a list, create a new paragraph and apply your list-intro style to it. If the list-intro style is for a "real" paragraph, type the text for that paragraph. Press Enter to switch to the list style and start the numbering.

> If your documents don't consistently use a particular style as the lead-in to a list, one option is to create a style that consists of a nonprinting frame in the left (or right) margin of the page. You can then use this style to start your lists and enforce correct numbering without adding an extra paragraph or space above the list. Turn on the display of paragraph marks to make sure that the frame is visible so that you don't delete it by accident.

Use SEQ fields to work around list numbering

A useful workaround for list numbering is to use SEQ fields to define a sequence, rather than using Word's Bullets and Numbering feature. This way, you tell Word explicitly where each list starts, so it can't really get confused. Entering SEQ fields manually is tedious, but you can create AutoCorrect entries that enable you to enter them almost effortlessly.

> The advantage—and disadvantage—of using SEQ fields is that what you're creating isn't a list in Word's standard sense, so Word doesn't treat it as a list. This means that you may need to force renumbering on the paragraphs in the sequence to get the numbering right. Of course, if you're used to having to force Word to restart (or continue) numbering, that shouldn't be too much of a hardship.

To create the AutoCorrect entries:

1. Start a new paragraph, and press Ctrl+F9 to insert the curly braces that designate the start and end of a field code: {}. (Don't try typing the braces—that won't work.)

2. Click inside the braces and type `SEQ numlist \r1` to start a sequence of numbered fields starting with 1. Click after the closing brace and type a period and a tab.

3. Press Shift+Home to select what you've entered—that is, `{ SEQ numlist \r1 }`. and the tab. Choose Tools → AutoCorrect Options (Tools → AutoCorrect in Word 2000) to display the AutoCorrect dialog box with your selection entered in the With box. Make sure the "Formatted text" option is selected (it should be selected by default), and type `1]` in the Replace box. Click the OK button to add the AutoCorrect entry.

4. Edit your SEQ field so that it reads `{ SEQ numlist \n }`, which will make it enter the next number in the sequence. Type a period and a tab after the closing brace, and press Shift+Home to select from the insertion point back to the beginning of the line. Choose Tools → AutoCorrect Options (Tools → AutoCorrect in Word 2000) to display the AutoCorrect dialog box with your selection entered in the With box. Make sure the "Formatted text" option is selected (it should be selected by default), and type `x]` in the Replace box. Click the OK button to add the AutoCorrect entry.

5. Close the AutoCorrect dialog box, Shift-click the File menu, and choose Save All to save these new formatted AutoCorrect entries in *Normal.dot*.

That probably seemed like pretty fair gibberish, but you can now create a numbered list by typing `1]` and a tab at the start of the first paragraph and then `x]` and a tab at the beginning of each subsequent paragraph. Word automatically displays the correct numbers for the fields. Note that if you later go back and insert a new paragraph in the list, the numbers after it will be wrong. To update them, select the list and press F9.

> To begin a list with the numbering continued from the previous list, start the first item of the continuation list with `x]` rather than `1]`.

Watch Out for Revision Marks Wrecking Numbered Lists

The Annoyance: When I use revision marks, my numbered lists go berserk. How can I restore normality?

The Fix: If you've read the previous Annoyance, you'll know that Word's list templates can get unstable when they're used extensively. Revision marks make things worse, because in addition to all the numbering that Word already has to track for each list, it has to track which items have been deleted and which added.

As you might guess, most of these problems go away if you stop using revision marks—but that's usually not an option. Your next best choice is to ignore the problems with the revision marks until you (or your colleague) have finished the editing process and cleared the revision marks out of the document. At that point, the numbered lists will most likely look much better, if not perfect. You can then decide between working your way through the document and restarting each numbered list manually, or trying one of the other methods described in the previous Annoyance for hammering the list templates into shape.

Fix "Page X of Y" Numbering

The Annoyance: I've put a "page 1 of 50" numbering feature in my document's header, but it's not working correctly.

The Fix: This problem is most likely to occur if you're using Word 2000 without any Service Releases applied to it. Upgrading to Word 2000 SR-1 or a later Service Release should fix this problem, as should upgrading to a later version of Word.

If for any reason (for example, company policy) you can't upgrade:

1. Press Ctrl+End to move to the end of the document and click to put the insertion point in the last paragraph. Choose Insert → Bookmark, type a name (starting with a letter and including no spaces, though underscores are okay), and click the Add button.

2. Choose View → Header and Footer to switch to the header. Place the insertion point where you want the numbering, and type Page and a space. Click the Insert Folio button on the Header and Footer toolbar to insert the current page number, then type a space, of, and another space.

3. Choose Insert → Reference → Cross-reference (in Word 2000, choose Insert → Cross-reference), select "Bookmark" in the "Reference type" drop-down list and "Page number" in the "Insert reference to" drop-down list, and click the bookmark in the "For which bookmark" list. Uncheck the "Insert as hyperlink" box. Click the Insert button, and then click the Close button.

This is a clumsy and ugly fix, but it works.

Tame Word's List Indentation

The Annoyance: The way Word indents lists—especially nested lists—is very frustrating. If you leave it at the default settings, you very quickly end up with very short lines. Trying to reformat a line within the list so that it aligns the way I want it to is next to impossible.

The Fix: I doubt that this is what you want to hear, but you need to adjust the styles you use for the lists (whether they are list styles or paragraph styles) so that they have the indentation you want. Don't leave the styles at their default settings, because Word indents the lines generously, as you say. See "Get Started with Styles" and "Stop a Style Change in One Document from Affecting Other Documents" in the next section for instructions on modifying existing styles in Word and creating new ones.

Make Outline Numbering Work

The Annoyance: I can't make outline numbering work properly. It used to number only the paragraphs that had a Heading style applied. Now it seems to number paragraphs indiscriminately.

The Fix: It sounds as though you've applied outline levels to some of the styles in your document that don't need them. Click in one of the paragraphs that shouldn't have a number, choose Format → Paragraph, and check the selection in the "Outline level" drop-down list on the Indents and Spacing tab of the Paragraph dialog box. If it says anything other than "Body text," modify the style and set the outline level to "Body text."

Create Custom Outline Numbering

The Annoyance: I write many lecture notes in Word (not in Outline view, because I include sections that don't fit into the regular outline format). I find it especially annoying that when I have Word set to generate the next line of an outline and I press Return, Word automatically decides which format of numbers and letters to assign to the next level of the outline. For example, I would like to have a level of Roman numerals, followed by capital letters at the next level, followed by Arabic numerals. Word decides to put lowercase letters and then Arabic numerals. I also prefer to use parentheses, but Word automatically puts periods after the letters/numerals.

The Fix: If I understand you right, you should be able to fix this problem by customizing the outline numbering in the template attached to the document:

1. Choose Format → Bullets and Numbering, and then click the Outline Numbered tab.

2. Click the outline format closest to your needs, click the Customize button to display the Customize Outline Numbered List dialog box, and then click the More button to display the full dialog box (see Figure 4-9).

3. In the Level list, select the level of outline numbering that you want to customize, and then use the other controls in the dialog box to apply the numbering and formatting you want. Repeat the process for the other levels of the list that you want to change.

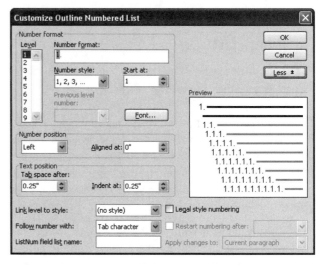

Figure 4-9. You can customize Word's outline numbered lists so that they automatically apply your preferred numbering formats to different list levels.

STYLES

Get Started with Styles

The Annoyance: Okay, I've got the hang of direct formatting: bold, italic, and all the font jazz; indents, line spacing, keep-with-next-and-don't-leave-it-hanging-out-alone-at-the-end-or-start-of-a-page, space before and after, and all that. But I can't get the hang of styles. How do I add them to the formatting I've applied?

The Fix: You don't—it's the other way around. Styles should be the basis of all the formatting you apply in Word. You'll be able to lay out your documents far faster, and with much less effort, by using styles rather than direct formatting.

Here's the best way to start using styles:

- Make a list of all the different paragraph types you'll need to use in a particular set of documents: headings, body text, various types of lists (numbered, bulleted, sublists, etc.), figures, tables, captions, notes, and so on. You will create paragraph, list, and table styles for each of these items.

- Make a second list of all the items within paragraphs that will need different formatting applied—for example, bold, italic, bold and italic, subscript, superscript, or underline. You will create character styles for all of these items.

- Create a new template for the documents (see "Templates" in Chapter 2). Save it, but don't close it.

- In the template, create a new paragraph, list, or table style (or modify an existing style) for each of the elements. See "Create a new style" and "Modify an existing style," next, for specifics.

- Still in the template, create a new character style for each of the character styles you identified.

- Turn off the "Update automatically" option for each style (more on this shortly).

- Test the template by entering text in it and applying the styles. Change the styles as necessary.

- Delete the text in the template, and set the remaining paragraph to the style with which you want each new document based on the template to start.

- Save the template, close it, and start a document based on it.

Create a new style

To create a new style, take the following steps:

1. With the template open, choose Format → Styles and Formatting to display the Styles and Formatting task pane, and then click the New Style button to display the New Style dialog box (see Figure 4-10). In Word 2000, choose Format → Style, and then click the New button in the Style dialog box.

2. In the New Style dialog box, type a descriptive name for the style and specify the style type: Paragraph, Character, Table, or List.

By giving your styles names that start with a word they have in common, you can make them appear close to each other in Word's style lists. For example, styles named "Body Italic" and "Body Special" will appear close to each other and be easy to apply, whereas "Italic Body" and "Special Body" will be widely separated and harder to find in the list.

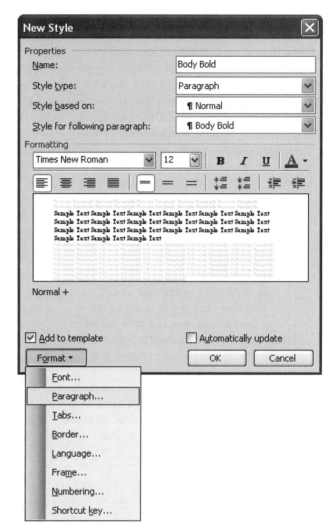

Figure 4-10. Set up the formatting of a new style in the New Style dialog box. The Modify Style dialog box offers almost exactly the same controls.

3. For a paragraph style or a table style, select the style on which the new style is based. The new style picks up all the formatting of the base style, which you can then change as needed. This enables you to create new styles quickly, but bear in mind that if you change the base style afterwards, the new style will inherit those changes. For a paragraph style, select the style for the following paragraph as well. For example, after a heading style, you might want a body text style.

4. Use the controls in the Formatting area to adjust the font formatting, alignment, spacing, and indentation. To make further adjustments, click the Format drop-down list and choose the appropriate item from the pop-up menu.

> The "Add to template" box controls whether a change you make to the style in a document is added to the document's template. When you're editing a style within a document, you must check this box to make Word save the changes back to the style in the template. When you're editing a style in the template itself, you don't need to check this box (although there's no harm in checking it).

5. If you want Word to update the style automatically when you change a paragraph that has the style applied, and then reapply the style throughout the document, check the "Automatically update" box. Usually it's best to uncheck this box and to update your styles manually. (This box doesn't apply to character styles.)

6. Click the OK button to close the New Style dialog box, and then save your changes to the template.

Modify an existing style

You can modify either one of the styles you've already created or one of Word's built-in styles. To do so:

- In Word 2003 or Word XP, choose Format → Styles and Formatting, click the style, click the drop-down arrow button, and choose Modify from the pop-up menu to display the Modify Style dialog box.

- In Word 2000, choose Format → Style to display the Style dialog box, select the style in the Styles list, and click the Modify button to display the Modify Style dialog box.

If you're working in a document rather than in the template itself, remember to check the "Add to template" box if you want Word to apply the change to the template as well as to the document in which you're working.

Remove Formatting with Default Paragraph Font/Clear Formatting

The Annoyance: Maybe I'm just dumb, but when I tried to apply the "Default Paragraph Font" to my body text paragraphs in Word 2000, the style didn't change. I tried it again, but still no good.

The Fix: The Default Paragraph Font item in the Style drop-down list and Style dialog box looks like a style, but in fact it's not: what it actually does is remove any additional formatting that has been applied to the paragraph so that it matches the current style definition. (You might also say that it simply reapplies the current style to the paragraph.)

> Press Ctrl+Spacebar to restore the font formatting of a selection to the style's default font formatting. Press Ctrl+Q to restore the paragraph formatting of a selection to the style's paragraph formatting.

Bypass the Styles and Formatting Task Pane

The Annoyance: The new task pane for styles in Word 2003 and Word XP is difficult to use, especially if you want to change the attributes of a large number of styles at the same time. The extra styles added when you bold a word become confusing. I think Word calls these "formats," but they appear in the same list.

The Fix: You can bypass the Styles and Formatting pane if you want. Choose Tools → Customize, click the Commands tab, and verify that the correct template (for example, *Normal. dot*) is selected in the "Save in" drop-down list. Click Format in the Categories list, then drag the Style... item (the one with the ellipsis after it, not the Style drop-down list) to a menu or toolbar. You can then go directly to the Style dialog box.

Make the Style Drop-Down List Show the Styles You Want

The Annoyance: Sometimes the Style drop-down list contains a really short list of styles, and usually the style I want isn't there. Other times, the list is way too long and I have to scroll for miles to find the style I want.

The Fix: Word is set to show only the styles used so far in the document—the idea being that these are the styles you're most likely to want to apply next. To display the full list, choose Format → Styles and Formatting and then select "All styles" in the Show drop-down list in the Styles and Formatting task pane. Click the X button to close the task pane, and then try the Style drop-down list again. To switch back to the shorter list of styles, choose "Available styles" in the Show drop-down list.

In Word 2000, the Style drop-down list shows only the styles used so far in the document. You can't change this setting, but you can force Word to display the full list by Shift-clicking the Style drop-down list.

> Even if you press Ctrl+Shift+S to select it, the Style drop-down list tends to be a clumsy way of applying styles to a document. To apply styles quickly, create a custom menu (perhaps called Style) or toolbar that contains the styles you use consistently. Also consider creating keyboard shortcuts for the styles you use the most.

Quickly Change One Style to Another

The Annoyance: Our annoying affiliate has sent us a slew of documents that use the wrong styles. I need to change all the styles to the right ones for our marketing communications template.

The Fix: Word's Replace feature can change the styles for you, and a macro using Replace can whip through all the documents in less time than it takes to make a cup of decent coffee. (Chapter 8 shows you how to record macros and edit them.) But Word 2003 and Word XP offer another possibility that you should know about: choose Format → Styles and Formatting, click the offending style name, click the drop-down arrow, and choose the "Select all instances" option. With all the instances of the style selected in the document, click the style to which you want to change these items. You probably won't want to use this feature for changing entire documents, but it's good for lighter-duty work.

Stop a Style Change in One Document from Affecting Other Documents

The Annoyance: I used to be able to redefine styles for the current document just by making a local formatting change, reapplying the style, and specifying that I wanted Word to update the style definition rather than reapply the existing definition. By default, that changed the style definition only in the current document; if I wanted the change to extend to all documents, I had to specifically say so by responding to a prompt asking whether I wanted the changes made to apply to all Word documents. Now it seems to do the latter by default, which is insane.

The Fix: I don't think that what you've described is actually happening, although the complex relationship between styles in documents and their templates, and the thorny issue of which styles get updated when, can make this appear to be happening. Let's take a look at how Word updates styles and how you can use styles most efficiently in your documents.

Update styles manually rather than "by example"

You can update styles in Word in two ways: "by example" (i.e., by changing the formatting of an instance of the style, and then reapplying the style, usually from the Style drop-down list), or by working in the Modify Style dialog box. Updating styles by example tends to be easier, because you can see the effects of the changes you make, but using the Modify Style dialog box is far less ambiguous, because you can specify whether to add the style change to the template and you can see whether the "Update automatically" box is checked or unchecked for the style. For this reason, it's best to always use the Modify Style dialog box to change styles.

If you *do* update a style by example and if the "Update automatically" box is unchecked for the style, Word displays a different Modify Style dialog box (see Figure 4-11) to let you decide whether to update the style or reapply it as it stands. You can also choose whether to automatically update the style from now on.

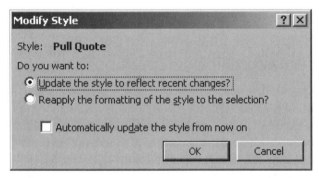

Figure 4-11. The Modify Style dialog box lets you choose whether to update the style with the formatting applied to the current selection or reapply the style as it stands to the selection.

Use styles efficiently

To use styles efficiently within your documents, follow these guidelines:

- Create styles only in your templates. Don't create styles in your documents—that's a recipe for confusion.

- Don't use the "Update automatically" option on your styles. Update them manually.

- Update styles only in the template.

- Standardize style names across your templates so that every style name has a consistent meaning and usage.

- If possible, avoid applying direct formatting on top of styles. Create further styles as necessary to achieve the same effect as the direct formatting would.

Redefine the Normal Style

The Annoyance: Why can't I redefine the Normal style by example like all the other styles?

The Fix: I don't know, but it sure is annoying. Perhaps it's because so many other styles are based on the Normal style; any change you make to the Normal style cascades down to each of the other styles based on it.

Here's how to redefine the Normal style:

- In Word 2003 and Word XP, choose Format → Styles and Formatting, right-click the Normal item in the Styles and Formatting pane, click the Modify button, and work in the Modify Style dialog box.

- In Word 2000, choose Format → Style to display the Style dialog box. Click the Normal item in the Styles list, click the Modify button, and work in the Modify Style dialog box.

> You can quickly access the Style drop-down listbox on the Formatting toolbar or the Style dialog box by pressing Ctrl+Shift+S. In Word 2003 and Word XP, press this key combination once to select the Style drop-down listbox if it's displayed, or to display the Style dialog box if the Styles drop-down list is not displayed. In Word 2000, press it once to select the Style dialog box.

Control the Style When You Paste

The Annoyance: I pasted a paragraph formatted with a Note style, and Word changed it into an item in the nearby numbered list. Hello?

The Fix: Word is trying to be friendly, but you need to train it to know your needs a bit better. I'm guessing that your Note style includes a bullet that causes Word to consider it part of a list. To fix the problem immediately, click the Paste Options Smart Tag and choose Paste List Without Merging. Word will restore the formatting of the paragraph you pasted.

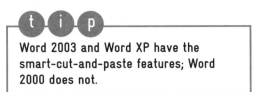

Word 2003 and Word XP have the smart-cut-and-paste features; Word 2000 does not.

To prevent Word from changing the style the next time you paste a list-like paragraph, choose Tools → Options, click the Edit tab, and then click the Settings button to display the Settings dialog box for smart cut and paste (see Figure 4-12). Uncheck the "Merge pasted lists with surrounding lists" box, and click the OK button to close each dialog box.

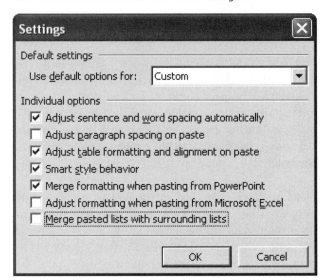

Figure 4-12. Uncheck the "Merge pasted lists with surrounding lists" box to prevent Word from changing the style of list paragraphs you paste into another list.

The other option you should know about here is the "Smart style behavior" box, which is useful when you're pasting text from one document to another. If you check this box, Word compares the style name of the text you paste with the style names in the destination document. If the names match, Word applies the style in the destination document. So, if you copy a Body paragraph from a document that uses 10-point font for that style to a document that uses 13-point font for Body, Word applies the 13-point style to the text. This behavior is usually helpful, but if you don't like it, uncheck the box.

Make the Pasted Text Take the Destination's Style

The Annoyance: When I add text from another document or web page into a Word document, I want the current style in my Word document to control the style of the pasted text. But instead, I end up with the pasted text being in "Normal (Web)" style or some other style with the wrong font.

The Fix: In Word 2003 and Word XP, you can click the Paste Options Smart Tag and choose Match Destination Formatting from the pop-up menu to make the pasted text take on the current style.

If you've turned off Smart Tags, or if you're using Word 2000, you're pretty much stuck using Paste Special to paste in the text without any formatting (choose Edit → Paste Special → Unformatted Text), unless you're prepared to create a macro for doing so. If you do a lot of pasting, creating a macro might be worthwhile (see "Create a 'Paste as Unformatted Text' Macro" in Chapter 8 for details). When you paste unformatted text, it receives the style currently applied to the paragraph in which you paste it.

Watch Out When Formatting Starts to "Slip"

The Annoyance: The formatting in my documents sometimes "slips"—for example, I applied boldface to some text, but it changed back to the regular font after I edited another section of the document and then returned to it.

The Fix: This isn't a fix, but an emergency warning. Formatting slipping like this means that the document is getting corrupted. Save the contents of your document in another format before the corruption gets worse. Choose File → Save As, select Rich Text Format in the "Save as type" drop-down list, and save the document as a rich text file. Close the document, and copy the rich text document to a backup medium. Then create a new Word document, choose Insert → File, insert the contents of the rich text file, and save the document. Check the document all the way through for missing text.

Avoid Layout Changes on Different Computers

The Annoyance: I created my report at home and formatted it to look great, with the graphics and page breaks in just the right places. But when I opened it at work, the layout had changed. All that work wasted!

The Fix: The problem is most likely that you're using different printer drivers on your home computer and work computer. If you need to ensure that a document's layout is exactly the same on two computers, use the same printer driver on both computers. If you need to be able to lay out the document at home and print it at work, check which printer driver your work computer is using, install that driver on your home computer too, and set that printer as the default printer while you create and work on the document. It doesn't matter if you don't *have* the printer, as long as you don't try to print the document to it.

> To set a printer as the default, choose Start → Printers and Faxes, right-click the printer, and choose "Set as Default Printer" from the shortcut menu.

If you need to ensure that a document's layout stays the same on computers on which you can't install printer drivers, your best bet is to save the document in PDF format. You'll need Adobe Acrobat or an application with similar capabilities (such as Jaws PDF Creator, available at *http://www.jawspdf.com*, or GhostWord, available from *http://source-forge.net/projects/ghostword* and other sources) to create the file, but people will then be able to view it exactly as you intended on most major operating systems.

> If creating a PDF isn't an option, you can avoid some potential changes in your documents by not using double tabs (set suitable tab stops instead) and hard page breaks (use the paragraph layout options instead). Your documents will still tend to look slightly different on different computers, though.

INSERTING AND POSITIONING GRAPHICS

Control the Size of a Pasted Graphic

The Annoyance: Whenever I paste in a bitmap graphic (e.g., a GIF or JPEG), Word decides for itself what size the image should be in my document. I would like for it to paste in the image at its natural size and then let me scale it if necessary. Lots of images only look good at their natural sizes, so I don't want Word messing around with the dimensions.

The Fix: Word is probably just trying to make sure that the picture fits within the margins or page size you're using. To force Word to display the picture at its full size, right-click the picture, choose Format Picture, click the Size tab, and set the Height and Width spinners to 100%.

Make Your Pictures Look Right

The Annoyance: I have trouble making pictures fit into my documents. There are so many steps for inserting pictures, with hidden formatting issues. How do I put a picture where I want it without messing up the entire document? Some pictures have even just disappeared!

The Fix: Inserting a picture in a document shouldn't be too much of a chore: choose Insert → Picture → From File and take it from there. Here are the six key points about positioning pictures:

- Word can put pictures either in line with the text or in the drawing layer (discussed in the next bulleted paragraph). A picture that's in line with the text moves the text around it. You can specify whether a picture is in line or not by right-clicking it, choosing Format Picture, clicking the Layout tab, and choosing "In line with text," "Square," or "Tight" to put the picture in line or "Behind text" or "In front of text" to put the picture in the drawing layer.

- The drawing layer is inaccurately named. It's actually a stack of sublayers, so you can put one picture or other graphical object on top of another. This can be useful for creating visual effects, but it can also explain why pictures sometimes disappear—something else is on top of them and blocking the view. You can rearrange the layers of objects by right-clicking a visible object and choosing the appropriate command from the Order submenu—for example, Send Backward or Bring in Front of Text.

- The drawing layer extends both in front of and behind the text layer, so you can put graphics behind the text or in front of it if you want.

- Pictures can be positioned either relative to a text object (for example, a paragraph) or relative to the page. To specify precise positioning, click the Advanced button on the Layout tab of the Format Picture dialog box and work on the Picture Position tab.

- The easiest way to resize a picture is by clicking it in the document and then dragging its sizing handles. For precise sizing, use the Size tab of the Format Picture dialog box.

- The basic way of putting a picture into a document is to *insert* it. This makes Word store all the picture information, so if you send the document to somebody else, the picture will be in the document. This is handy, but it increases the document's size. To keep down the size of a document (especially one that contains many pictures), you can *link* the picture instead of inserting it. The document then stores only a link to the picture and reads the picture in from the picture file. If the picture file is moved, or if you send the document to someone who can't access the picture file, the picture doesn't appear. Word also offers a hybrid option: insert the picture *and* link it back to its source. Word then uses the linked picture when it's available, which is useful for making the document show the latest picture available, and falls back on the inserted picture when the link is not available. To insert (or insert and link) a picture, click the arrow by the Insert button and choose the appropriate command from the pop-up menu.

Crop Pictures Outside Word

The Annoyance: The lads in the Sales department put together a nice brochure, complete with graphics they'd borrowed from the manufacturer's web site. They cropped the graphics in Word so that the manufacturer's name was hidden. But when the VP accidentally reset one of the graphics on his copy of the brochure, the manufacturer's name popped up, and the trouble started.

The Fix: The fix is simple enough: don't crop graphics in Word! If you need to make sure that a part of a graphic isn't visible in your document, crop the graphic before putting it into Word. Word's "cropping" just hides the specified amount at the edge of the picture.

Any graphics application worth having can crop pictures. (Even Paint, which is arguably barely worth having, can do rudimentary cropping: choose Image → Attributes and enter smaller measurements to crop parts of the south and east edges off a graphic.) The freeware IrfanView (*http://www. irfanview.com*) offers good cropping, along with a wealth of other features.

Get Rid of the Drawing Canvas

The Annoyance: When I click the icon to create a text box in the Mac version of Word, I get a nice, discreet box that I can resize as needed. But when I ask Word XP for a text box, it creates a half-page-sized box that takes over the document, and I have to spend a fair amount of time resizing the box and reformatting the text to get everything under control.

The Fix: Welcome to the Drawing Canvas, Word 2003 and Word XP's tool for helping you put together drawings consisting of AutoShapes. Word 2000 doesn't offer this annoyance—and, as you've discovered, neither do Word X and Word 2004 for the Mac.

To turn off the Drawing Canvas, choose Tools → Options, click the General tab, and uncheck the "Automatically create drawing canvas when inserting AutoShapes" box. You should then get a more manageable text box when you click the Text Box button on the Drawing toolbar.

Rotate Text to the Angle You Want

The Annoyance: When manipulating text in a table cell in Word, I can only rotate it 90 degrees one way or the other. In WordPerfect, I can rotate text 90, 180, 270, or 360 degrees. Obviously, I don't generally want to rotate 360 degrees, but it's helpful to have the 180-degree option.

The Fix: As you say, the Format → Text Direction command is limited to producing vertical text (either a 90-degree rotation or a 270-degree rotation)—and it works only for table cells.

If this isn't sufficient, what you need to do is create a graphic that contains the text you want to rotate. Create the text in Word, and then use a utility such as IrfanView (*http://www. irfanview.com*) to capture a graphic of the text and crop it down to the section you want. Insert the graphic, position it in front of or behind the text, and rotate it to the angle you want (see Figure 4-13).

Q. How many Word programmers does it take to change a light bulb?
A. None—that's a hardware problem.

Figure 4-13. For upside-down text, such as the answers to riddles or "Fold this sheet here" instructions, you need to use a graphic showing the text you want.

Wrap Text Around a Picture

The Annoyance: I'm trying to put a picture in my document with the text wrapping around it. But every time I insert the picture, Word puts it in line with the text.

The Fix: The immediate fix for this picture is to right-click it, choose Format Picture, click the Layout tab, and select the "In front of text" option. You can specify the horizontal alignment by clicking the Advanced button and choosing the appropriate positioning and wrapping settings in the Advanced Layout dialog box. Alternatively, drag the graphic to the desired position.

If you want to make Word always place pictures in a different way than in line with the text, choose Tools → Options, click the Edit tab, and choose the appropriate option (for example, "Behind text") in the "Insert/paste pictures as" drop-down list. Word 2000 doesn't offer this option.

Make Graphics Visible in Print Layout View

The Annoyance: Why is there a difference between page view and print view as far as graphics are concerned? I want to see all the graphics all the time, in any view.

The Fix: It sounds as though you've got Word's "Picture placeholders" option turned on. (The usual reason for turning on picture placeholders is to make the document scroll faster.) When this option is on, Print Layout view displays only placeholders—empty rectangles—to indicate where pictures appear. This option doesn't apply to Print Preview, so when you switch to Print Preview, your pictures appear.

To turn off placeholders, choose Tools → Options, click the View tab, and uncheck the "Picture placeholders" box. Word will then display all pictures in every view.

Display Object Anchors

The Annoyance: I deleted some text in a document—and Word deleted an unrelated graphic along with the text.

The Fix: What's happened is that the text you deleted included the object anchor for the graphic. The object anchor is a logical connector that links a floating graphic (or other floating object) to the text of the document.

Undo the deletion at once by pressing Ctrl+Z or choosing Edit → Undo. Then turn on the display of object anchors so that you can see where objects are anchored: choose Tools → Options, click the View tab, check the "Object anchors" box, and click the OK button. Select the graphic and check where the anchor is (see Figure 4-14) before deleting adjacent text.

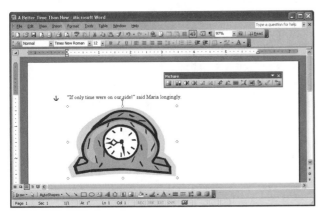

Figure 4-14. Object anchors add to the clutter in a document window, but they can help you avoid accidentally deleting graphics and other objects.

Position the Graphic Relative to the Page

The Annoyance: I found the perfect graphic, inserted it in my document, and sized it just right. But as soon as I start to edit the text of the document, the graphic goes walkabout.

The Fix: The problem is that the graphic is anchored to something that's moving—probably a paragraph. Right-click the graphic and choose Format Picture, click the Layout tab, click either the "Behind text" option or the "In front of text" option (whichever seems best for this picture), and then click the Advanced button. On the Picture Position tab, uncheck the "Move object with text" box. Select each of the "Absolute position" options (there's a horizontal one and a vertical one) and choose Page in the drop-down lists alongside these options.

> **Warning**
> If an anchor is contained in a table, you can position the object only relative to the table, not relative to the page.

Lock the Anchor When the Graphic Is in Place

The Annoyance: My object anchors are moving as I edit the text of my document. How can I get the anchors to stay where I cast them, even if I need to move the objects?

The Fix: Choose Format → Picture, click the Layout tab, and click the Advanced button. Check the "Lock anchor" box on the Picture Position tab to make the anchor stay in place. Uncheck the "Move object with text" box if you want to prevent the object from moving when you move the text to which the anchor is attached.

Create a Watermark

The Annoyance: I need to stamp "DRAFT" in red across each page of my report. I can put a floating graphic on each page, but they tend to move even if I try to anchor them.

The Fix: Word considers this to be a watermark. Choose Format → Background → Printed Watermark and use the options in the Printed Watermark dialog box.

To create a watermark, Word uses the header-and-footer layer. If the canned options in the Printed Watermark dialog box don't give you enough flexibility, you can tweak the watermark by choosing View → Header and Footer and working with the watermark directly. The header-and-footer layer is a special layer that enables you to position text or graphics anywhere on the page, not just in the areas conventionally reserved for headers and footers.

Position Lines Where You Need Them

The Annoyance: I have real problems with Word's line-drawing capabilities. For example, it's extremely difficult to create a "form" in Word with a bit of text (Name, Address, etc.) followed by a line extending to the right margin of the page.

The Fix: The easiest solution is not to use a drawing object for this; instead, set a tab at the right margin and use underscores as tab leaders. Type the introductory text and press Tab, and you'll get a line of underscores that extends from the last character to the right margin. Figure 4-15 shows an example.

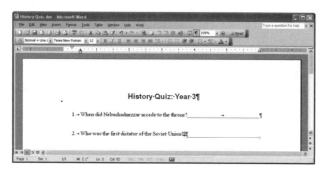

Figure 4-15. To create a line from the end of text to the right margin, you can either use a tab with underscores as the tab leader (as in the top example) or draw a line drawing object (as in the bottom example). If you draw a line, use absolute positioning relative to the character and paragraph, and lock the anchor.

If you choose to stick with a drawing object, you'll need to specify absolute positioning for it. Before you start, turn off the Drawing Canvas in Word 2003 and Word XP (see "Get Rid of the Drawing Canvas," earlier in this chapter). You may also want to display the object anchors: choose Tools → Options, click the View tab, and check the "Object anchors" box. Also on the View tab, check the "Text boundaries" box so you can see exactly where the right margin is.

See "Position the Graphic Relative to the Page," earlier in this chapter, for more details on positioning drawing objects.

Draw the line, then right-click it and choose Format AutoShape from the shortcut menu. Click the Layout tab in the Format AutoShape dialog box, click the Advanced button, and then click the Picture Position tab. Select the "Absolute position" option in the Horizontal area, enter a small mea-

surement such as 0.1" in the measurement box, and choose "Character" in the "To the right of" drop-down list. Select the "Absolute position" option in the Vertical area and choose "Paragraph" in the "Below" drop-down list. Check the "Move object with text" box, and then click the OK button to close each of the dialog boxes.

Back in the document, drag the line's anchor so that it's positioned just after the last character in the sentence, and then drag the line to the correct position if necessary. Revisit the Advanced Layout dialog box and tweak the settings if necessary. When you're satisfied with the line's position, check the "Lock anchor" box to prevent yourself from accidentally moving the anchor.

HYPERLINKS

Stop Word from Automatically Inserting Hyperlinks

The Annoyance: Every time I type anything that looks like a web address or email address, Word creates a hyperlink for me. I can get rid of the hyperlink with Undo, but how do I stop Word from doing this?

The Fix: In Word 2003 or Word XP, if you can see a Smart Tag under the start of the hyperlink, click the Smart Tag and choose Stop Automatically Creating Hyperlinks from the pop-up menu.

If there's no Smart Tag, choose Tools → AutoCorrect Options (in Word 2000, choose Tools → AutoCorrect), click the Auto-Format As You Type tab, and uncheck the "Internet and network paths with hyperlinks" box.

See Where a Hyperlink Will Really Take You

The Annoyance: I've been sent a document with a hyperlink in it, but when I click the hyperlink, my browser displays a page with a different address than the one in the hyperlink.

The Fix: You might find this annoying, but it's not a glitch. The anchor text for a hyperlink—the text that appears in the document to indicate the presence of the hyperlink—doesn't have to be related to the URL used in the hyperlink. Thus, you can create a hyperlink with descriptive text (for example, "Click here to display the brochure") rather than the address of the hyperlink.

Where this gets confusing is when, for example, someone pastes a URL or email address into a Word document. Word automatically creates the appropriate type of hyperlink (for example, an *http://* hyperlink for a URL and a *mailto:* hyperlink for an email address) and displays the pasted text as the anchor text. If someone then accidentally (or intentionally) edits the anchor text, it will be different from the target URL or email address to which it is linked, but the link will still be correct, as long as it was correct in the first place.

If you need to edit the target address of a hyperlink, or you just want to see where it will take you, right-click it and choose Edit Hyperlink. (In Word 2000, right-click and choose Hyperlink → Edit Hyperlink.) From the Edit Hyperlink dialog box, you can edit the text of the hyperlink and the URL to which it links.

Bring Hyperlinks to Heel

The Annoyance: What bugs me? You see a hyperlink embedded in a document, and you want to correct something within it. You put the cursor at the end of the hyperlink and begin to backspace over it to the offending character, and, lo and behold, the whole thing is automatically highlighted and deleted. Worse still, you try to click in a hyperlink to either edit the text or select it so you can move or delete it, and you're suddenly launched into cyberspace.

The Fix: Most people agree that you can help maintain the sum total of happiness in the universe by not embedding hyperlinks in your documents, but the message hasn't caught on universally.

To add to the problem, Word 2003 and Word XP handle hyperlinks in a different way than Word 2000 does. In Word 2000, you click a hyperlink to trigger it and Ctrl-click to edit it; in Word 2003 and Word XP, by default, the actions are the other way around. To change the default behavior in Word 2003 and Word XP, choose Tools → Options, click the Edit tab, and clear the "Use CTRL + Click to follow hyperlink" box.

> ### Warning
> If you get the click or Ctrl-click right, you can edit the text of hyperlinks directly in your document, but doing so is rarely a good idea. It's much better to display the Edit Hyperlink dialog box so that you can easily see whether you're editing both the hyperlink and the URL to which it is linked, or just the hyperlink.

The only safe way to approach a hyperlink is to right-click it and choose the appropriate command on the shortcut menu. For example, right-click and choose Edit Hyperlink to open the hyperlink in the Edit Hyperlink dialog box. (In Word 2000, right-click and choose Hyperlink → Edit Hyperlink.)

TABS

Stop Word from Turning Tabs into Indents

The Annoyance: Sometimes a tab gives me an indent instead of the tab I want. Arrgh!

The Fix: Did I mention that Word is trying to be helpful? In word processing, you should almost never need to use a tab. See the sidebar "Stubbing Out Tabs" for details on this way of thinking.

If you insist on using tabs, though, you can. If you're using Word 2003 or Word XP, choose Tools → AutoCorrect Options, click the AutoFormat As You Type tab, and uncheck the "Set left- and first-indent with tabs and backspaces" box. That will stop Word from creating a first-line indent when you press Tab. It'll also prevent you from using Backspace to reduce the left indent or move the left margin further to the left, but that's the price you pay for progress.

If you're using Word 2000, choose Tools → Options, click the Edit tab, and uncheck the "Tabs and backspace set left indent" box. Same feature, different name and location.

Use Tabs Effectively

The Annoyance: I've used tabs to lay out columns of data. But when my husband opens the document on his PC, the tabs have all shifted to different positions. My first guess was that his computer was from Mars, but it's actually a Dell. How can I make the tabs display consistently?

The Fix: If you're using tabs to align columns of text, consider using a table instead (see Chapter 7). But if you're convinced that tabs are the way to go, here's what you must know to use them effectively.

To work easily with tabs, you need to be able to see where you've put them—or (worse) where someone else has put them in the document you're trying to fix. You can toggle the display of all formatting marks by clicking the Show/Hide button on the Standard toolbar or pressing Ctrl+Shift+8 (or Ctrl+*, if you prefer to think of it that way). To see just tabs, choose Tools → Options, click the View tab, check the "Tab characters" box, and click the OK button. Each tab then appears as a small arrow pointing to the right.

Word starts you off with built-in tabs at half-inch intervals. These are fine for occasional use, but if you want to align columns of text precisely, you should set the tabs manually instead. If you use the built-in tabs to align text, the positioning will change if you change the margins or the font, or if you paste the aligned text into another document that has different settings. Your husband's computer may have substituted a font for one you used, or it may have applied his version of a template that has different tab settings from your version.

You can change the default tab interval by choosing Format → Tabs and setting the interval you want in the "Default tab stops" text box.

You can set tabs manually by using either the horizontal ruler or the Tabs dialog box (Format → Tabs). On the ruler, drag an existing tab mark to move it (hold down Alt as you drag to see exact measurements in the ruler), or drag it downward off the ruler to delete it. To set a new tab, click the Tab button at the left end of the ruler so that it shows the type of tab you want (hover the mouse pointer to display the ScreenTip for the tab type if you're not sure which type it's indicating, as shown in Figure 4-16), and click at the appropriate point in the ruler to place the tab there.

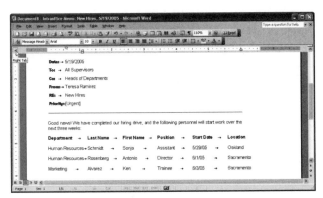

Figure 4-16. Click the Tab button at the left end of the horizontal ruler to change the type of tab. Hover the mouse pointer to identify the current type of tab.

All of Word's tabs are largely self-explanatory, except for the bar tab, which creates a thin vertical line at the specified position. It's not really a tab, because you don't have to press Tab to set it: the line simply appears in the paragraphs for which you've set the bar tab. Depending on what type of documents you create, you may find bar tabs occasionally useful or simply a puzzling waste of time.

If you want to see exactly where you're putting your tabs, select the paragraphs you want to affect, and then choose Format → Tabs. The Tabs dialog box appears (see Figure 4-17). Type the position for the tab in the "Tab stop position" text box, select the appropriate option button in the Alignment area, choose the appropriate option button in the Leader area (the default is None), and click the Set button. You can also clear a tab you've selected in the "Tab stop position" listbox, or clear all tabs set so far.

To type a tab in a table, press Ctrl+Tab rather than plain Tab (which moves the selection to the next cell in the table).

Figure 4-17. The Tabs dialog box enables you to position tabs precisely as needed.

Align Numbers with Decimal Tabs

The Annoyance: I need to get columns of numbers aligned on a decimal point. Tabs aren't much use, because I have to put just the right amount of spaces after them to get the alignment right.

The Fix: Use a decimal tab—a tab that aligns figures on a decimal point. You can set a decimal tab by using either the Tabs button on the ruler or the Tabs dialog box (Format → Tabs).

To lay out extra-wide tabular data, you can set tabs beyond the left and right margins of a page.

Convert Tabs and Spaces to Just Tabs

The Annoyance: My boss creates complex tables that look beautiful but turn out to be painstakingly aligned with a mixture of tabs and spaces. I've tried showing her how to change the default tab stops, but she's got better things to worry about. So I need to remove the spaces, leaving the tabs; reduce each set of multiple tabs to a single tab; and then fix the tab stops. Madness beckons.

The Fix: Find and Replace can knock out the spaces and extra tabs for you. Choose Edit → Replace, enter ^w (whitespace) in the "Find what" box and ^t in the "Replace with" box, and then click the Replace All button.

You'll then need to fix the tab stops manually, but that shouldn't take you long.

HEADERS, FOOTERS, AND SPECIAL LAYOUT

Create Different Headers on Different Pages

The Annoyance: I need to use different headers on different pages, but I can't find the options I need.

The Fix: Word's headers and footers are plenty confusing to start with, but once you've learned what the different options are and where they hide, you can create a wide range of headers and footers.

Choose File → Page Setup and click the Layout tab (see Figure 4-18). Check the "Different first page" box if you just want a different header or footer on the first page. (This box is also useful when you want headers and footers on every page except the first.) Check the "Different odd and even" box to use different headers or footers on facing pages, as is done in most books.

If different headers on the first page or on odd and even pages is all you need, close the Page Setup dialog box, choose View → Header and Footer, and enter suitable text. But what you'll often need to do is divide your document into sections (by using Insert → Break). Each section can then have its own header and footer. By default, each section after the first picks up the header and footer from the first section (assuming that section has a header and footer). Click the "Link to Previous" button on the Header and Footer toolbar (see Figure 4-19) to break the link with the previous section, and then create the new header or footer for the section you're in.

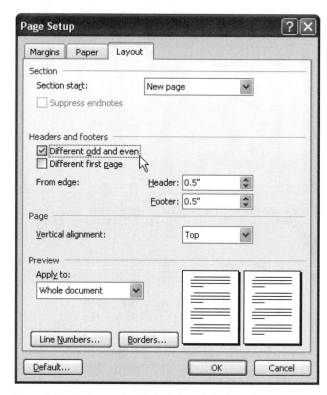

Figure 4-18. The Layout tab of the Page Setup dialog box is the place to start arranging complex headers and footers.

Figure 4-19. To create a different header or footer in a section, you must break the default link to the previous section's header or footer.

Another option that's often useful is to use the same header or footer throughout a document, but insert in it the closest heading of a particular level. See the next Annoyance for details.

Create a Header from a Heading Paragraph

The Annoyance: I need to set up a document that uses the text from the current Heading 1 paragraph as part of the header.

The Fix: Easy enough. Choose View → Header and Footer, position the insertion point where you need the text, and choose Insert → Field to display the Field dialog box. In the Categories drop-down list, select Links and References, and then select StyleRef in the "Field names" list. Choose the style in the "Style name" list (see Figure 4-20), and click the OK button. In Word 2000, you need to click the Options button in the Field dialog box, click the Styles tab, and then select the style.

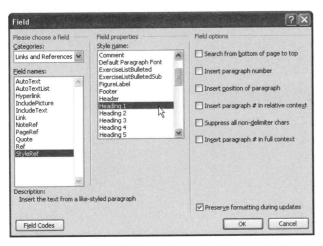

Figure 4-20. Use a StyleRef field to put the text from the nearest heading of a specified level in the header or footer.

Divide a Page into Multiple Pages

The Annoyance: I can't divide a page into multiple pages in Word (e.g., quarters: 4 "pages" to an 8.5" x 11" page), as can easily be done in WordPerfect. I can create a "custom size," but to divide a page into quarters, I have to create a table with multiple columns to create the interior margins and adjust the page margins for the outside margins—a royal pain.

The Fix: How satisfactory a fix this is will depend on exactly what you're doing, but one possibility is to create one page to a page and then print multiple pages on the same piece of paper: choose File → Print and specify your other printing options as usual, but then choose "4 pages" (or another suitable setting) in the "Pages per sheet" drop-down list before you click the OK button.

Forms, Revising, Proofing, and Finalizing

Most of us reckon that Sartre was wrong about other people being the very definition of hell—but working with other people in Word can sure be annoying as heck. They meddle with your forms and don't fill in the bits you want them to. They make changes without using revision marks, so you have to pore through the documents to see what they've messed up. And they put comments directly into the text rather than using Word's Comments feature. Their spelling may leave a lot to be desired, too—but perhaps not as much as their grammar, which they may allow Word's grammar checker to "improve" with its suggestions.

As you probably know, Word offers a slew of features to help keep your colleagues under control and fix problems with documents they've edited—but these features bring their own annoyances, too. This chapter walks you through annoyances brought on by both your colleagues and Word itself. You can often kill two annoyances with one stone—double the satisfaction in half the time. We'll start with a quick look at Word forms, then take a look at two features most of us love to hate: Track Changes and the spelling and grammar checkers.

FORMS

Prevent a User from Accessing Parts of a Document

The Annoyance: Our office is moving from paper-based forms to online forms as part of our "Drive to Save the World." I've created online versions of most of the forms now, with plenty of space for people to fill in the relevant information. The trouble is, they tend to delete areas of the form that they think don't apply to them.

The Fix: What you need is a Word form: a document that has fields for filling in information, and in which you can protect the areas that you don't want users to change.

To create a form, follow these general steps:

1. Create a document as usual, entering the necessary text, leaving gaps for the form fields that the users will fill in, and formatting the contents as needed.

> You can also create a form in a template rather than in a document and then make it available to your colleagues in a workgroup templates folder shared on the network. However, a document kept on the network is usually easier to keep updated than a template. Chapter 2 discusses how to create templates.

2. Right-click the menu bar or any displayed toolbar and choose Forms from the pop-up menu to display the Forms toolbar (or choose View → Toolbars → Forms).

3. Use the three leftmost buttons on the Forms toolbar to insert text boxes, checkboxes, and drop-down lists as needed. Word puts a bookmark around each form field, so if you have bookmarks displayed, each form field appears within brackets. (To display bookmarks, choose Tools → Options, click the View tab, and check the Bookmarks box.) You can toggle field shading on and off by clicking

the Form Field Shading button on the toolbar. Having the shading displayed while you're laying out the form helps you avoid deleting form fields by accident.

4. Double-click a form field (or select the field and click the Form Field Options button on the toolbar) to display the Form Field Options dialog box for the form field. Figure 5-1 shows the Text Form Field Options dialog box; the Check Box Form Field Options dialog box and the Drop-Down Field Options dialog box include checkbox- and drop-down-specific options but are otherwise almost identical. They include similar fields for running a macro on entry to and exit from the form field, the bookmark name for the field, a checkbox for specifying whether the field is enabled, and a checkbox for controlling whether Word calculates the field when the user leaves it.

> You can add help text to a form field by clicking the Add Help Text button and working in the Form Field Help Text dialog box. You can choose between two forms of help text: text displayed in the status bar when the user accesses the field, and text displayed when the user presses F1 when the field is selected. This help can be useful for complex forms, but you should try to explain the contents of fields in the body of the form so that users don't need to rely on the help text, which they may not be savvy enough to access.

5. To test your form, click the Protect Form button (the button with the lock icon) on the Forms toolbar. Word then makes only the form fields accessible. You can move the selection from one field to another by pressing Tab, Page Down, or ↓ to move forward, or Shift+Tab, Page Up, or ↑ to move backward. Click the Protect Form button again to remove the protection.

6. When the form is complete, protect it with a password so that others can't change it. Choose Tools → Protect Document. In Word 2003, check the "Allow only this type of editing in the document" box in the Protect Document task pane; choose "Filling in forms" in the drop-down list;

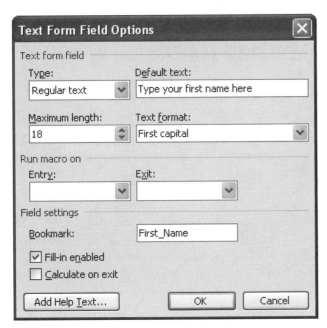

Figure 5-1. Use the Form Field Options dialog box to control whether the form field is enabled (so that the user can fill it in) and to set the name of the bookmark that refers to it. The other options available depend on the type of form field: a text box (as shown here), a checkbox, or a drop-down list.

click the Yes, Start Enforcing Protection button; and enter a password in the Start Enforcing Protection dialog box. In Word XP or Word 2000, select the Forms option in the Protect Document dialog box, type a password, and click the OK button.

7. Save the document, and then make it available to the users who need to fill in the form. When a user opens the form, she can move quickly from one field to another, fill in the necessary information, and save the form under a name other than its current name (because the form is password-protected).

> Word uses the term "form" to describe a document (or template) with areas that you fill in, but there's no reason to restrict your use of Word forms to documents that are considered to be forms in the conventional sense of the word. Word's form capabilities can be useful for many other sorts of documents, from business invoices to personal letters.

Force a User to Fill In Certain Fields

The Annoyance: Right, protecting the form has prevented my colleagues from deleting the sections that don't apply to them. But they're still leaving some vital fields blank and filling in others incorrectly.

The Fix: For a text form field, you can control what the user enters to some extent by specifying the type of text ("Regular text," "Number," "Date," "Current date," "Current time," or "Calculation") in the Type drop-down list in the Text Form Field Options dialog box. You can also control the default entry, the length of the entry, and the format in which it is entered.

For any form field, you can run a macro on entry (when the user moves the selection to the form field), on exit (when the user moves the selection to another form field), or both. An exit macro is especially useful for checking that the contents of the field are suitable and for displaying a message box explaining any problems to the user. (Chapter 8 discusses how to create macros.)

Exit macros are almost ideal for ensuring that the user fills in all the required fields in the form—but only almost. If the user uses the keyboard to move from field to field, the exit macros can validate each field. But if the user moves about the form with the mouse, he can skip fields altogether. When the user skips a field, the exit macro doesn't run, and there's no validation.

A straightforward approach is to force the user to work through the fields in the form in turn, validating the result of each field as the user leaves it. This approach has the advantage of alerting the user immediately to a problem with a field, but it means the user must work through the fields in order.

To validate each field as the user leaves it, create an exit macro for each field. Perform suitable validation (for example, check the `Result` property of a text `FormField` object to make sure that it's not an empty string) and display a message box explaining any problems that the user must fix before leaving the field. For each field except the last, make the exit macro, after finding the field's contents satisfactory, select the next form field (e.g., `ActiveDocument.FormFields("FullName")`. `Select` selects the field with the bookmark name *FullName*).

The user can then fill in the next field. If the user tries to leave a field without completing it, the exit macro runs and tells him the problem.

If you're reluctant to constrict users to working through the form in order, validate the form's contents when the user submits it or saves it. If you add a Submit button from the Control Toolbox (choose View → Toolbars → Control Toolbox), you can attach to it a macro that performs the validation and notifies the user of any fields that were left blank. If you rely on the user saving the form, either create a macro named FileSave in the form that performs the validation, identifies any problems, and saves the form if all is well; or use the DocumentBeforeSave event to perform the validation.

Capture Only the Data from a Form

The Annoyance: Okay, I've got my colleagues filling in the form now—and they're filling in all the fields more or less correctly, which is great. The problem is, I need to extract the data from the form and dump it into our database. I guess I could write a macro to do so, but I don't know how.

The Fix: Nor do you need to. Word can strip the data out of the form for you. Open the form template (or document), choose Tools → Options, click the Save tab, and check the "Save data only for forms" box.

Once you've done this, Word selects the "Plain text" item in the "Save as type" drop-down list when the user displays the Save dialog box. When the user clicks the Save button, Word displays the File Conversion dialog box, allowing the user to check the encoding of the text file before saving it. The resulting text file, which is in comma-separated value (CSV) format, contains only the text entered in the form and the values of any checkboxes (1 if checked, 0 if unchecked).

COMMENTS AND REVISION MARKS

Deflate Comment Balloons

The Annoyance: I use the Comments feature all the time. It worked fine in Word 2000, but it Word 2003 it drives me nuts. In Word 2000, the comment appeared in a pop-up balloon above the word to which it was anchored. When you printed the document with comments, they appeared on a separate page at the end of the file. In Word 2003, when you add a comment in Print Layout view, Word reduces the zoom level and creates a wide right margin where the comments appear. This makes it harder to edit the text—and when you print, the whole page image is smaller, so it's hard to read, too.

The Fix: Word XP offers the same annoyance. To stop Word from using right-margin balloons for comments and tracked changes, choose Tools → Options, and click the Track Changes tab. In Word 2003, choose "Never" in the "Use Balloons (Print and Web Layout)" drop-down list. In Word XP, uncheck the "Use balloons in Print and Web Layout" box. Word then displays each comment in a balloon when you hover the mouse pointer over the text to which it's connected, as in Word 2000.

If getting rid of the balloons altogether is too drastic, use the "Preferred width" setting on the Track Changes tab to reduce the amount of space Word uses for the balloons.

Shrink the Comment Window

The Annoyance: If you add a comment in Normal view, Word opens an absurdly large comment window at the bottom of the screen. It takes up far too much screen real estate, even on my 19" monitor. To make matters worse, you can't close the window by clicking on an X. You have to go to the menu bar and find the option to close it.

The Fix: As you say, Word does tend to display the Reviewing Pane at far too large a size. Drag its split bar to slim it down a bit. To close the Reviewing Pane quickly, drag its split bar all the way to the bottom of the screen, or simply double-click the split bar. You can also press Alt+Shift+C to close this pane (or any other pane except the task pane, which requires Ctrl+F1).

Turn On and Use Track Changes

The Annoyance: I have to circulate my reports around half the department for helpful suggestions. Comparing each of their documents with my copy and integrating the changes takes forever.

The Fix: You should be able to save plenty of time by turning on Word's Track Changes feature. Either double-click the TRK indicator on the status bar so that it goes black instead of being grayed out, or choose Tools → Track Changes (in Word 2000, the menu option is more involved: choose Tools → Track Changes → Highlight Changes, check the "Track changes while editing" box, and click OK). Word will start tracking the changes you make. Teach your colleagues how to turn on Track Changes, and you'll be able to see the changes they've made.

For the best effect, circulate a single copy of the document around to each of your colleagues in turn, rather than letting each person loose on a separate copy. By default, Word tracks insertions, deletions, and formatting changes, and it shows each person's changes in a different color (for up to eight different people). To change what's marked and how, choose Tools → Options and click the Track Changes tab (see Figure 5-2).

With Track Changes on, you'll be able to see easily who has changed what in your document and to accept or reject changes (see Figure 5-3). The Display for Review drop-down list on the Reviewing toolbar lets you switch among four views of your document: Final Showing Markup, Final, Original Showing Markup, and Original. You can even print out the document with the change balloons if you need to keep an audit trail.

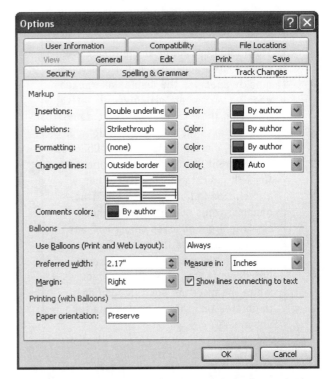

Figure 5-2. The Track Changes tab of the Options dialog box lets you decide which changes to mark and which colors to use.

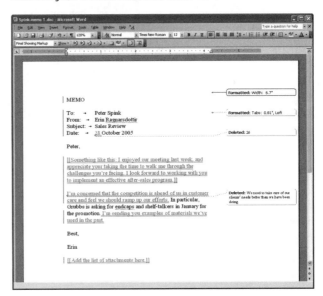

Figure 5-3. Track Changes makes reviewing the changes to a document a breeze.

Turn Off Revision Marks for Formatting

The Annoyance: Format changes are always tracked if tracking is on. Sometimes it's useful to track them, but in the kind of work I do, it's usually not. Is there any way to make tracking these changes optional instead of inevitable?

The Fix: No, but you can at least hide the marks for formatting changes. Choose Tools → Options, click the Track Changes tab, and select None from the Formatting drop-down list (or, in Word 2000, the "Changed formatting" drop-down list).

Toggle Revision Marking Quickly

The Annoyance: Where the heck do I turn off that stupid document revision control thing?

The Fix: Word offers you three ways of toggling Track Changes on and off:

- Press Ctrl+Shift+E.

- Double-click the TRK indicator in the status bar.

- Choose Tools → Track Changes (or, in Word 2000, choose Tools → Track Changes → Highlight Changes, check the "Track changes while editing" box, and then click the OK button).

See Only the Revision Marks for Some Reviewers

The Annoyance: Okay, now tell me how this is supposed to work. Half the department has been hacking at our yearly report with revision marks on, and I need to get it cleaned up. There are so many changes and comments that I can't see the wood for the leaves. I really want to see only the changes made by my boss; she's the one whose name goes on the report.

The Fix: If you're using Word 2000, now's the time to upgrade to Word 2003, because Word 2003 and Word XP offer just the feature you want. Display the Reviewing toolbar if it's hidden (choose View → Toolbars → Reviewing), click the Show button, choose Reviewers, and then choose the name of the reviewer whose changes you want to see (see Figure 5-4). Choose All Reviewers to see all the changes.

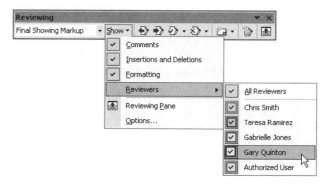

Figure 5-4. Word 2003 and Word XP let you see just the revisions made by a particular reviewer.

Get Rid of the Reviewing Pane Quickly

The Annoyance: I often edit Word 2003 files with Track Changes, using the Final setting in the Reviewing toolbar so I can see what the edited version will look like. Sometimes when I'm in the midst of editing, I want to insert a comment. After I've done so, Word changes the setting from Final to

Final Showing Markup, so I have to change it back again. But here's the real annoyance: when I change back to Final, Word sometimes decides to open the Reviewing Pane at the bottom of the window.

The Fix: Word has to switch to Final Showing Markup when you insert a comment, because otherwise you won't be able to see the comment. If you're using Print Layout view or Web Layout view and you've selected the "Use balloons in Print and Web Layout" box on the Track Changes tab of the Options dialog box (Tools → Options), Word displays the balloons in your preferred margin. Otherwise, Word displays the Reviewing Pane for you to enter the comment.

There's no real fix, but here are two quick ways to get rid of the Reviewing Pane: either double-click the bar that splits the Reviewing Pane from the document area or press Alt+Shift+C.

Use "Compare and Merge Documents" to Highlight Untracked Changes

The Annoyance: My colleagues helpfully turned off Track Changes before editing the document—or maybe I forgot to turn it on. Either way, I've got four versions of a document without revision marks, and I need to integrate all the worthwhile changes.

The Fix: In Word 2003 and Word XP, you have several options for merging documents. Open the original version of the document, and choose Tools → Compare and Merge Documents. In the Compare and Merge Documents dialog box, select the first of the other versions of the document, click the drop-down arrow on the Merge button, and choose "Merge into Current Document." Word merges the documents and marks the changes with revision marks. If the results of the merge look okay, repeat the procedure to merge the next of the edited versions of the document. Check the results again, and then finish the merges.

If you don't want to merge the selected version of the document into the open version of the document, you can press the Merge button to merge the open document into the selected document, or you can click the drop-down arrow on the Merge button and choose "Merge into New Document" to merge the documents into a new document.

If your colleagues have made extensive changes to the document, the merged version will look like the site of a major editing battle, but it beats manually integrating the changes in each of the versions of the document.

Check the Legal Blackline box in the Compare and Merge Documents dialog box to turn the Merge button into a Compare button and remove the drop-down list from the button. Legal blackline uses revision marks just like the compare-and-merge commands, but it always creates a new document to ensure that neither of the documents you're comparing gets changed.

In Word 2000, you don't have so many options for merging documents. Open the original version of the document, choose Tools → Merge Documents, and select the first of the other versions to merge it into the open version. Repeat as many times as necessary.

Prevent Other People from Turning Off "Track Changes"

The Annoyance: I'd like to force my boss to use Track Changes for the edits she makes to a report, but she claims that seeing the changes "impacts" her creativity and spontaneity.

The Fix: Good for her, I guess. Have you tried protecting the document for tracked changes, but turning off their display? Your boss then won't be able to turn off Track Changes unless she knows your password. To set this up, in Word 2000, choose Tools → Protect Document, check the "Allow only this type of editing in the document" box; select "Tracked changes" in the drop-down list; click the Yes, Start Enforcing Protection button; and enter a password. In Word XP or Word 2003, choose Tools → Protect Document, select the "Tracked changes" option, type a password, click the OK button, and confirm the password.

If your boss is being suitably creative and spontaneous, she may not look at the TRK telltale on the status bar, which will be the main indication that changes are being tracked.

If tracking changes semi-surreptitiously isn't a go, just let her edit the document without protection and use the Compare and Merge Documents command to spotlight the spontaneity for you. See the previous Annoyance, "Use 'Compare and Merge Documents' to Highlight Untracked Changes," for details.

SPELLCHECKING

Choose or Lose the Red and Green Squiggles

The Annoyance: The red and green squiggles drive me nuts.

The Fix: If the squiggles offend you, turn them off. Choose Tools → Options, click the Spelling & Grammar tab (see Figure 5-5), and uncheck the "Check spelling as you type" box (to turn off the red squiggles), the "Check grammar as you type" box (to turn off the green squiggles), or both. You can then check spelling and grammar manually at your convenience.

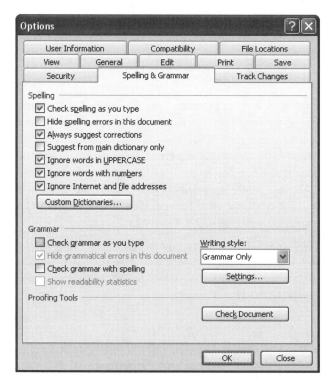

Figure 5-5. Word checks your spelling and grammar by default. Turn off either form of checking on the Spelling & Grammar tab of the Options dialog box.

> **tip**
>
> You can also suppress the red and green squiggles by checking the "Hide spelling errors in this document" and "Hide grammatical errors in this document" boxes. This removes the visual annoyance but is otherwise pointless, as your computer continues to waste processor cycles on checking spelling and grammar. If you want to get rid of the squiggles, it's better to leave these boxes unchecked and to uncheck the "Check spelling as you type" and "Check grammar as you type" boxes, thereby removing the burden of spelling and grammar checking from your computer.

Spellcheck Your Documents in Your Preferred Way

The Annoyance: I turned off the green squiggles, but the red squiggles are stacking up in my document—it's enough to distract me from writing new material.

The Fix: Your first option is to turn off the red squiggles (the spelling queries) as well: choose Tools → Options, click the Spelling & Grammar tab, and uncheck the "Check spelling as you type" box. You can then check spelling whenever you want by clicking the Spelling and Grammar button on the Standard toolbar, pressing F7, or choosing Tools → Spelling and Grammar. From there, you can work in the Spelling and Grammar dialog box (see Figure 5-6).

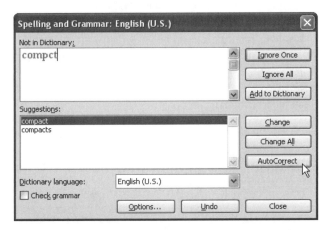

Figure 5-6. Use the Spelling and Grammar dialog box to check the spelling (and, if you choose, grammar) of your entire document at once. Create AutoCorrect entries for any typos you think you'll repeat. Click the Add to Dictionary button to add the queried word to the current dictionary and prevent Word from querying it again.

If you don't want to turn off the red squiggles, deal with them one at a time: right-click a word and choose the correct substitute from the pop-up menu (see Figure 5-7). Alternatively, use the AutoCorrect submenu to create an AutoCorrect entry for the word, which will fix the same problem automatically in the future. You can also choose the Ignore All option to prevent Word from querying the word again in this document, or you can choose Add to add the queried word to the current dictionary.

Figure 5-7. To check one spelling issue at a time, right-click the word and choose the appropriate option from the shortcut menu. If you think you might make this mistake again, create an AutoCorrect entry directly from the menu.

Watch Out for Mistakes Missed on Porpoise…

The Annoyance: The spelling checker doesn't alert you to the possibility that a word may be the *wrong* word, even though it's spelled correctly. Purpose or porpoise? Mourning or morning? These mistakes make me look real dumb.

The Fix: You said it. The spelling checker actually does catch a few correctly spelled problems of word choice and grammar—for example, it'll suggest "must have" instead of "must of" and "there are" instead of "their are," because these examples are always wrong. But beyond that, the spelling checker can't help you if you've got the wrong word. This is a job for a dictionary, a helpful colleague or friend, or a professional editor.

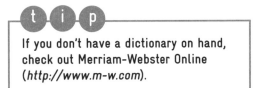

If you don't have a dictionary on hand, check out Merriam-Webster Online (*http://www.m-w.com*).

...and Missed on Purpose

The Annoyance: But I spellchecked my document all the way through! How can you tell me it still has mistakes? Vile pedant!

The Fix: You need to tweak the settings for the spelling checker. Choose Tools → Options and click the Spelling & Grammar tab. See whether the "Ignore words in UPPERCASE" box is checked. If you use uppercase much in your documents (for example, for headings), uncheck this box to make sure that the spelling checker checks the uppercase words as well.

The "Ignore words with numbers" option (which is also checked by default) can also leave typos in your documen5ts—I mean, *documents*—if you strike the number keys by mistake.

> If the spelling checker still fails to catch obvious mistakes, check the language formatting of the mistakes. If someone has applied the "Do not check spelling or grammar" option to the text, the spelling checker will glide right past it. Select the text, choose Tools → Language → Set Language, make sure the correct language is applied, and verify that the "Do not check spelling or grammar" box is unchecked.

Prevent Word from Spellchecking Code

The Annoyance: I'm writing a programming paper, and Word is driving me nuts. I've added a bunch of terms to the custom dictionary, but each time I run the spelling checker, it queries almost everything in the blocks of code in the paper.

The Fix: Apply the "Do not check spelling or grammar" option to your code. The best way to do this is to modify the style that you use for the code. Display the Modify Style dialog box for your code style, check the "Add to template" box, click the Format button, and choose Language from the pop-up menu. In the Language dialog box, check the "Do not check spelling or grammar" box and click the OK button to close each of the dialog boxes in turn.

Use Custom Dictionaries for Special Terms

The Annoyance: I need to add a heap of special terms to the custom dictionary for my current project and then remove them when it's finished.

The Fix: You can do this by adding words to the dictionary and then deleting them manually (as described in the next Annoyance, "Remove Mistakes from a Dictionary"). However, it's much easier to create a new custom dictionary for the project, add the words to it, and then stop using the dictionary (or remove it) when the project is over. Here's how to create new custom dictionaries:

1. Chose Tools → Options, click the Spelling & Grammar tab, and click the Custom Dictionaries button (the Dictionaries button in Word 2000). The Custom Dictionaries dialog box appears (see Figure 5-8).

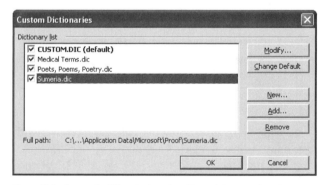

Figure 5-8. Segregate different categories of terms into separate custom dictionaries that you can use only when you need them.

2. Click the New button to display the Create Custom Dictionary dialog box. Navigate to the folder in which you want to store the dictionary (the default is your *%userprofile%\Application Data\Microsoft\Proof* folder), type a descriptive name, and click the Save button. Dictionary files use the *.dic* extension.

> See the upcoming Annoyance "Share a Dictionary with Other Users" for instructions on sharing a custom dictionary with other users of your computer or across a network. In this case, you'll need to store the dictionary in a shared folder, not in *%userprofile%\ Application Data\Microsoft\Proof*.

3. Check the box for each dictionary that you want to use.

4. Click the dictionary to which you want to add new terms when checking spelling, and then click the Change Default button.

5. Add further dictionaries if necessary, or click the OK button in each dialog box to return to your document.

> If you've already created a dictionary file, or acquired one, you can add it to the list in the Custom Dictionaries dialog box by clicking the Add button. Use the Add Custom Dictionary dialog box to navigate to and select the dictionary file, and then click OK.

Remove Mistakes from a Dictionary

The Annoyance: I was clicking my way through a spell-check to meet a deadline, and I accidentally added a couple of misspellings to the dictionary instead of making Word ignore them. How can I get these misspellings out of the dictionary so that Word doesn't keep accepting them?

The Fix: Choose Tools → Options, click the Spelling & Grammar tab, and click the Custom Dictionaries button (Dictionaries button in Word 2000). In the Custom Dictionaries dialog box, select the appropriate dictionary and click Modify to open a dialog box showing the contents of the dictionary. Scroll down to the word (or type the first few letters in the Word text box to scroll automatically to it), select the word, and click Delete. Repeat this maneuver to delete all the other misspellings in the dictionary, and then click the OK button in each of the three open dialog boxes to return to your document.

> ### ADDING WORDS TO A CUSTOM DICTIONARY
>
> You can also use the dictionary's dialog box (which you display by selecting it and clicking the Modify button in the Custom Dictionaries dialog box) to add words to a dictionary one by one, but doing so tends to take more effort than adding them when the spelling checker queries them in your documents.
>
> If you need to add a whole list of terms to a dictionary, open the dictionary file in a text editor such as Notepad so that you can add the terms easily. Open a Windows Explorer window to the folder containing the dictionary and double-click the dictionary file to open it in Notepad (or your default text editor, if you have set a different one than Notepad). You can then type or paste in the words, one to a line. Save the dictionary file as usual, making sure that it retains its *.dic* extension.

Share a Dictionary with Other Users

The Annoyance: I've added all the words I need to a custom dictionary. Now I need to share it with the other users of my computer so that we agree on our spelling.

The Fix: You can do this by placing the dictionary in a shared folder. The best place is probably a subfolder in the *Shared Documents* folder, as files you place here are automatically shared with all users of the computer. But if you've set up another shared folder, you may choose to use that instead.

To move the dictionary from its current folder to the shared folder:

1. Remove the dictionary from the Custom Dictionaries list. Choose Tools → Options, click the Spelling & Grammar tab, and click the Custom Dictionaries button (Dictionaries button in Word 2000). Select the dictionary and click the Remove button. (This removes the dictionary from Word's list but doesn't delete it.) Leave the Custom Dictionaries dialog box open.

2. Use Windows Explorer or your preferred file-management application to navigate to the folder where you stored your custom dictionary (the default is your *%userprofile%\Application Data\Microsoft\Proof* folder), and move it to the shared folder.

3. Switch back to Word, click the Add button in the Custom Dictionaries dialog box, and add the dictionary from its new location.

If you're on a network, you can share a dictionary among two or more computers by placing the dictionary in a shared folder. Unless two or more users happen to add a word to or delete a word from the dictionary at precisely the same moment, there should be no problem with sharing the dictionary.

Create a Custom Dictionary Quickly

The Annoyance: Adding words to a custom dictionary one by one is fine for casual use, but I've got a whole list of terms that I'd like to lump into a custom dictionary all at once. Isn't there a faster way?

The Fix: Indeed there is. A dictionary file is just a text file saved with the *.dic* extension that contains a list of acceptable words, one to a line. You can create a new dictionary file using a text editor such as Notepad, WordPad, or Word itself. For example:

1. Choose Start → All Programs → Accessories → Notepad. Notepad opens with a new text document.

2. If you have an existing list of words for the dictionary, paste it in. Alternatively, type the list of words. Either way, make sure there's only one word to a line.

3. Choose File → Save, and then navigate to the folder in which you want to save the dictionary file.

4. In the File Name text box, type the name for the dictionary, including the *.dic* extension, inside a pair of double quotation marks—for example, `"Icelandic Monarchs.dic"`. Then click the Save button.

5. Load the custom dictionary in Word, as described in "Use Custom Dictionaries for Special Terms," earlier in this chapter.

Solve the "Custom Dictionary Is Full" Error

The Annoyance: When I try to add a word to my custom dictionary, Word tells me the custom dictionary is full.

The Fix: There are three possible causes for this error: the custom dictionary file has reached its maximum size (64 KB), the custom dictionary file is corrupted, or your spelling-checker files are corrupted.

First, find out where the dictionary is located (unless you already know). Choose Tools → Options, click the Spelling & Grammar tab, and click the Custom Dictionaries button (Dictionaries button in Word 2000). Select the dictionary and view the "Full path" readout to see which folder it's in. Open a Windows Explorer window to that folder.

Check the dictionary file's size (for example, choose View → Details and look at the Size column). If it's 64 KB or more, it's too big for Word to add any more words, but you can still add more words by using Notepad, WordPad, or another application. If you want to be able to add words to the dictionary from Word, you must reduce the dictionary's size by removing some words. Your best bet is to split the dictionary into two or more custom dictionaries based on theme. Alternatively, create a new custom dictionary and set it as your default dictionary, so that Word adds new words to it instead of to the previous custom dictionary.

If your dictionary file is smaller than 64 KB, it may be corrupted. You may not be able to tell whether it's corrupted, though, so the next step is to create a new dictionary anyway:

1. Open a Windows Explorer window to the folder containing your custom dictionary. Rename your dictionary file, changing its *.dic* extension to a *.txt* extension, and then double-click it to open it in Notepad.

2. Right-click in the Windows Explorer window and choose New → Text Document to create a new text document. Type the name of your possibly corrupted dictionary (with the *.dic* extension) and press Enter to apply the name. Press Enter again to open the new dictionary file in another Notepad window.

3. Copy the contents of the old dictionary file (with the *.txt* extension) to the new dictionary, omitting any parts that show obvious signs of degeneration (such as gibberish characters instead of recognizable words).

4. Save the new dictionary file, and close both Notepad windows.

Now check to see if Word can add new words to your custom dictionary. If not, your spelling-checker files are probably corrupted. To replace them with pristine versions:

1. Open a Windows Explorer window to your *%programfiles%\Common Files\Microsoft Shared\Proof* folder.

2. Delete the files *msspell3.dll* and *mssp3en.lex*.

3. Open your CD drive, insert your Office CD, hold down the Shift key (to prevent the installation routine from starting), close the drive, and then release the Shift key.

4. Start Word, type a deliberate misspelling, and start a spelling check. Word will prompt you to install the spelling- and grammar-checking features (see Figure 5-9). Click the Yes button, and the Windows Installer will install them.

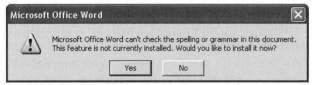

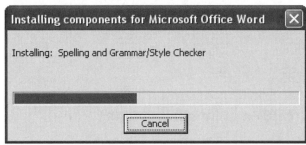

Figure 5-9. The "custom dictionary is full" error message may mean that your spelling files are corrupted. If so, make Word reinstall them.

Protect Your Custom Dictionary

The Annoyance: Word seems to have deleted almost all the words I've been painstakingly adding to my custom dictionary. Help!

The Fix: This behavior is enough to drive even reasonable people up the wall. It occurs when the word you add to the custom dictionary takes the dictionary over its size limit of 64 KB. To get the dictionary's size down, Word deletes most of the dictionary's existing content—without even telling you.

To avoid this problem, keep backups of your custom dictionaries together with backups of all your key files. (See "Move Word to Another Computer" in Chapter 1 for details on which files to save.) Check the size of your custom dictionaries regularly and prune or split any that are nearing the 64 KB line of death.

Unstick the Spelling Checker

The Annoyance: Every now and then, the spelling checker has trouble with a particular word and checks it repeatedly until I cancel the spelling check.

The Fix: This normally happens only when you click the Change All button in the Spelling and Grammar dialog box, the queried word isn't in the main dictionary or a custom dictionary, and the document contains multiple instances of the word.

The easiest solution is to cancel the spelling check and use Replace (Edit → Replace) to replace all the instances of the offending word. Alternatively, if the word is correct, add it to the main dictionary or a custom dictionary.

Create an Exclusion Dictionary

The Annoyance: Gasp of horror! I just handed out a document about Pubic Health in Cincinnati! Now, where's the Resume Wizard?

The Fix: The Resume Wizard is on the Other Documents tab of the Templates dialog box (in Word 2003 and Word XP) or the New dialog box (in Word 2000). Best of luck to you.

"Pubic" is, of course, spelled just fine, but you probably don't want to use it in most of your documents—and certainly not when you meant to type "public." To prevent this from happening again, you need to tell Word that you want it to query instances of this word, even though the spelling is fine. To do so, you create an *exclusion dictionary*: a list of the terms that you want to exclude from Word's spelling dictionaries. Here's how:

1. Determine the name for the exclusion dictionary. It must have the same name as your main dictionary, but with the *.exc* (exclusion) extension instead of the *.lex* (lexicon) extension. The name of the dictionary depends on the language you're using in Office. For American English, the main dictionary file is named *mssp3en.lex*, so the exclusion dictionary must be named *mssp3en.exc*. If you're not sure which dictionary you're using, choose Start → Search and search for `mssp3*.lex` files. The last two or three letters indicate the language: *mssp3fr.lex* for French, *mssp3es.lex* for Spanish, and so on.

There are two differences if you're using Office 97. First, the dictionary file will be Version 2 rather than Version 3 (for example, *mssp2en.lex* rather than *mssp3en.lex*). Second, you must save the exclusion dictionary in the same folder as the dictionary file, rather than in your own *Proof* folder, so it applies to all users of the computer.

2. In Word, choose Tools → Options, click the Spelling & Grammar tab, and then click the Custom Dictionaries button (Dictionaries button in Word 2000) to display the Custom Dictionaries dialog box.

3. Click the New button to display the Create Custom Dictionary dialog box, type the appropriate name in double quotation marks in the File Name text box (for example, `"mssp3en.exc"`), and click the Save button.

4. Select the new dictionary in the Custom Dictionaries dialog box, and click the Modify button to open the dialog box for modifying the dictionary. Type the first word that you want to add and press Enter (or click the Add button). When you've finished adding words, click the OK button to close each of the three open dialog boxes.

5. Restart Word to make it read your exclusion dictionary. Type one of the excluded words to double-check it's working correctly.

After you've added a word to an exclusion dictionary, you can't return it to use by using the Add to Dictionary command during a spelling check; you must edit the exclusion dictionary and remove the word manually.

Turn Off Grammar Checking

The Annoyance: No matter what I write, Word's grammar checker finds something wrong—or potentially wrong. I don't think my English is *that* bad.

The Fix: If it bugs you, turn off the grammar checker. Choose Tools → Options, click the Spelling & Grammar tab, and uncheck both the "Check grammar as you type" box and the "Check grammar with spelling" box. The former controls whether the grammar checker runs in the background the whole time you work, looking for words and phrases it can put squiggles under. The latter controls whether the grammar checker rides along when you run a spelling check.

You can also turn on or off grammar checking during spelling checks by checking or unchecking the "Check grammar" box in the Spelling and Grammar dialog box. This box toggles the setting of the "Check grammar with spelling" box on the Spelling & Grammar tab of the Options dialog box.

Automated spellchecking is a great boon, because spelling is one of the things a computer can get right almost all the time. But English grammar includes so many rules, exceptions, and pitfalls that suggestions from Word's grammar checker are often confusing (if not plain wrong), while properly constructed sentences of gibberish pass the check with flying colors.

If you know your grammar needs help, consult a colleague or (better) an editor.

If you can't face turning off the grammar checker altogether, customize its behavior. First, choose Tools → Options, click the Spelling & Grammar tab, and choose "Grammar Only" instead of "Grammar & Style" in the "Writing style" drop-down list. That will cut down a swath of grammatical grievances. Then click the Settings button to display the Grammar Settings dialog box (see Figure 5-10) and choose the settings that suit you.

Figure 5-10. If you use the grammar checker, customize its settings to suit your preferences and reduce avoidable queries.

Make Sense of Word's Readability Statistics

The Annoyance: I know I can turn off the readability statistics by unchecking the "Show readability statistics" box on the Spelling & Grammar tab of the Options dialog box, but I think I would find them interesting—if I only knew what they meant.

The Fix: The information in the Readability Statistics dialog box (see Figure 5-11) is largely useless, but it can have a cult appeal, especially if you're trying to straighten out someone else's report.

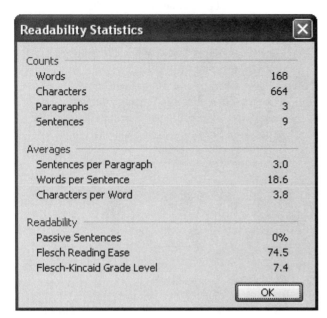

Figure 5-11. Readability statistics provide crude metrics of how your document is composed. Trust your own judgment—or, better, that of your editor.

The readouts in the Counts area—Words, Characters, Paragraphs, and Sentences—are straightforward enough. The readouts in the Averages area—Sentences per Paragraph, Words per Sentence, and Characters per Word—are simply computed from those counts. The averages can help you identify if your sentences or paragraphs are too long or your proportion of 50-cent words too high, but bear in mind that a suitable style will depend on your material and your audience. If you're writing an advanced biochemistry tract, you'll probably need all the long words you can shoehorn into your sentences.

Anyway, you're probably wondering more about the readouts in the Readability area:

- *Passive sentences* are sentences that use passive verbs rather than active verbs. For example, "Jack was painted by Jane" is passive, whereas "Jane painted Jack" is active. Passive sentences are widely thought—I mean, *many experts think* that passive sentences make writing less dynamic and appealing.

- *Flesch Reading Ease* is a measure of the relative difficulty of reading a sentence. The scale runs from 0 (incomprehensible) to 100 (easy to understand). If a document intended for mass consumption scores below 70, it probably needs revision.

> Word XP and Word 2003 use different rules than Word 2000 to calculate Flesch Reading Ease and may produce lower scores for the same sentence than Word 2000 does.

- *Flesch-Kincaid Grade Level* provides the U.S. school grade level at which a typical student would be able to read the text. For example, 7.0 represents the seventh grade. To ensure that a document is as comprehensible as possible, aim for a score around 7.0 or 8.0.

> Both Flesch Reading Ease and Flesch-Kincaid Grade Level are calculated on the average number of words per sentence and the average number of syllables per word.

Upgrade the Thesaurus

The Annoyance: Word's Thesaurus feature is so lame. If it were a horse, I'd have to shoot it.

The Fix: Get out the captive bolt, then. The only fix is to use a better thesaurus. For a quick fix, turn to the Merriam-Webster Online Thesaurus (*http://www.m-w.com*). For a more comprehensive and local solution, check out the free Word-Web (*http://wordweb.info*) or the $19 WordWeb Pro, a powerful dictionary, thesaurus, and word-finding program.

Printing, Faxing, and Scanning

If you've been following along through the annoyances discussed so far in this book, by this stage you should have documents ready to print or fax. You might think your annoyances will soon be at an end, and they might be—but chances are you'll find that Word has different ideas.

This chapter shows you how to deal with the worst printing annoyances that Word throws at you, starting with serious annoyances (Word crashes whenever you print, or printing simply fails) and moving along to tips for printing ranges of pages, printing in reverse order or draft quality, and performing complex duplexing for recalcitrant photocopiers. You'll also learn how to deal with "Bizarre Swelling of the Right Margin Syndrome," how to respond when your printer slices off your footer, and how to create a print file.

Faxing is usually less annoying than printing, even though Word hides the Fax command and incoming faxes aren't ideal candidates for inclusion in your documents. To the rescue comes Microsoft Office Document Scanning, which can save you a heap of time (and save your fingernails) when you need to include either text or pictures from hardcopy sources in your documents.

PRINTING

Stop Word 2003 from Crashing When You Print

The Annoyance: The upgrade to Word 2003 was a cinch, until I tried to print a document. Word crashed. I tried it again. Word crashed again. The document I'm trying to print is nothing exciting—just a one-page report with a handful of cells from an Excel spreadsheet.

The Fix: This is a bug in Word 2003's handling of documents that contain OLE (Automation) objects, such as cells from a spreadsheet or slides from a presentation.

The temporary fix is to choose Tools → Options, click the Save tab, uncheck the "Allow background saves" box, click the OK button, save the document, and then print it. Leave background saves turned off unless you prize them for your other documents.

The longer-term fix is to install Microsoft Office 2003 Service Pack 1, which fixes the problem. Go to *http://support. microsoft.com*, download the Service Pack, and run it to install its contents.

Stop Word XP from Crashing When You Print

The Annoyance: I opened my document in Word XP, checked the header, chose File → Print, clicked the OK button, and *boom*! Word flatlined, and I got an apology for the "inconvenience." I tried it again, and the same thing happened. What's going on here?

The Fix: When background printing is switched on, Word XP is a mite sensitive to your editing headers and footers, working with comments, or running macros that return document information (for example, the number of pages) before printing. Having text boxes or multiple sections in the document makes things worse.

The immediate solution is to turn off background printing: choose Tools → Options, click the Print tab (see Figure 6-1), and uncheck the "Background printing" box. Save the document and try printing again. For a more long-term fix, install Office XP Service Pack 3—or better still, upgrade to Office 2003, which is less buggy as a whole.

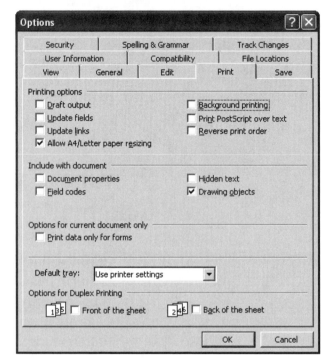

Figure 6-1. Turning off background printing means you have to wait longer before resuming your work, but it helps you avoid certain crashes in Word XP.

Troubleshoot Word's Refusal to Print

The Annoyance: I'm royally stuck. Word 2003 won't print anything at all. I know the printer is fine, because I can print from Excel, the Photo Printing Wizard, Notepad, and every other application I've tried.

The Fix: Take a deep breath, and then try Plan A:

1. Quit Word, restart it, and try printing again.

2. If that didn't help, shut down your PC, restart it, open Word, and try printing again.

Still no good? Never mind. It's just as well to start with the easy solutions in case they work, but you can fall back on Plan B:

1. Create a new document, type a few characters, and try printing it. If it prints, your problem is most likely confined to the template on which the offending documents are based. Create a new template, attach the documents to it, and see if they'll print. If not, continue with the next step.

2. Quit Word, rename *Normal.dot* (see "Word Hangs on Startup" in Chapter 1) to a harmless name such as *old-Normal.dot*, and then restart Word. Word automatically creates a new *Normal.dot*. See if you can print now.

3. No? The printer driver may have become corrupted, and Word has revealed the problem first because it works the printer driver harder than your other applications do. Quit Word again, choose Start → Printers and Faxes, right-click the printer, choose Delete, and click the Yes button in the confirmation dialog box. Click the "Add a printer" link in the Printer Tasks list, and reinstall the printer.

4. *Still* no good? Bad news: You will need to get rid of customizations you've made, which means you'll need to make them again if you want to restore them. Close Word, choose Start → Run, type `regedit`, and press Enter to launch the Registry Editor. Navigate to the *HKEY_CURRENT_USER\Software\Microsoft\Office\11.0\Word* subkey, right-click the *Data* subkey under it, choose Delete, and confirm the deletion. Choose File → Exit to close the Registry Editor, and then restart Word. Word will automatically re-create the *Data* subkey, which should resolve the printing problem.

> If you can print from neither Word nor other applications, the problem most likely lies with the printer driver. See Step 3 in the solution for the fix.

Identify Fields That Change When You Open and Print a Document

The Annoyance: All I did was open the document and print it. Why is Word asking me if I want to save changes when I close the document?

The Fix: The document contains one or more fields that were updated automatically either when the document was opened or when it was printed. Often, the field that changes is a date field that changes to the current date, so check that the printout contains the date you want it to have. For an older document of which you're printing a new copy, you probably will neither want the date to change nor want to save the changed version of the document. To prevent Word from updating the field when you print, choose Tools → Options, click the Print tab, and uncheck the "Update links" box.

If you can't immediately identify the field, choose Tools → Options, click the View tab, choose "Always" in the "Field shading" drop-down list, click the OK button, and then look for the shading in the document.

Make the Print Button on the Standard Toolbar Display the Print Dialog Box

The Annoyance: The Print button on the Standard toolbar prints the whole document on the default printer without displaying the Print dialog box. The other Print commands (File → Print, Ctrl+P) display the Print dialog box. Aargh!

The Fix: "This behavior is by design," as Microsoft has been known to say all too often, but that doesn't mean you have to like it. Presumably somewhere there are Word users who always want to print a full copy of the document on the default printer without seeing the Print dialog box. For everyone else, the Print button is a prime target for customization:

1. Choose Tools → Customize, click the Commands tab, and make sure *Normal.dot* is selected in the "Save in" drop-down list.

2. Drag the Print button off the Standard toolbar into the document area. Drop it, and it will vanish.

3. With File selected in the Categories list, scroll down to the Print... item (*not* the Print item without the ellipsis—that's the one you just disposed of), and drag it to the Standard toolbar. Click the Close button to close the Customize dialog box.

4. Shift-click the File menu and choose Save All. If Word prompts you to save *Normal.dot*, click the Yes button.

Now when you click the Print button on the Standard toolbar, the Print dialog box will appear.

Print a Range of Pages

The Annoyance: I know how to print separate pages or ranges of pages by entering 1,6,8-20 or whatever in the Pages text box in the Print dialog box. But now I need to print only some sections of a document—or, better yet, only some pages within particular sections.

The Fix: You can tell Word which sections you want to print by using s and a number to represent each section. For example, s1 prints Section 1, s1-s3 prints Sections 1 through 3, and s2,s4 prints Sections 2 and 4.

To create sections within your documents, choose Insert → Break and select the appropriate type of section break.

If you need to print only some pages within a section, use p and a number to represent the page and s and a number to represent the section. For example, p2s4 refers to Page 2 in Section 4. The easiest way to get the designation correct is to move the insertion point to the page you want to print and then look at the Page *X* Sec *Y* readout at the left end of the status bar.

To print a range that spans sections, type the starting point, a hyphen, and the ending point in the Pages text box. For example, p2s2-p6s4 prints from Page 2, Section 2 to Page 6, Section 4.

By default, the Print dialog box appears with the All option selected in the Page Range group box. See "Display the Print Dialog Box with Current Page Option or Pages Option Selected" in Chapter 8 for a way of making Word select the Current Page option or the Pages option by default.

Print in Reverse Order

The Annoyance: I'm pretty much cool on printing, except that I have to run the printouts through our copier in reverse order to get the copies into the right order for stapling. (No, I don't understand our copier either.) It would be handy if Word offered a setting for this.

The Fix: It does, but not in the main Print dialog box. Choose File → Print, click the Options button, and check the "Reverse print order" box on the Print tab. (If this dialog box looks familiar, that's because it's the Print tab of the Options dialog box in drag.) Click the OK button to return to the regular Print dialog box, and you'll be ready to go.

Print Double-Sided Pages Without a Duplex Printer

The Annoyance: Okay, here's the problem. I need duplex printing—but all I've got is a single-side laser printer. The copier wants the first page facing forward, the second page facing backward, the third page facing forward, and so on.

The Fix: You've got me turned around too—but you should be able to achieve the effect you need by playing around with the "Odd pages" and "Even pages" options in the Print drop-down list in the regular Print dialog box and the "Front of the sheet" and "Back of the sheet" boxes on the Print tab (click the Options button in the regular Print dialog box). Print out one set of pages, print out the other, and then shuffle the two in your best casino manner and deal them to the copier.

Print in Draft Quality

The Annoyance: Back when the dinosaurs were staggering to extinction, I used to edit manuscripts on paper in the evenings, often with a horn of mead and a dino-drumstick to crunch on. Old habits die hard, and in Word 2, I used to print what it called "drafts"—manuscripts with minimal formatting—for editing manually. I'd like to try that again, with Gewürz and chicken wings now that the kids are asleep, but the option seems to have disappeared.

The Fix: Draft output hasn't actually disappeared in recent versions of Word; it's just hidden. Choose Tools → Options, click the Print tab, and check the "Draft output" box. Be warned that not all printers support draft output, so you may not succeed. But it's worth a try.

Turn Off Background Printing

The Annoyance: When I print a long document, Word 2003 seems to bog down completely. The hourglass cursor disappears, and I can click in the Word window, but Word takes an eon to register each character I type.

The Fix: It sounds as though you've got background printing turned on. Background printing (in theory) lets you get working again in Word more quickly, but it takes more memory, so if your computer is struggling to run Word and print, it's best to turn off background printing. To do so, choose Tools → Options, click the Print tab, uncheck the "Background printing" box, and then click the OK button. When you print a long document, get up and stretch, shadowbox with the watercooler, or bug your colleagues for a few minutes, rather than watching the document print.

Print Colored Text as Black on a Monochrome Printer

The Annoyance: My colleagues keep sending me documents formatted in all sorts of colors that print in varying shades of gray on my wretched (I mean, trusty) old laser printer. How can I make them print in black?

The Fix: Choose Tools → Options, click the Compatibility tab (see Figure 6-2), choose the version of Word that you're using in the "Recommended options for" drop-down list, and then check the "Print colors as black on noncolor printers" box. Click the OK button.

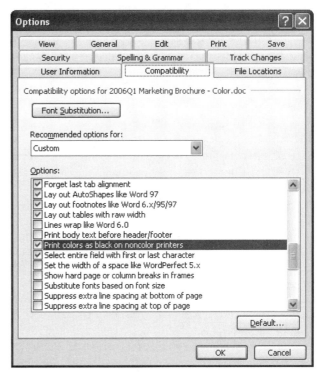

Figure 6-2. Select the "Print colors as black on noncolor printers" box to make colored text print darker on a black-and-white printer.

Print the document on your trusty old printer, and the colored text will print firmly in black rather than gray. If in the future you want to return to printing the colors in shades of gray, go back and uncheck the box.

If you need to be able to print a document quickly in black and white without messing with the settings in the Compatibility dialog box, create a macro that switches the print settings for you. See "Print a Document in Monochrome" in Chapter 8 for details.

Adjust Your Margins for Printing

The Annoyance: I get really annoyed when I receive a Word document via e-mail or on disk, try to print it, and get the message "Your margins may exceed the printable area, do you wish to continue?" Sometimes it prints okay, sometimes it cuts off a portion of the words on the top or bottom, and sometimes it takes one page and turns it into two. Why, why, why? The document was fine on the PC that created it. Why doesn't Word keep the same parameters, or at least import the settings the document was created with into my copy of Word?

The Fix: The problem is that different printers can print to different distances from the edge of the page. Some modern photo-capable printers can print right up to the edges of the page, but most laser printers and inkjets leave a margin of 0.2", 0.4", or more. Chances are that the document was laid out by someone whose printer can get closer to the edges of the paper than your printer can. You may also find that this occurs with a document you create yourself if you switch from one local (or network) printer to another that uses wider margins.

The fix is easy enough: if Word offers you a Fix button, click it to fix the problem automatically. Otherwise, choose File → Page Setup, click the Margins tab (see Figure 6-3), and adjust the offending margin or margins. Unless you're creating intricate layouts, it's usually a good idea to leave large margins on your documents anyway; they look less crowded, and people can scribble notes on them more easily.

Stop the Printer from Cutting Off the Bottom of the Page

The Annoyance: My printer keeps lopping off the bottom of the page. I wouldn't care, except that's where the footer is supposed to be.

The Fix: The short fix is to choose File → Page Setup, click the Margins tab (see Figure 6-3), and adjust the bottom margin. But if you're frequently getting this problem, make sure that you're using the same paper size as the person who set up the document.

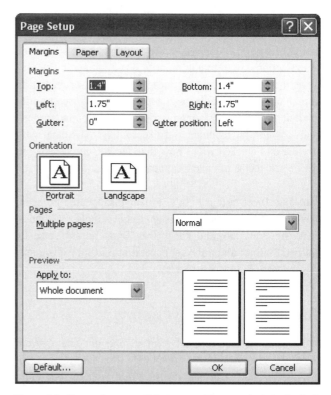

Figure 6-3. If your printer cuts off the bottom of the page, check the depth of the bottom margin.

If you're working with Britons, the problem might be that they're setting up the documents for A4 paper rather than letter-size (8.5" X 11") paper. A4 is longer than letter-size paper, so the bottom of the page is apt to suffer when you print an A4 document on letter-size paper. Word includes a built-in feature for correcting this problem automatically: choose Tools → Options, click the Print tab, and check the "Allow A4/Letter paper resizing" box. You'll still need to check your documents in Print Preview (choose File → Print Preview) before printing them, but this should take the edge off the problem.

Handle "Bizarre Swelling of the Right Margin Syndrome"

The Annoyance: Okay, tell me what's going on. I printed the first few pages of the new sales report we've been working on, and the right margin is about two inches fatter than it should be. The bottom margin is bigger too. Did I hit a secret keystroke for the Insert → Pork → At East and South command while my espresso was kicking in?

The Fix: It sounds as though the document contains tracked changes (or comments), the view is showing "Final with markup" or "Original with markup" rather than "Final," and the pages you printed don't have any tracked changes or markup on them. Word is reserving space in the right and bottom margins for the change balloons and notes, even though there aren't any on these pages.

To fix this problem, either get rid of the tracked changes (accept them or reject them, as appropriate) or switch the view to "Final" in the "Display for review" drop-down list on the Reviewing toolbar.

Create a Black Background with White Text

The Annoyance: I need to print white text against a black background. I've changed the font color to white, but I'm just getting white text on a white background—in other words, sweet flatulent alpacas.

The Fix: You need to set the background color of the paragraphs involved to black. Drag down the left margin to select the paragraphs, choose Format → Borders and Shading, click the Shading tab, and click the black square in the Fill list. (The color name rectangle will show "Black" when you click the right square.) Choose "Solid (100%)" in the Style drop-down list, and click the OK button.

If you set the background to black, you can leave the font color set to Automatic, and Word will automatically make the font color white so that it contrasts with the background.

Print to a File

The Annoyance: My supervisor wants a full-color, glossy printout about the size of a barn door of our annual report. I called the local print-o-rama, and they can do it, but they don't have Word on their computers, and I can't install a copy there just to print. So I'm stuck unless I hike over to Kinko's in the city.

The Fix: What you need to do is print to a file (that is, save the print output to a file), take the file along to the print shop on a CD or memory card, and print it there. For best results, find out which printer you'll use at the print shop, and then install the driver for that printer on your PC. Choose File → Print, select that printer, check the "Print to file" box, choose any other settings (for example, specify which pages to print), and click the OK button. In the Print to File dialog box, specify the name and location of the file. Copy the file to a CD or memory card and hop along to the print shop. Remember to switch back to the appropriate printer before you try printing another document.

FAXING

Find Where Word Hides the Fax Command

The Annoyance: Okay, so how do I send a fax? It's not as if Word has a "Fax This Document" command anywhere—least-ways, not that I can see. I've even looked in the Customize dialog box.

The Fix: About 99 out of 100 people would agree with you that Word's faxing could be easier. Windows itself, and most Windows applications, considers sending a fax to be a form of printing: instead of sending the document to a printer, you send it to a fax, which "prints" it across the wires to the recipient's fax. Intuitive, huh? Better yet, the fax components may not be installed on your PC yet, so you may need to set them up.

Here's how to fix faxing:

1. Make sure there's a fax modem installed on your PC. If your PC is halfway modern, it'll have one already. Otherwise, plug in a USB or serial-port fax modem (or a PC Card fax modem if you're using a notebook PC).

2. Install Fax Services if they're not already installed. Insert your Windows XP CD in an optical drive, choose Start → Control Panel → Printers and Other Hardware → Printers

and Faxes, and click the Set Up Faxing link in the Printer Tasks list. Follow the resulting wizard to install Fax Services.

3. Choose Start → All Programs → Accessories → Communications → Fax → Fax Console to run the Fax Configuration Wizard. Work your way through the wizard, specifying your name, fax number, phone numbers, email address, and so on, and designating the fax device to use (your fax modem). Choose whether to receive faxes and (if so) whether to store incoming faxes, print them, or send them to an email address.

4. In Word, open the document that you want to fax, choose File → Print, and select the appropriate fax item in the Name drop-down list. If you need to change the resolution of the fax, click the Properties button and work on the Fax Performs tab of the Fax Properties dialog box. Otherwise, verify that the page range, number of copies, and so on are correct, and then click the OK button. Word "prints" the document to the fax and starts the Send Fax Wizard, which walks you through the process of specifying the recipient, adding a cover page (if needed), and deciding when to send the fax and what priority to assign it. You can preview the fax to double-check that it is correct before you transmit it.

If you don't have a fax modem, one alternative is to use an Internet fax service such as eFax (*http://www.efax.com*) or Fax1.com (*http://www.fax1.com*).

Get a Fax into a Word Document

The Annoyance: My computer is receiving faxes just fine. In fact, my boss has just sent through a three-page report from Toledo. I'm impressed by his faith that I can somehow magically put the fax into a Word document in time for the big meeting in 10 minutes, but I don't share that faith.

The Fix: It can be awkward when the real world intrudes on a belief system.

Anyway, the brief answer to your problem is to ask your boss to resend the document in some other form, pronto. Any other method of transferring the text is preferable. If your boss can send you a fax, he can surely send the text as an attachment to a message from his Hotmail account, can't he? If an attachment is beyond him, have him lump the text into the body of an email message. Fixing the line breaks and stripping out Hotmail's ludicrous attempts at formatting will be preferable to retyping it.

Still, if you're stuck with a fax, you can try either of two tacks:

- Try OCR on the fax. If it's not too grubby, you should be able to get most of the text. You'll need to check it and correct any errors, but that's better than retyping it. See the next Annoyance, "Scan and OCR a Document," for details.

- If the fax is clean enough, or if you must use it as is in your document, insert each page as a graphic and crop off the transmission data at the top and bottom. The resolution will be low, and your mileage will vary, but it's worth a try. If you're going to print the document, you can use Word's cropping feature. If you're going to distribute it in electronic form and you don't want others to be able to see the cropped areas, use a graphics application to crop the fax before inserting it in the Word document.

SCANNING

Scan and OCR a Document

The Annoyance: Well, you can congratulate me on my new job, for a start. I'm the Senior Archivist at ACME, Inc. Not bad, huh? But here's what I've got to do: transfer three storage rooms full of boxed documents into an electronic library that everyone can access through their PCs using Word 2003. I've got plenty of time, but I think my patience will wear through before too long if I spend all day copy-typing documents. Still, I need the money.

The Fix: Quell any thoughts of arson that have strayed through your mind. First, you need a clear policy on which documents to keep and which to shred immediately. This book can't help you on that, but anything more than a few years old is unlikely to be of much use. Did you know that Microsoft encourages its employees to clear out their email when it reaches the ripe old age of three months? Heck, even some cheeses are older than that.

Second, you need to get to work with a decent scanner and the Microsoft Office Document Scanning feature that lurks, frequently unnoticed, on the Office Tools menu for Office 2003 and Office XP. In the Scan New Document dialog box (Figure 6-4), choose the preset to use—try "Black and white" to start—and then click the Scan button. When the scan is completed, the Microsoft Office Document Imaging window opens. From here, you can choose File → Save to save the scanned picture under either the default name that Microsoft Office Document Scanning has assigned (note that the document isn't saved yet, even though it appears to have a filename) or a name of your choosing, or choose Tools → Send Text to Word to send the text to a document in a new Word session. You'll probably need to clean up the text in Word before saving it. Arrange the windows so that you can see both the scan of the document and the OCRed text, and make the text match the original.

Figure 6-4. Office 2003 and Office XP include built-in scanning and optical character recognition (OCR) capabilities. You provide the scanner.

Use a Scanned Picture in a Word Document

The Annoyance: I'm creating our company's latest brochure—actually, probably the last before we get bought by one of our shark-nosed competitors. Anyway, we've got this dusty old photo on the wall of the Founder shaking hands with some dusty old politician, and I need to put that front and center in the brochure to show how old and worthy we are.

The Fix: Microsoft Office Document Scanning can help you out here too. Get the photo off the wall and out of its frame, and wipe off as much of the dust as possible. Lay it flat and square on your scanner, choose Start → All Programs → Microsoft Office → Microsoft Office Tools → Microsoft Office Document Scanning, choose the Color option in the "Select a preset for scanning" list, and click the Scan button.

When the Microsoft Office Document Imaging window opens, click the Select button, drag to select the area of the picture you want, and choose Edit → Copy Image. Right-click in the thumbnails column on the lefthand side, and choose Paste Page to create a new page with just your selection. Right-click the thumbnail for the original page, and choose Delete Page to delete it. Then choose File → Save, save the picture, and exit Microsoft Office Document Imaging.

Switch back to Word, position the insertion point at the appropriate place, choose Insert → Picture → From File, and insert the picture in the document.

Tables, Columns, and Text Boxes

Tables are a great tool for positioning data precisely in your documents without resorting to such horrors as groups of text boxes. Tables mostly behave pretty well, provided that you know what you're doing with them—but their complexities and occasional outré habits can be extremely annoying.

In this chapter, you'll learn how to quell these various annoyances. We'll look at how to decide whether to use Word's fancy drawing features for tables; how to position tables and their contents exactly where you want them and prevent Word from adjusting column widths without your consent; how to use header rows, borders, and formulae; and many other table-related issues.

Compared with tables, columns and text boxes provide more moderate levels of annoyance—but the end of the chapter shows you how to deal with the curve balls these features can throw at you.

TABLES

Choose Whether to Draw Tables or Just Insert Them

The Annoyance: What's the point of the Tables and Borders toolbar? All it does is complicate the process of creating tables, which I've been doing just fine using the Insert Table dialog box for 10 years now. I started back with Word 2, whenever that was.

The Fix: If you can create the effects you need using the Insert Table dialog box, don't bother with the Tables and Borders toolbar.

How useful the Tables and Borders toolbar is to you will probably depend on the types of tables you create. If all you need are straightforward tables with the same number of cells in each column, simply use the Insert Table dialog box (Table → Insert → Table) to create your tables. But if you need to create complex tables that use cells with different widths or heights, drawing may be a better option. Start by drawing the outline of the table so that it occupies the amount of space you want to devote to it, and then draw the internal lines to create the columns, rows, and cells.

Another approach to creating a "complex" table is to insert a standard table, click the Eraser button on the Tables and Borders toolbar, and then knock out individual borders to create differently sized cells.

Prevent Word from Resizing a Table

The Annoyance: I can't stand the "artificial intelligence" built into Word's table feature. You can define how wide the table and/or each column should be in the Table Properties dialog box, but Word then changes the widths according to the text put in the cells.

PRODUCING COLUMNS OF DATA IN WORD

Word offers three ways to lay out material in columns:

- **You can use tabs to create columns. This works okay for short items, particularly those that require decimal tabs (see "Align Numbers with Decimal Tabs" in Chapter 4).**

- **You can use Word's columns (Format → Columns) to create snaking, "newspaper-style" columns. See "Create Newspaper-Style Columns" at the end of this chapter for details.**

- **You can use tables to create columns of cells. Tables work especially well for longer items that wrap from one line to the next, but they're also good for short items. You can easily create running headers for multipage tables (see "Repeat a Header Row," later in this chapter).**

The Fix: Word always wants to help as much as it can, and resizing columns automatically to fit their contents must have seemed like a good idea. Unfortunately, AutoFit tends to give people fits automatically.

To prevent Word from resizing the columns, insert a table by using the Insert Table dialog box (see Figure 7-1) rather than by clicking the Insert Table button on the Standard toolbar and "painting" out a table grid. Choose Table → Insert → Table or click the Insert Table button on the Tables and Borders toolbar. Specify the number of columns and rows, select the "Fixed column widths" option, specify a width in the spinner box if you choose, and click the OK button.

If the table is already inserted in your document with AutoFit turned on:

1. Right-click in the table, choose Table Properties, and click the Table tab if it's not already displayed.

2. Click the Options button, uncheck the "Automatically resize to fit contents" box, and then click the OK button to close each dialog box (see Figure 7-2).

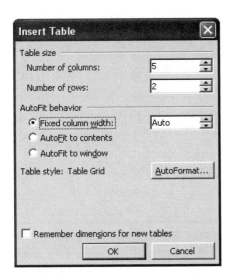

Figure 7-1. To prevent Word from resizing your table columns, select the "Fixed column width" option in the Insert Table dialog box.

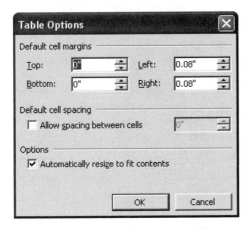

Figure 7-2. You can also turn off AutoFit in an existing table.

Place a Table at the Top of a Page

The Annoyance: I want to place a table at the top of a new page, but I don't want a paragraph mark to appear before it. Sometimes I can get this to work, but usually not.

The Fix: Click in the first row of the table, choose Format → Paragraph, click the Line and Page Breaks tab, and check the "Page break before" box. Don't put a hard page break (Ctrl+Enter) before the table, or you'll get that unwanted paragraph mark.

Get a Table Away from the Start of a Document

The Annoyance: I created a new document and began a table right at the top of the page, and now I can't shift it. There must be an obvious way of moving it, but I'm not seeing it.

The Fix: Position the insertion point in the first row of the table and choose Table → Split Table or press Ctrl+Shift+Enter. Alternatively, enter a few carriage returns after the table (by pressing the Enter key), click in the table and choose Table → Select → Table, and then drag the table down a paragraph or two.

Position a Table Correctly on a Page...

The Annoyance: I'm struggling to get the tables in my document positioned just right on the page. I can drag the left and right borders to where I want them on the ruler, but I have to set the zoom level really high to get them exactly right. Too much coffee, and I tend to drag too far.

The Fix: You can hold down Alt while resizing a column to display exact measurements in the ruler, but you'd probably be better off working in the Table Properties dialog box (see Figure 7-3). Right-click in the table and choose Table Properties from the shortcut menu to display the dialog box. Use the "Indent from left" spinner box on the Table tab to control how far from the left margin the table appears (set a negative indent if you want the table to start in the margin). Use the Alignment settings to specify the alignment for the table.

Figure 7-3. Use the Table Properties dialog box to set the indentation and alignment for a table.

...and Position the Table's Contents Correctly

The Annoyance: Okay, the table is in place, and I've got most of the text in the cells. Now all I need to know is how to lay out that text properly.

The Fix: The Table Properties dialog box is also the key to positioning the contents of the table accurately:

- Right-click in the table and choose Table Properties from the shortcut menu to display the dialog box. Click the Table tab, click the Options button, and specify the default cell margins and any default cell spacing in the Table Options dialog box (see Figure 7-4, top).

- To override those default settings in a cell, select the cell, click the Cell tab of the Table Properties dialog box, click the Options button, and work in the Cell Options dialog box (see Figure 7-4, bottom). You can also turn off text wrapping from here, on those rare occasions when you want to prevent the text from wrapping within a cell.

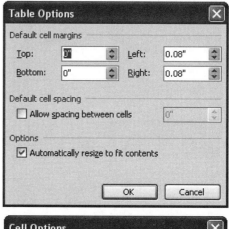

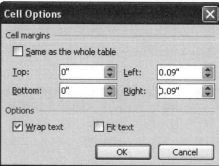

Figure 7-4. The Table Options dialog box lets you set default top, bottom, left, and right cell margins. The Cell Options dialog box lets you override the cell margins for particular cells.

- To change the vertical alignment of a cell, choose the appropriate "Vertical alignment" option on the Cell tab of the Table Properties dialog box.

- Within the cell, you can apply many types of standard paragraph formatting by using the controls on the Formatting toolbar or in the Paragraph dialog box (Format → Paragraph). For example, you can change the horizontal alignment, the indentation, and the line spacing.

Make a Table the Full Width of the Text

The Annoyance: I'd like my table to take up the full text width of the page. But whenever I change the page margins, I need to change the width of the table manually to match.

The Fix: Right-click the table, choose Table Properties, click the Table tab, check the "Preferred width" box, choose

"Percent" in the "Measure in" drop-down list, and specify 100% in the middle drop-down list. Word will then change the table's width automatically when you change the margins of the page.

Restore the Cell Height and Width Dialog Box

The Annoyance: I guess I'm still stuck in the Dark Ages of Word 97, because I miss the Cell Height and Width dialog box that you could use to—well—control the height and width of a cell. It didn't offer all the fancy options of the Table Properties dialog box, but it was easy enough for me to understand.

The Fix: You can still use the Cell Height and Width dialog box (see Figure 7-5) if you want. To pop it up just once for old times' sake and see if it matches up to your memories, choose Tools → Macro → Macros, type `tableformatcell`, and press Enter. To use it more frequently, choose Tools → Customize, click the Commands tab, check that *Normal.dot* is selected in the "Save in" drop-down list, click All Commands in the Categories list, and drag the TableFormatCell item from the Commands list to your Table menu or other preferred location. After closing the Customize dialog box, Shift-click the File menu, choose Save All, and save the changes to *Normal.dot* if prompted.

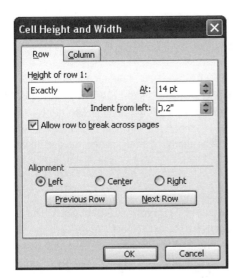

Figure 7-5. Word 2000 and later versions suppress the Cell Height and Width dialog box, but dissenters like you can liberate it if you choose.

Repeat a Header Row

The Annoyance: Today's report has an ugly six-page table in it. I'm cleaning it up, and every time I make an edit—even applying or removing formatting—the rows bounce from one page to the next. That means the heading rows on the second and subsequent pages are now in the wrong place. I moved them back the first time I noticed it, but they keep jumping around. I guess I'd better leave 'em until I finish editing.

The Fix: If they're moving around, they're not real heading rows: they're just normal rows formatted to look like heading rows. Word can automatically repeat one or more heading rows for you when the table goes to a second or subsequent page. Set up the row (or rows) on the first page, select it (or them), and choose Table → Heading Rows Repeat. When rows walk from one page to another, Word keeps the header row or rows in the right place.

Delete a Table, Not Just Its Contents

The Annoyance: Call me anal, but I hate inconsistency in the Windows interface. Over the last couple of months, I've grown used to selecting what I want to delete and then pressing the Delete key to off it. (Yes, I've offed the Recycle Bin already.) It works in Explorer, works in Excel, and works in Word...but not for tables. When I try to delete the selected part of a table, all Word does is delete the contents of the cells. Pavlov would be rolling in his kennel.

The Fix: There's no real fix, but understanding the rationale for Word's behavior might help you feel better. Word's designers decided to draw a distinction between deleting all or part of a table's contents and all or part of its structure. So a standard Delete command deletes contents, while the easiest way to delete the table's structure (with any contents that remain) is to select the appropriate part of the table and then press Backspace. You can also choose Table → Delete and choose Table, Columns, Rows, or Cells (as appropriate) from the submenu.

Work Smart with Table Columns

The Annoyance: Changing the width of one column affects all the other columns, too. Just when I get one column perfect, I need to change another column, and that screws up the perfect column. It'd be great to lock a column's width so it won't change unless I explicitly say so.

The Fix: Your wish is granted—to some extent. Word tries to maintain the table width you specified, so if you drag one column border to widen or narrow a column, Word automatically adjusts the column to the right to compensate. To override this behavior, Shift-drag the column border. This makes Word maintain the width of the column to the right, but it means that your table's overall width will change.

> To set column widths precisely, right-click in the first column, choose Table Properties, click the Column tab, and use the "Preferred width" spinner box to set the column width. Click the Next Column button to move to the next column and set its width.

Use Different Cell Widths in Different Rows

The Annoyance: What I need is to be able to change the widths of the cells in one row without affecting all the other rows in the table. But there doesn't seem to be any way to do this other than merging cells, which isn't what I want to do.

The Fix: You can do this with minimal effort. If you want the cell widths in each row to be different, create each set of rows as a separate table, and then join them. When you create separate tables, it's usually best to put one or more blank paragraphs between them to ensure that Word doesn't get confused and start treating them as a single table when you drag a column border in one table close to the column border in another table. When your tables are finished, delete the blank paragraphs to bring them together. Word then treats the tables as a single table.

If you need different cell widths in only one set of rows, create a separate table for the row or rows that you want to have different cell widths. Select that table (Table → Select → Table), right-click it, and choose Cut from the shortcut menu. Right-click the appropriate cell in the main table, and choose Paste Rows from the shortcut menu. Make sure that you don't choose Paste as Nested Table, unless you want to nest the rows in the cell.

Rearrange Table Columns

The Annoyance: After struggling with this table for a couple of hours, I've realized that the second column should really be the first column. Please tell me I don't have to retype both columns!

The Fix: It's okay, you needn't retype anything. You can move table columns either by dragging or by using Cut and Paste. Getting the hang of dragging columns can take a little practice, so if you have time, create a sample table in a new document and play around with moving the columns. The easiest way to select a column is to move the mouse pointer just above the topmost cell in the target column so that the pointer changes into a black arrow pointing downward, and then click; alternatively, you can click in the column and choose Table → Select → Column. Click anywhere in the selected column, and drag it to the column before which you want it to appear.

Convert Text to Tables

The Annoyance: I get long membership lists—database dumps—that I need to convert into Word tables. If they were separated with tabs, I could just use the Table → Convert → Text to Table command, but they're separated with regular old spaces—as many of them as are needed to line up the columns.

The Fix: You can fix this easily. Choose Edit → Replace and replace ^w (whitespace) with ^t (a tab). Select the list, choose Table → Convert → Text to Table, make sure the Tabs option is selected and that the "Number of columns" box shows the right number of columns, and click the OK button to perform the conversion.

Print Table Gridlines

The Annoyance: I can't print the gridlines in my table.

The Fix: The table gridlines are there only for reference. They never print unless you apply borders. If you don't need to see the gridlines on screen, choose Table → Hide Gridlines to remove them from the display and help eliminate any confusion.

If you want to print gridlines, add borders to the table. Right-click in the table, choose Borders and Shading from the shortcut menu, select the borders you want on the Borders tab (see Figure 7-6), and click the OK button. The key control here is the "Apply to" drop-down list, which lets you specify whether to apply the current border to the entire table, the current cell or selected cells, or the current paragraph.

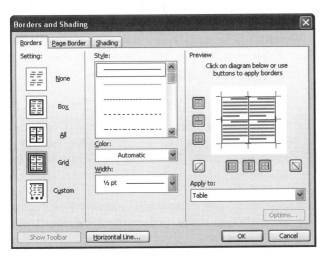

Figure 7-6. Use the Borders and Shading dialog box to add a border to any gridlines that you want to print.

Get Rid of Table Gridlines

The Annoyance: I chose Table → Hide Gridlines, but they're still hanging around—even through the Table menu now has the Show Gridlines command instead.

The Fix: Here's another reason why Microsoft isn't renowned for its design brilliance. What you're seeing are actually the text boundaries for the table. You're seeing boundaries for the page's margins as well, aren't you? Choose Tools → Options, click the View tab, and uncheck the "Text boundaries" box. That'll do the trick.

Make All Your Table Borders Print

The Annoyance: The right and bottom borders of my table don't print, even through the other borders print okay.

The Fix: It sounds as though you've placed the right and bottom borders outside the printable area for your printer. Most printers can print up to 0.2" or 0.4" from the edge of the paper, but some need wider margins. Try bringing the table borders back into the land of the living.

Wrap Text Around a Table

The Annoyance: I need to use a table like a graphic. Can I put it behind the text in my document?

The Fix: No, but you can make the text wrap around it. Right-click the table, choose Table Properties, and click the Table tab. Choose the appropriate alignment option—Left, Center, or Right—and then click the Around option in the "Text wrapping" area. Click the Positioning button to display the Table Positioning dialog box (see Figure 7-7), which offers options similar to those for positioning pictures (see "Position the Graphic Relative to the Page" in Chapter 4).

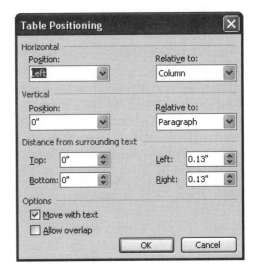

Figure 7-7. When you wrap text around a table, use the Table Positioning dialog box to position the table precisely where you want it.

Create Formulas in Tables

The Annoyance: I know how to embed an Excel spreadsheet in a Word document, but that seems like overkill when all I need is a simple formula to sum the contents of a column in a table.

The Fix: What you can do is create a table formula in Word. Table formulas aren't very powerful (especially if you're used to Excel's capabilities), but they're powerful enough to prove handy in a pinch. Position the insertion point in the appropriate cell, choose Table → Formula, and then choose the formula, number format, and any other options in the Formula dialog box (see Figure 7-8).

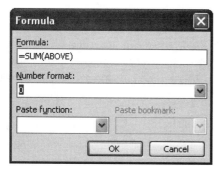

Figure 7-8. Simple formulas in Word's tables can save you from having to embed spreadsheet fragments in your documents.

The formulas you're most likely to want are =SUM(LEFT), which adds the cells to the left of the active cell, and =SUM(ABOVE), which adds the cells above the active cell. You can also use =SUM(RIGHT) and =SUM(BELOW) if needed, or create custom formulas by referring to specific cells in "row, column" format (for example, R1C2 refers to row 1, column 2) or by assigning bookmarks to cells and referring to those.

Each formula is a field, so it appears within the braces that Word uses to denote fields—for example, { =SUM(BELOW) }. Word inserts these braces, so you don't need to type them manually when using the Formula dialog box. You can also insert a formula quickly by pressing Ctrl+F9 to insert the braces and then typing the formula between them. Don't try typing the braces; that doesn't work, because they're special field braces rather than simply {} characters.

Speed Up Word's Handling of Tables

The Annoyance: Tables in Word XP are slooooow! I don't remember this problem in Word 97—even before I upgraded from my ancient 486. What's the problem?

The Fix: Well, it's pretty much as you say: tables in Word XP (not to mention Word 2000 and 2003) *are* slower to load and redraw than tables in Word 97 and previous versions of Word. This is because the later versions of Word have to be able to create HTML tables, so they use a different (and slower) table engine. Nested tables slow things down even more, simply because they're more complex.

To minimize this annoyance, try the following:

- Turn off automatic cell resizing if you've left it on for any table. Right-click the table, choose Table Properties, click the Options button, and uncheck the "Automatically resize to fit contents" box.

- Keep tables short, if possible. If you have the choice of creating 10 short tables or a monster table with 10 subheadings, go for the 10 short tables. Eliminate merged cells if possible; they're useful for subheadings, but they slow down Word's handling of tables.

- When editing tables for content rather than layout, work in Normal view rather than in Print Layout view or Print Preview. Also try turning off background repagination: choose Tools → Options, click the General tab, and uncheck the "Background repagination" box.

- Keep rows shallow if possible. Instead of putting a dozen paragraphs in a row, create a dozen rows. Use borders to differentiate them.

- Keep your tables as simple as possible. Don't wrap text around tables unless you must—and if you must, do so when you've finished creating and editing the tables. Use as few graphics as possible in your tables, and when you do, put the graphics inline rather than having them float.

Avoid Vertically Merged Cells in Word 2000

The Annoyance: Our catalog is in an absurdly big table. It lists hundreds of parts, most of which have subcomponents. Each part takes up a row, and if there are subcomponents, the part is in a vertically merged cell, so that all the subcomponents are "under" it. Anyway, all was well until I was putting the finishing touches on the catalog. Then Word 2000 locked up, "experienced an error," and exploded the catalog into virtual shrapnel.

The Fix: I'm guessing you touched on a sensitive nerve in Word 2000's handling of tables that have vertically merged cells (two or more cells in the same column merged together vertically) spanning two or more pages. Such cells make tables a minefield that you can set off by doing something as innocuous as moving from page to page in Print Layout view.

The fix is to update to the latest Office 2000 Service Pack you can find, or to update to a later version of Office.

COLUMNS

Create Newspaper-Style Columns

The Annoyance: More of a grumble, really: text in columns is difficult to control, and there aren't many changes you can make to the settings to make the text look the way you want.

The Fix: It could be worse. The Columns dialog box (Format → Columns) lets you choose the number of columns; control the width of each column, and the spacing between it and the column to its right; and choose whether to put a line between each column. If you're looking for more complex effects, you should probably be using a page-layout application rather than Word. But if you're stuck with Word, try the following:

- Use heading styles and text styles as usual to differentiate the paragraphs in your columns.

- To end a column early, choose Insert → Break, select the "Column break" option, and click the OK button.

- Use a text box overlapping one or more columns to add variety or impact to your layout.

- You can insert a picture in a column as usual (Insert Picture → From File), and you can wrap text around it or even run text through it.

- To put a table in a column, choose Table → Insert Table, as usual.

Mix Different Numbers of Columns in a Document

The Annoyance: I need to create a newspaper-style layout with a masthead across the top of the page, blurbs on the five top stories below that, and then a three-column layout for the rest of the page. But when I change the number of columns, everything I've laid out so far goes screwy.

The Fix: This shouldn't happen unless you're selecting all of the text before you change the number of columns.

To fix this problem:

1. Select the first part of the text to which you want to apply a different number of columns, choose Format → Columns, specify the number of columns, make sure that "Selected text" rather than "Whole document" is selected in the "Apply to" drop-down list, and click the OK button.

2. Select the next part of the text that needs a different number of columns, choose Format → Columns, and specify the number of columns for that text. Word automatically inserts a continuous section break between each section that has a different number of columns.

Press Alt+ ↑ to move to the top of the previous column on the page, and Alt+ ↓ to move to the top of the next column.

Prevent Columns from Vanishing When You Save as a Web Page

The Annoyance: I got my columns just perfect in the document—but when I saved it as a web page for my site, Word lumped them together into a single column. Am I doing something wrong?

The Fix: It depends on how you define "wrong." But no, not really. Microsoft designed Word to do this, even if you don't like it. What you need to do is use a table to create your columns rather than using newspaper-style columns. Word will maintain the table's columns when you save the document as a web page.

TEXT BOXES

Use Text Boxes for Complex Layouts

The Annoyance: This is probably going to sound stupid, but never mind. I've been using Word for seven years now: letters, reports, even laying out a couple of novellas for a friend. I've used tables, pictures, frames, and more wizards than you can shake a staff at. But I've never used a text box—nor have I needed one. So I gotta ask: what are they for?

The Fix: As you've figured out, text boxes are a fairly specialized item. They're most useful for laying out awkward little bits of text (pull quotes, teasers, jokes, you name it) that require precise placement. With the work you've described, you probably haven't needed them—and you won't need them unless you start working with different types of documents.

Should you start creating more complex layouts in Word, such as newsletter or magazine pages that require carefully positioned boxes holding text—or should curiosity overcome you—here's how to proceed:

1. Lay out the rest of your document. The best time to place your text boxes is when the rest of the document is close to its final state.

2. Choose Insert → Text Box. Word changes the insertion point to a crosshair, and if you're in Normal view, Word changes to Print Layout view so that you can see what you're doing. Click where you want one corner of the text box, and drag in any direction to specify the size and proportions.

> As with most other drawing objects, you can hold down Shift to constrain the text box to a square instead of a rectangle, hold down Ctrl to draw the text box centered on the point you click rather than placing a corner there, and hold down Ctrl+Shift to do both.

3. To format the text box, right-click its frame, choose Format Text Box, and work in the Format Text Box dialog box.

4. To format the contents of the text box, select the contents (or part of them) and use standard formatting commands (for example, Format → Font or Format → Paragraph).

Create a Series of Linked Text Boxes

The Annoyance: I'm using a set of six text boxes to present a case study alongside the main text of my report. The trouble is, I'm still writing the report, so the size of the text boxes keeps changing, and I'm forever having to bump text along from one of them to the next—or back to the previous one. It feels like I'm never going to get the darn thing finished.

The Fix: The finishing is up to you, but Word can handle flowing the text from one text box to another if you link them together:

1. Create the text boxes (It sounds like you've done this step already.)

2. Enter the text in the first text box. In most cases, it's easiest to create and edit the text in a separate document in which you can see it all at once, and then paste it into the first text box when it's complete.

3. Right-click the frame of the first text box, and choose Create Text Box Link from the shortcut menu. The mouse pointer changes to a pouring jug. Click the next text box in the sequence to establish the link. Word flows the text to this text box.

4. Right-click the frame of the second text box, and repeat the linking procedure for the following text box. Repeat as necessary.

Once you've linked text boxes, you can navigate from one to another by right-clicking and choosing Next Text Box or Previous Text Box from the shortcut menu, or by using the Next Text Box and Previous Text Box buttons on the Text Box toolbar. To unlink a text box from the next text box, right-click its frame and choose Break Forward Link from the shortcut menu.

Automate Away Annoyances with Macros

8

In this chapter, I'll show you how to eliminate 15 or so common annoyances by using macros. Some of these annoyances are specific ones that you may share: for example, it may irk you that Word doesn't automatically return to the last editing position when you open a document, that it indiscriminately capitalizes the first letter of every word when you apply title case to selected text, or that you have to mess with the Paste Options dialog box or the Paste Options Smart Tag if you want to paste in text with no formatting.

We'll also look at a few more general issues, such as having Word perform a series of mechanical steps for you automatically, putting a message box or input box on a recorded macro so that you can control it better, and performing Find and Replace operations that are too complex to do through the user interface.

When you first start to work with macros, you'll face a steep learning curve in getting to know the Visual Basic Editor's interface and Visual Basic for Applications (VBA) at the same time. This chapter provides a gentle introduction to the power of macros and the complexities of the Visual Basic Editor. If you need to get up to speed, you'll get the best results in this chapter by starting at the beginning and reading (or working) through all the sections in order. If you're already comfortable with the Visual Basic Editor, feel free to skip around as usual. This chapter isn't a course in using VBA and the Visual Basic Editor, but it shows you how to get started creating code that can sweep many annoyances from your path.

MACROS

Record a Macro to Repeat a Task

The Annoyance: I spend half the day creating the same type of document over and over again. I've streamlined things as much as possible with templates, AutoText, and AutoCorrect, but it's still duller than watching asphalt dry.

The Fix: This sounds like a job for a macro or two. In short, you switch on the Macro Recorder, perform the series of actions that you want to be able to repeat at the touch of a button, and then stop the Macro Recorder. You can then play back the macro as often as needed. Here's how it works:

1. Start Word and set up the document you want to automate.

2. Choose Tools → Macro → Record New Macro to display the Record Macro dialog box (see Figure 8-1). Type a name for the macro (no spaces, but underscores are okay) in the "Macro name" box and provide a description in the "Description" box. In the "Store macro in" drop-down list, make sure that "All Documents (Normal.dot)" is selected, unless you specifically want to store the macro in a different document or template. (If you do, the macro will be available only when that document, that template, or a document based on that template is open.)

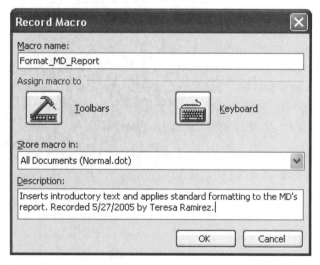

Figure 8-1. Assign a descriptive name and a detailed description to each macro you record—otherwise, your list of macros can quickly become confusing.

> **Warning**
> The Record Macro dialog box also lets you choose a way of running the macro in the future: click the Toolbars button and use the Customize dialog box to assign the macro to either a toolbar button or a menu command, or click the Keyboard button and use the Customize Keyboard dialog box to assign a keyboard shortcut. Although this functionality is convenient, it's best not to use it, because you'll often need to move your recorded macros from the default location into which Word records them to a more permanent location. Moving them breaks any way you've assigned of running the macro, so it's best to move the macro before you assign it to a toolbar, menu, or keyboard shortcut.

3. Click the OK button to start recording the macro. Word displays the Stop Recording toolbar, which contains a Stop Recording button and a Pause Recording/Resume Recording button. The mouse pointer displays an audio-cassette icon to indicate that recording is on.

4. Perform the actions that you want the macro to repeat. You can perform almost all keyboard actions—for example, moving the insertion point and selecting objects—and you can execute most commands from the menus. You cannot use the mouse to select objects or to drag the selection, although you can use the context menu to execute commands (for example, Cut or Paste).

5. If you need to perform an action that you don't want to record in the macro, click the Pause Recorder button on the Stop Recording toolbar, perform the action, and then click the Resume Recorder button.

6. When you've finished all the actions you want to record, click the Stop Recording button or double-click the REC indicator on the status bar to stop recording. (You can also double-click this indicator to start recording a macro.)

To play back the macro, open or activate the document you want to affect, choose Tools → Macro → Macros, select the macro in the listbox, and click the Run button. If you can't see the macro in the list, check the setting in the "Macros in" drop-down list. Choose "All active templates and documents" to see the full list of available macros.

Remove Unnecessary Commands from a Recorded Macro

The Annoyance: Hey, that was easy! I recorded a long macro that sets up the tedious bits of the proposal to a client. The trouble is, I got so carried away that I saved the document and closed it without stopping the Macro Recorder, so now each time I run the macro, it tries to save the active document under the same name.

The Fix: Right: time for you to bite the bullet and come to grips with the Visual Basic Editor. Don't worry, it doesn't bite; it tries to be friendly, and it threatens you with neither Auto-Correct nor AutoFormat As You Type.

You can quickly toggle into the Visual Basic Editor by pressing Alt+F11 from Word, but it's usually best to display the Macro dialog box, select the macro you want to edit, and then click the Edit button. That makes the Visual Basic Editor open the macro you want to edit, so you don't have to navigate to reach it. Figure 8-2 shows the Visual Basic Editor with a recorded macro open.

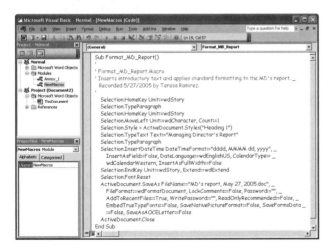

Figure 8-2. The Visual Basic Editor interface is fairly easy to come to grips with.

In the upper-left corner of the Visual Basic Editor window is the Project Explorer, which you use to navigate among open projects. A *project* is the VBA component of a document or template. Word places all recorded macros in the NewMacros module in the *Normal* project—the VBA component of *Normal.dot*. A *module* is a container for VBA code.

Below the Project Explorer is the Properties window, which shows the available properties (attributes) of the selected item. In this case, the NewMacros module is selected, and the only available property is its (Name) property.

The main area of the Visual Basic Editor is the Code window, which shows either the code for the selected item (here, the NewMacros module) or the selected user form. (A *user form* is a custom dialog box.) Each macro begins with a Sub line that shows the name of the macro followed by empty parentheses—for example, Sub Format_MD_Report()—and ends with an End Sub line.

To change your recorded macro, you edit the appropriate commands in the Code window. In this case, look for the commands for saving the document (the lines starting with ActiveDocument.SaveAs; an underscore at the end of a line indicates that the following line is a continuation) and closing it (the ActiveDocument.Close command). Select these lines using the mouse or the keyboard, and press the Delete key to delete them.

If you're satisfied with your changes, save them (click the Save button on the Standard toolbar, press Ctrl+S, or choose File → Save), and then choose File → Close and Return to Microsoft Word to close the Visual Basic Editor and return to Word. Alternatively, press Alt+F11 to flip back to Word, leaving the Visual Basic Editor open so that you can return to it later if you need to make further changes.

Control a Macro with a Message Box

The Annoyance: I've recorded a handful of complex macros, and boy, do they save me a bunch of time formatting and tweaking my documents! But sometimes I hit the hotkey for a macro by mistake, and it makes a whole bunch of changes to my document that I didn't need. It's my fault for being clumsy, but I'd sure like to be able to keep this from happening.

The Fix: You can stop a macro while it's running by pressing Ctrl+Break. (Depending on your keyboard, you may find Break on the front face of the Pause key rather than on a key of its own.) But unless you're extremely quick off the mark, the macro will likely have executed many commands by the time you realize your mistake.

The best solution is to build a confirmation message box into each macro, telling you what the macro is going to do and giving you the chance to cancel it if you've run the macro by mistake or chosen the wrong macro.

To add a confirmation box to a macro, open it in the Visual Basic Editor (choose Tools → Macro → Macros, select the macro, and click the Edit button) and click in the Code window just after the comment lines if they are present, or after the Sub line if they are not. (The comment lines are the lines of text at the beginning of the macro that start with an apostrophe and are colored green by default. These are usually set off with a blank line above and below. You can use the comment lines to give the macro's name and a brief description of what it does.)

Press Enter to create a new line, press ← to move back to the new line, and type the code for a message box (see Figure 8-3), which should look like this:

```
If MsgBox(Prompt:="Format this document?",
Buttons:=vbYesNo + vbQuestion, _
    Title:="Format MD Report") = vbNo Then
    Exit Sub
End If
```

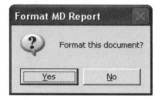

Figure 8-3. Use a message box to make sure neither you nor your colleagues runs a macro by mistake.

This MsgBox statement uses three arguments, named items that denote information used in the statement: Prompt, Buttons, and Title. Prompt receives a text string in double quotation marks (here, "Format this document"), which is displayed in the body of the message box. Title receives another string ("Format MD Report"), which appears in the titlebar. The Buttons argument controls both the buttons displayed in the message box and the icon (if any). vbYesNo makes the message box display a Yes button and a No button. vbQuestion makes the message box display a question-mark icon.

The If condition makes VBA check which button the user clicks in the message box. If the user clicks the No button, the result of the message box is vbNo. In this case, the Then statement comes into effect, and the Exit Sub command makes VBA exit the subprocedure—in other words, skip the rest of the code in the macro. If the user clicks the Yes button, the result of the message box is vbYes; the Exit Sub command doesn't run in this case, so the rest of the macro does run. The End If statement marks the end of the If condition.

As you type the code for the message box, the Visual Basic Editor will help you out with prompts. When the Visual Basic Editor displays a drop-down list of possible options, you can choose from it by "typing down" (continuing typing) to reach your selection, by using ↓ and ↑, or by using the mouse.

To test your message box, *step into* the macro by clicking anywhere between the Sub and End Sub lines and then pressing F8 to execute one command at a time. The Visual Basic

Editor displays a yellow highlight on the command it's currently executing so you can track what's happening. When the message box is displayed, click the Yes button or the No button to dismiss it so you can continue executing the code.

Return to the Last Editing Position When Opening a Document

The Annoyance: I began word processing using a Mac application called WriteNow. When you saved a document in which you were working, WriteNow also saved where you were (that is, where your cursor was positioned in the document). When you opened the document again to continue, the cursor started off where you had left it at the end of the previous session. It frustrates me with Word, especially with a *loooong* document, to always find myself back at the first character of the file when I reopen it.

The Fix: A macro can make Word return to the last editing position. If you assign the macro the predefined name AutoOpen, it will run automatically when you open a document.

PREDEFINED MACRO NAMES

Word recognizes five predefined names for macros that run automatically:

- AutoExec **(when Word starts)**
- AutoExit **(when Word quits)**
- AutoNew **(when you create a new document based on a template containing an** AutoNew **macro)**
- AutoOpen **(when you open a document that contains an** AutoOpen **macro, or a document based on a template that contains one)**
- AutoClose **(when you close such a document)**

By assigning these names, you can make macros run automatically. You can also make an automatic macro run another macro if needed. To do so, include the other macro's name on its own line. For example:

```
Sub AutoOpen()
    Configure_Document_for_Editing
End Sub
```

If you don't want to create a macro, you can return to the last editing position by pressing Shift+F5 after you open the document; see "Return to Your Last Three Edits" in Chapter 3.

Here's how to create the macro:

1. Open the Visual Basic Editor and create a new module for storing your macros. (Word puts recorded macros in the NewMacros module by default, but you'll do better to keep your macros separate.) Right-click the Normal item in the Project Explorer and choose Insert → Module. The Visual Basic Editor creates a new module called Module1. Press F4 to move the focus to the Properties window, type a distinctive name for the module (again, no spaces, but underscores are okay), and press Enter to apply it.

2. With your new module still selected in the Project Explorer, click in the Code window. Create the stub of a macro by typing the Sub keyword and the AutoOpen name:

   ```
   Sub AutoOpen
   ```

3. Press Enter at the end of the line. The Visual Basic Editor automatically adds the parentheses after the macro name, a blank line, and the End Sub line:

   ```
   Sub AutoOpen()

   End Sub
   ```

4. Type the statement Application.GoBack between the Sub line and the End Sub line.

It's as easy as that. If you don't always want to return to the last editing position when you open a document, add a message box to let you choose whether to do so, as shown in Example 8-1.

To prevent a line of code from growing too long, you can break it by typing a space and an underscore at the appropriate point. The break must be between VBA terms rather than inside them, and it cannot be within a string.

Example 8-1. An AutoOpen macro to return to the location of the last edit after soliciting confirmation

```
Sub AutoOpen()
    If MsgBox(Prompt:="Return to the last edit?", Buttons:=vbYesNo + vbQuestion, _
        Title:="Return to Last Edit") Then
        Application.GoBack
    End If
End Sub
```

Make Print Preview Open in Editing Mode

The Annoyance: Call me weird, but I've taken to editing in Print Preview. But it takes three steps to switch to Print Preview, enter Edit mode, and zoom the window how I want it. I'd like to make it one step.

The Fix: Easy enough. Actually, this is a good candidate for a recorded macro. Choose Tools → Macro → Record Macro, type a name (for example, **PrintPreviewEdit**), type a description, and then click the OK button. Choose File → Print Preview, and click the Magnifier button to enter editing mode. Choose View → Toolbars → Print Preview to toggle off the Print Preview toolbar (to save the space it takes up). Choose View → Zoom, select your preferred zoom settings, and click the OK button. Click the Stop Recording button on the Stop Recording toolbar to stop the Macro Recorder.

If you open the macro in the Visual Basic Editor, it should look something like Example 8-2.

Here's what's going on in this macro:

- The `ActiveDocument.PrintPreview` statement technically applies the `PrintPreview` method to the `ActiveDocument` object. The `ActiveDocument` object represents the active document—that is, the document you're working with in the user interface. A *method* is a command or action that you can take with an object.

- The `CommandBars("Print Preview").Visible = False` statement turns off the display of the Print Preview toolbar. A `CommandBar` object is either a toolbar (as it is here) or a menu bar. VBA groups similar objects into groups called *collections* to simplify access to them. To reach an object in a collection, you specify its name (as here: the object called "Print Preview" in the `CommandBars` collection) or its index number (for example, `CommandBars(1)` indicates the object with the index number 1 in the `CommandBars` collection). Objects have properties (attributes) that control how they behave. This statement sets the `Visible` property of the `CommandBar` object to `False`, making it invisible—in other words, hiding the toolbar.

- `With... End With` is a structure for applying multiple methods, properties, or a combination of the two to the same object. By using a `With` statement, you tell VBA that you're referring to a particular object until you start referring to another object. (This enables VBA to work faster than if it has to work out the target object each time.) This `With` statement works with the `Zoom` object contained in the `View` object within the `ActivePane` object (the active pane) within the `ActiveWindow` object. The statements contained in the `With` statement set the number of page columns to `2` and the number of page rows to `1`—in other words, the equivalent of clicking the Many Pages button in the Zoom dialog box and choosing two pages wide by one page deep.

```
Example 8-2. A macro that opens Print Preview in editing mode

Sub PrintPreviewEdit()

' PrintPreviewEdit Macro
' Macro recorded 5/14/2005 by Teresa Ramirez

    ActiveDocument.PrintPreview
    ActiveDocument.ActiveWindow.View.Magnifier = False
    CommandBars("Print Preview").Visible = False
    With ActiveWindow.ActivePane.View.Zoom
        .PageColumns = 2
        .PageRows = 1
    End With
End Sub
```

If you want this macro to supplant the built-in Print Preview command, rename it `FilePrintPreview`. You cannot record a macro with the name of a built-in command, but you can rename a recorded macro in the Visual Basic Editor so that it replaces a built-in command.

You can also create a macro with the name of a built-in command by working in the Visual Basic Editor. A quick way to start such a macro is to press Alt+F8 to display the Macros dialog box, choose "Word Commands" in the "Macros in" drop-down list, select the command you want to replace, choose "Normal.dot" in the "Macros in" drop-down list, and then click the Create button. Word enters the code equivalent to the command in the Visual Basic Editor, providing a good starting point.

Make Outline View Open Expanded to a Specified Level

The Annoyance: Word opens in Outline view with everything expanded, including the text. (See "Expand and Collapse Outline View Quickly" in Chapter 3 for more on this annoyance.) I only want it to show Level 1 headings.

The Fix: Create the macro shown in Example 8-3 to replace Word's built-in `ViewOutlineMaster` command, which is used for the View → Outline command and for the Outline View button on the horizontal scrollbar.

```
Example 8-3. A macro to make Outline view open
expanded to Heading Level 1

Sub ViewOutlineMaster()
    ActiveWindow.View.Type = wdOutlineView
    ActiveWindow.View.ShowHeading (1)
End Sub
```

The first statement changes the view of the active window to Outline view. The second statement collapses the outline so that it shows only Level 1 headings. Change the heading number if you want to display a different level of headings—for example, `ActiveWindow.View.ShowHeading (3)` displays Level 1, Level 2, and Level 3 headings.

Copy and paste the macro in the same module you created in "Return to the Last Editing Position When Opening a Document," but change the name of the copy to "ViewOutline." This replaces the built-in Word command assigned to the Ctrl+Alt+O shortcut for switching to Outline view. (If you need to get the built-in Word command back, rename or delete your macro.)

Still in the Visual Basic Editor, click the Save button, or choose File → Save, to save your changes.

Switch the Active Document to Read-Only Status

The Annoyance: I receive lots of documents that I need to read but that I'm not supposed to change. I know I could open them as read-only from the Open dialog box by using the drop-down on the Open button, but I usually open them directly from email or from Explorer, so I don't have that choice. What I'd like is a box to check that tells Word I want to handle a document as "read only" after I've already opened it.

The Fix: As you say, there's no simple checkbox—or other control—to switch an open document to read-only status. But you can create a macro that does this well enough (see Example 8-4). Also, from Windows Explorer, you can right-click a Word document and choose "Open as Read-Only" from the shortcut menu.

Example 8-4 probably looks impenetrable, but once you get the hang of the `If... Then` statements, it's pretty straightforward. Here's what's happening:

Example 8-4. A macro to switch the active document to read-only status

```
Sub Reopen_Active_Document_As_Read_Only()

    'close the active document and reopen it as read-only
    'store the page number and return to it when the document is reopened

    Dim strDocName As String
    Dim strDocFullName As String
    Dim strTitle As String
    Dim intPage As Integer

    strDocName = ActiveDocument.Name
    strDocFullName = ActiveDocument.FullName
    strTitle = "Reopen Document As Read-Only"
    intPage = Selection.Information(wdActiveEndPageNumber)

    If MsgBox(Prompt:="Close " & strDocName & " and reopen as read-only?", _
        Buttons:=vbYesNo + vbQuestion, Title:=strTitle) = vbYes Then
        If ActiveDocument.Path = "" Then
            MsgBox Prompt:="This document has never been saved." & vbCr & vbCr _
                & "Please save it now.", _
                Buttons:=vbOKOnly + vbExclamation, Title:=strTitle
        If Dialogs(wdDialogFileSaveAs).Show = 0 Then
            Exit Sub
        End If
        strDocFullName = ActiveDocument.FullName
    End If

    If Not ActiveDocument.Saved Then
        If MsgBox(Prompt:="The document contains unsaved changes." & vbCr _
            & vbCr & "Click Yes to save the changes; " & _
            "click No to discard the changes.", Buttons:=vbYesNo + vbQuestion, _
            Title:=strTitle) = vbYes Then _
        ActiveDocument.Save
    End If

    ActiveDocument.Close SaveChanges:=wdDoNotSaveChanges
    Documents.Open FileName:=strDocFullName, ReadOnly:=True
    Selection.GoTo What:=wdGoToPage, Which:=wdGoToAbsolute, Count:=intPage
    End If
End Sub
```

- The first few lines are comments explaining what the macro does.

- The second group of lines uses `Dim` statements to declare *variables*, or storage slots for data used in the macro. The format is `Dim variablename As variabletype`. The first three declarations create String variables, which are variables that can hold text characters. The fifth declaration creates an Integer variable, which is a variable that can contain only a whole number (either positive or negative).

- The third group of lines assigns information to the variables. The `strDocName` variable receives the document's name (without the path). The `strDocFullName` variable receives the document's name and path. The `strTitle` variable receives the text to be displayed in the titlebar of each message box. The `intPage` variable gets the page number of the end of the current selection. (This will be used for the macro to display this page again after reopening the document.)

- The first `If` statement displays a message box to confirm that the user wants to run the macro. If the user clicks the Yes button, returning the value `vbYes`, the rest of the macro runs; if not, execution branches to the `End If` statement just before the `End Sub` statement, and the macro ends without taking any action.

- Provided the user has clicked the Yes button in the first message box, the next `If` statement checks whether the active document's path is an empty string (`""`—double quotation marks with no characters between them). If so, that means the document has never been saved, so the macro displays a notification message box (with just an OK button) followed by the Save As dialog box, which is the object named `wdDialogFileSaveAs` in the `Dialogs` collection. If the value returned by the Save As dialog box is `0`, the user has clicked the Cancel button rather than saving the document, so the `Exit Sub` statement exits the macro. Otherwise, the `strDocFullName = ActiveDocument.FullName` statement assigns the document's name and path (now that it has one) to the `strDocFullName` variable.

- The next `If` statement checks whether the document contains unsaved changes (`If Not ActiveDocument.Saved` translates to "if the active document has not been saved") and, if so, displays a message box asking the user to click the Yes button to save the changes or the No button to discard the changes. If the user clicks the Yes button, the `ActiveDocument.Save` statement saves the changes.

- After all those preliminaries, it's time for action. The `ActiveDocument.Close SaveChanges:=wdDoNotSaveChanges` statement closes the document without saving changes. (If the user chose to save unsaved changes, they've already been saved.) The `Documents.Open` statement then uses the `strDocFullName` variable to open the document again, this time as read-only. The `Selection.GoTo` statement displays the page whose number is stored in the `intPage` variable—that is, the page that was displayed when the macro was run.

Close All Documents Except the Current One

The Annoyance: I tend to end up with a stack of documents open and need to close all except the one I'm working on. Clicking the Close button gets tedious, even though it could hardly be easier.

The Fix: You can easily create a macro (see Example 8-5) to close all the documents except the current one. To do so, you use a *loop*, a structure that tells VBA to repeat an action as long as a condition is true or until a condition is met.

```
Example 8-5. A macro that closes all documents except the active document

Sub Close_All_Except_Active_Document()

    Dim i As Integer
    Dim strKeepOpen As String

    strKeepOpen = ActiveDocument.Name

    For i = Documents.Count To 1 Step -1
       If Documents(i).Name <> strKeepOpen Then Documents(i).Close
    Next i

End Sub
```

As you can see, this macro is short and friendly: it even lacks comments about what the macro does (add them at the beginning if you like) and a message box to confirm that the user wants to take the action (you could add this too). Here's how it works:

- The first group of lines declares an Integer variable named i and a String variable called strKeepOpen. The next line then assigns to strKeepOpen the name of the active document, which is the document the macro will leave open.

- The For... Next loop uses the variable i as its counter and runs from Documents.Count (which returns the number of open documents) to 1, decrementing the counter by 1 (Step -1) at each iteration. (By default, loops increment the counter by one unless you specify otherwise. This loop needs to run backwards because each time the macro closes a document, the number of documents in the Documents collection decreases by one.) The If state-

ment compares the name of the current document with strKeepOpen and closes the document if the name doesn't match. For example, if you have 12 documents open, Word starts with Documents(12)—the twelfth document in the Documents collection—and closes that document if its name does not match the value of strKeepOpen. The Next i statement indicates the end of the loop, making execution return to the For statement. The loop continues to execute until the counter reaches 1.

Create a "Paste as Unformatted Text" Macro

The Annoyance: I often have to create documents that are cobbled together from various sources, and I need to strip out all the existing formatting.

The Fix: As you saw in Chapter 3, pasting material as unformatted text can save you plenty of formatting annoyances. To automate the process, all you need is a single line of VBA code (see Example 8-6).

Example 8-6. A macro that pastes as unformatted text

```
Sub Paste_As_Unformatted_Text()
    Selection.PasteSpecial Link:=False, DataType:=wdPasteText, _
        Placement:=wdInLine, DisplayAsIcon:=False
End Sub
```

See Which Keyboard Shortcuts Are Assigned

The Annoyance: Our systems people have customized our main work template so that we can all use company-standard keyboard shortcuts for applying styles and running macros. The problem is that I was ahead of them on this and have been using my own shortcuts—which aren't all the same as the new ones. So now some of my shortcuts work, while others run commands I'm not expecting. How can I see what's assigned where? I'm sick of combing through the Customize Keyboard dialog box in the hope of identifying the apparently random command they've assigned to my shortcut.

The Fix: Good news—you can print out a list of assignments. Choose Tools → Macro → Macros, type `listcommands`, and press Enter or click the Run button. In the List Commands dialog box (see Figure 8-4), choose the "Current menu and keyboard settings" option (to see the full list of commands, choose the "All Word commands" option). You can print out the resulting table for reference, search through it, or sort it by the column that interests you (using Table → Sort).

Figure 8-4. The List Commands command produces a table of the keyboard shortcuts currently assigned in Word.

Remove Typed Numbering from Lists and Headings

The Annoyance: My boss emails me numbered lists of tasks for everyone in the office. When I put them into our Assignment template, I need to delete all the numbers he's typed in, because the lists get automatic numbering from the styles. I know I can go through selecting each list and then clicking the Numbering button on the Formatting toolbar twice, once to remove the numbers and once to reapply them, but that messes up the list templates.

The Fix: Create the short macro shown in Example 8-7 to remove the manually applied numbers from a selected list.

WordBasic was the programming language used in early versions of Word, before Microsoft applied VBA to Word. VBA includes a `WordBasic` object that enables you to use WordBasic commands, such as this one, via VBA.

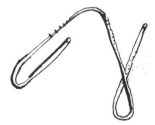

```
Remove_Manual_List_Numbering()
    WordBasic.ToolsBulletsNumbers Replace:=0, Type:=1, Remove:=1
End Sub
```

Apply Proper Capitalization

The Annoyance: The Title Case option in the Change Case dialog box (Format → Change Case) makes the first letter of each word uppercase and the remaining letters lowercase. But conjunctions and short prepositions (five letters or fewer, according to the magazine I work for) should be all lowercase.

The Fix: A macro can fix most of these errors, although you will need to check prepositions that need initial capitals because they are part of a verb. Example 8-8 shows the macro.

If you're familiar with VBA, you'll probably find the extended Or condition cumbersome—not to mention a lot of typing. You can make the code more compact by using a Select Case statement instead of the If statement, using Case "a", "above", "after", "an", and so on.

The code in the macro is fairly straightforward:

- In the first group of statements, the macro declares two variables: a String variable named strL and an Integer variable named i.

- In the second group of statements, the macro selects the appropriate paragraph. The first statement compares the selection type to wdInsertionPoint—the "selection" being a point in the text rather than an actual selection of characters or other objects. If the selection is not an insertion point, the macro collapses the selection to an insertion point. The second statement selects the first paragraph of the (collapsed) selection—in other words, the paragraph in which the insertion point is located. Selecting the paragraph also selects the paragraph mark at its end, and this paragraph mark counts as a "word." So, to work with only the real words, the third statement shortens the selection by one character to the left, deselecting the paragraph mark.

- The third group of statements applies title case (first letter capitalized) to the first and last words in the selection, because the first and last words in a heading must always be capitalized even if they're short prepositions or conjunctions.

- The fourth group of statements uses a For... Next loop to check each of the remaining words in the selection against a list of short prepositions and conjunctions. (Adjust this list to meet your company's style demands.) The loop runs from 2 (the second word) to Selection. Words.Count - 1, or the number of words in the paragraph minus 1 (so as not to affect the last word, to which title case has already been applied). The second statement assigns to strL the lowercase (LCase) version of the currently selected word, with any leading or trailing spaces trimmed off it (when you double-click to select a word, VBA includes any spaces after the word). Using the lowercase version of the word is necessary because the comparison is case-sensitive. The If statement then compares strL to the list of prepositions and conjunctions. If there's a match, Word applies lowercase to the word; if not, the Else statement applies title case to the word.

- Finally, the Selection.Collapse statement collapses the selection to its end, which is equivalent to pressing → to deselect a selection.

Example 8-8. A macro to apply proper capitalization to a title

```
Sub Apply_Proper_Capitalization()

  'applies proper capitalization to the first paragraph in the selection

    Dim strL As String
    Dim i As Integer

    If Selection.Type <> wdSelectionIP Then Selection.Collapse
    Selection.Paragraphs(1).Range.Select
    Selection.MoveLeft Unit:=wdCharacter, Count:=1, Extend:=wdExtend

    Selection.Words(1).Case = wdTitleWord
    Selection.Words(Selection.Words.Count).Case = wdTitleWord

    For i = 2 To Selection.Words.Count - 1
        strL = LCase(Trim(Selection.Words(i)))
        If strL = "a" Or strL = "above" Or strL = "after" Or strL = "an" Or _
        strL = "and" Or strL = "as" Or strL = "at" Or strL = "below" Or _
        strL = "but" Or strL = "by" Or strL = "down" Or strL = "for" Or _
        strL = "from" Or strL = "in" Or strL = "into" Or strL = "of" Or _
        strL = "off" Or strL = "on" Or strL = "onto" Or strL = "or" Or _
        strL = "out" Or strL = "over" Or strL = "the" Or strL = "to" Or _
        strL = "under" Or strL = "up" Or strL = "with" Then
            Selection.Words(i).Case = wdLowerCase
        Else
            Selection.Words(i).Case = wdTitleWord
        End If
    Next i

    Selection.Collapse Direction:=wdEnd

End Sub
```

t i p

This macro isn't perfect, as it ignores the possibility of periods or other punctuation requiring prepositions or conjunctions to be title case in the middle of a paragraph. You might adapt the macro to take care of this need. You might also add a list of uppercase terms (for example, XP) or intercapitalized terms (for example, iPod) that require special treatment.

Double-Save a Document

The Annoyance: Call me paranoid, but I think Word may really be out to get me—or perhaps it's just that I'm working with master documents. Anyway, Word seems unstable, and I want to keep a backup copy of each document I'm working with while I'm working with it. It seems to me that Word's automatic backup copy would be just about ideal, if it were a copy of my most recent save rather than the last-but-one save. With the speed at which I'm trying to make progress on my documents, even losing a couple of minutes' worth of changes is painful.

The Fix: Create a macro to force Word to save the document twice in immediate succession. Call the macro **FileSave** so that it replaces Word's built-in Save command and picks up its keyboard shortcut (Ctrl+S).

If you simply want to double-save the document, all you need is the macro shown in Example 8-9.

Example 8-9. A macro to save the active document twice in succession

```
Sub FileSave()

    Options.CreateBackup = True

    ActiveDocument.Save
    ActiveDocument.Saved = False
    ActiveDocument.Save

End Sub
```

The `Options.CreateBackup = True` statement ensures that the "Always create backup copy" feature is on (you can also set it by choosing Tools → Options, clicking the Save tab, and checking the "Always create backup copy" box).

But if you really need to safeguard your work, you can adapt the macro so that it automatically copies the backup document to a safe location—for example, a network drive, as in Example 8-10.

This macro declares three String variables to store the text it uses for naming the documents. It assigns to `strDocName` the name of the active document and assigns to `strWordBackupDoc` a string consisting of the full name (including the path) that Word gives the backup document for the active document. For example, if the active document is named *Example.doc* and is located in the *C:\Samples* folder, its backup document is named *C:\Samples\Backup of Example.wbk*.

The macro assigns to `strMyBackupDoc` the path and name for the backup document that you want to create. In this example, the macro assigns the backup document the path *Z:\Public\Backups* (change it as needed, and use the notation *\\server\folder* if the drive isn't mapped to a letter), the basic filename, the word "backup," the date in *yyyy-mm-dd* format, and the time in *hh-mm-ss AMPM* format. In other words, the backup document for *Example.doc* will have a name such as *Example backup 2005-05-27 04-14-38 PM.doc*.

Finally, the `FileCopy` statement copies the file specified by `strWordBackupDoc` to `strMyBackupDoc`. If there's already a file with that name in the backup folder, it will be overwritten, but unless you save twice within a second, this shouldn't happen.

```
Example 8-10. A macro to back up the active document's default backup copy to a network drive

Sub FileSave()

    Dim strDocName As String
    Dim strWordBackupDoc As String
    Dim strMyBackupDoc As String

    Options.CreateBackup = True

    ActiveDocument.Save
    ActiveDocument.Saved = False
    ActiveDocument.Save

    strDocName = ActiveDocument.Name

    strWordBackupDoc = ActiveDocument.Path & "\Backup of " & _
      Left(strDocName, Len(strDocName) - 3) & "wbk"

    strMyBackupDoc = "Z:\Public\Backups\" & Left(strDocName, _
        Len(strDocName) - 4) & " backup " & Format(Date, "yyyy-mm-dd") & _
        " " & Format(Time, "hh-mm-ss AMPM") & ".doc"

    FileCopy strWordBackupDoc, strMyBackupDoc
End Sub
```

Print a Document in Monochrome

The Annoyance: Changing the Compatibility settings in the Options dialog box so that I can legibly print a document that contains color text on my monochrome printer (see "Print Colored Text as Black on a Monochrome Printer" in Chapter 6) is getting kinda old. Automate it for me already!

The Fix: Right you are. Create a macro that looks like Example 8-11.

This macro creates two Boolean variables, which are variables that can only be True or False. It then checks to see if the number of open documents is 0; if so, it stops running the macro so as to avoid the error that results from trying to print without a document open.

Example 8-11. A macro to print the active document in monochrome

```
Sub Print_Active_Document_in_Monochrome()

    Dim blnBWOn As Boolean
    Dim blnDocClean As Boolean

    If Documents.Count = 0 Then Exit Sub

    With ActiveDocument
        blnDocClean = .Saved
        blnBWOn = .Compatibility(wdPrintColBlack)
        .Compatibility(wdPrintColBlack) = True
        Dialogs(wdDialogFilePrint).Show
        .Compatibility(wdPrintColBlack) = blnBWOn
        .Saved = blnDocClean
    End With
End Sub
```

For the bulk of its code, the macro uses a `With` statement referring to the active document. It stores the current state of the document's `Saved` property (`True` if the document contains no unsaved changes, `False` if it does contain some) in the `blnDocClean` variable, and the state of the `Compatibility` (`wdPrintColBlack`) setting (whether the "Print colors as black on noncolor printers" checkbox on the Compatibility tab of the Options dialog box is checked) in the `blnBWOn` variable.

The macro then sets `Compatibility(wdPrintColBlack)` to `True` and displays the Print dialog box so that the user can print the document. Finally, the macro restores `Compatibility` (`wdPrintColBlack`) and `Saved` to the values stored in the two variables.

Display the Print Dialog Box with the "Current Page" or "Pages" Option Selected

The Annoyance: When I'm working on a document, I often want to finish editing a page, print it, check it, and then print another page. But the Print dialog box always appears with the All option selected in the Page Range group box.

The Fix: With a short macro (see Example 8-12), you can make the Print dialog box appear with the Current Page option, the Pages option, or the Selection option selected instead. If you select the Pages option, you can specify the range of pages to print, as in the example.

Example 8-12. A macro to display the Print dialog box with print options preselected

```
Sub Display_Print_Dialog_Custom()
    With Dialogs(wdDialogFilePrint)
        .Range = wdPrintRangeOfPages
        .Pages = "3,5,7-11"
        If .Show = -1 Then .Execute
    End With
End Sub
```

The `With` statement works with the `wdDialogFilePrint` member of the `Dialogs` collection—in other words, the Print dialog box. The commands inside the `With` statement control the options selected:

- To select the Current Page option, use this statement:

  ```
  .Range = wdPrintCurrentPage
  ```

- To select the Pages option and specify a simple range of pages, use these statements, substituting suitable numbers on the `From` and `To` lines:

  ```
  .Range = wdPrintFromTo
  .From = "2"
  .To = "4"
  ```

- To select the Pages option and specify a complex range of pages, use these statements, substituting suitable numbers on the `Pages` line:

  ```
  .Range = wdPrintRangeOfPages
  .Pages = "3,5,7-11"
  ```

The `Show` method displays the dialog box and returns a value for the button the user clicks. If the value is `-1`, which indicates that the user clicked the OK button, the `Execute` command executes the instructions contained in the dialog box. If the user clicks the Cancel button, VBA does not execute the instructions.

Perform Find and Replace Operations with Complex Formatting

The Annoyance: I tried the replace-with-subscript trick mentioned in Chapter 4 (see "Replace with a Subscript"), and it's fine as far as it goes. But what I need to do is find each table caption; check to see if the paragraph before it uses a boxed style; and, if it doesn't, apply a top border to the table caption. I can't do that with Replace, now can I?

The Fix: Not as you describe it, no. But a macro using Find can locate the table captions, check them, and apply the border as needed. The macro shown in Example 8-13 searches for each paragraph using the Table Caption style and applies a top border to that paragraph if the previous paragraph doesn't have a bottom border. You'll need to adapt the specifics, but the principle should work for you.

Example 8-13. A macro to search for specific formatting and check nearby formatting

```
Sub Check_Table_Captions()

    'go through the document for paragraphs in the Table Caption style
    'check if the paragraph before has a bottom border
    'if not, apply a top border to the Table Caption paragraph

    Dim i As Integer
    Dim strMTitle As String

    On Error GoTo ErrorHandler

    strMTitle = "Apply Upper Border to Table Caption Style"

    If MsgBox(Prompt:="Apply the upper borders to the Table Caption style?", _
        Buttons:=vbYesNo + vbQuestion, Title:=strMTitle) = vbNo Then
        Exit Sub
    End If
    For i = 2 To ActiveDocument.Paragraphs.Count
        With ActiveDocument.Paragraphs(i)
            .Range.Select
            If .Style = "Table_Caption" Then
                If .Previous.Borders(wdBorderBottom).LineStyle <> _
                    wdLineStyleSingle Then
                    .Borders(wdBorderTop).LineStyle = wdLineStyleSingle
                    .Borders(wdBorderTop).LineWidth = wdLineWidth100pt
                    .Borders(wdBorderTop).Color = wdColorBlack
                End If
            End If
        End With
    Next i

ErrorHandler:
    If Err.Number = 5834 Then
        MsgBox Prompt:="This document doesn't use the Table Caption style.", _
            Buttons:=vbOKOnly + vbInformation, Title:=strMTitle
        Exit Sub
    Else
        MsgBox Prompt:="The following error has occurred:" & vbCr & vbCr & _
            "Error Number: " & Err.Number & vbCr & vbCr & _
            "Error Description: " & Err.Description, _
            Buttons:=vbOKOnly + vbInformation, Title:=strMTitle
        Exit Sub
    End If
End Sub
```

Much of this macro is straightforward if you've been follow-ing along through this chapter, but the following points are worth noting:

- The `On Error GoTo ErrorHandler` line tells VBA to trap errors and directs them to an error handler (a section of code designed to deal with errors). Unhandled errors in your macros usually display error message boxes, which are confusing for users, as many of the errors are hard to interpret. The error this macro is most likely to encounter is the active document not containing the Table Caption style. If this happens, the code after the `ErrorHandler:` label at the end of the macro runs, checking the error number against the number for a missing style (`5834`); if it matches, the error handler displays a message box explaining what has happened and then exits the macro. If there's a different error, the `Else` statement makes the macro display a message box giving the error's number and description. This information tends to be neither intelligible nor helpful, but it's preferable to having an error message box named Microsoft Visual Basic appear unexpectedly on the screen.

- The `For` loop uses a counter (`i`) and runs from `i = 2` to `ActiveDocument.Paragraphs.Count`, which is the number of paragraphs in the document. This loop enables the macro to check every paragraph in the document (skip-ping the first paragraph, which doesn't have a paragraph before it) for the Table Caption style.

- The `With` statement works with the paragraph the loop is currently examining (`ActiveDocument.Paragraphs(i)`). If the paragraph's style is Table Caption, the nested `If` statement checks to see if the previous paragraph (`.Previous`) is lacking a bottom border. If it is, the three `.Borders` statements apply the necessary border.

Print Samples of Each Font Installed on Your PC

The Annoyance: I need a printout of all the fonts that Word can offer me. I'm sick of scrolling through the font list trying to find one that looks okay.

The Fix: Try the macro shown in Example 8-14.

Here's what the macro does:

1. First, it declares two String variables, one to store the current font name and the other to store the sample text string.

2. It then displays an input box prompting the user to enter the sample text string that she wants to use, providing her with default text that she can accept. If the input box returns an empty string (`""`), the user either clicked the Cancel button, or deleted the default string and failed to replace it. Either way, the macro quits without further ado.

3. Next, the macro creates a new document (`Documents. Add`) and uses a `For... Next` loop that runs once for each font (i.e., for each item in the `FontNames` collection). The loop resets the font, types the font's name followed by "parahere," applies the font, and types the sample text string. The word "parahere" is a placeholder that enables the macro to separate the font names from the sample text that follows; you can use any other unique text string instead.

4. The macro then selects all the content of the document and sorts it alphabetically by paragraph.

5. The `With Selection.Find` structure clears formatting and options that might cause problems and then performs two replace operations. Some Find properties may already be set in Word, so it's best to clear formatting, specify a zero-length text string, and turn off options such as "Match case," "Use wildcards," and "Find all word forms." The `Execute` command executes each search. The first replace operation replaces the placeholder text "parahere" with "parahere" and an extra paragraph, which splits each font name from its sample text. The second replace operation replaces "parahere" with a Heading 2 paragraph. This has the effect of applying the Heading 2 style to the para-graphs that contain the font names.

6. The three `Selection` statements collapse the selection, apply the Heading 1 style to the first paragraph in the document, and enter a heading for the list in that para-graph.

7. The message box tells the user what the macro has done and prompts her to save the document if she wants to keep it.

Example 8-14. A macro to list all the fonts available to Word, with a sample of each font

```
Sub List_All_Fonts()
    'Lists all the fonts available to Word with the current printer driver

    Dim strFont As Variant
    Dim strText As String

    strText = InputBox(Prompt:= _
        "Type the sample text you want to use in the font listing:", _
        Title:="List All Fonts", _
        Default:="The five boxing wizards jump quickly.")
    If strText = "" Then Exit Sub

    Documents.Add
    For Each strFont In FontNames
        Selection.Font.Reset
        Selection.TypeText strFont & "parahere"
        Selection.Font.Name = strFont
        Selection.TypeText strText & vbCr
    Next

    ActiveDocument.Content.Select
    Selection.Sort FieldNumber:="Paragraphs", _
        SortFieldtype:=wdSortFieldAlphanumeric

    With Selection.Find
        .ClearFormatting
        .MatchCase = False
        .MatchAllWordForms = False
        .MatchWholeWord = False
        .MatchSoundsLike = False
        .MatchWildcards = False
        .Forward = True
        .Wrap = wdFindContinue
        .Text = "parahere"
        .Replacement.Text = "parahere^p"
        .Execute Replace:=wdReplaceAll

        .Text = "parahere"
        .Replacement.Style = "Heading 2"
        .Execute Replace:=wdReplaceAll
        .Replacement.ClearFormatting
        .Replacement.Text = ""
        .Execute Replace:=wdReplaceAll
        .Text = ""
    End With

    Selection.Collapse Direction:=wdCollapseStart
    Selection.Paragraphs(1).Style = "Heading 1"
    Selection.TypeText "List of Fonts Available to Word"

    MsgBox "The macro has created a list showing the fonts currently " _
        & "available to Word." & vbCr & vbCr & _
        "Please save this document if you want to keep it.", _
        vbOKOnly + vbInformation, "List All Fonts Macro"

End Sub
```

ADMINISTERING MACROS

Move a Macro from One Template to Another

The Annoyance: I reckon I've more or less gotten the hang of the Visual Basic Editor by now—at least, I can create and edit macros in different projects. But do you mean to tell me that I need to use Cut and Paste to move a macro from one project to another?

The Fix: You've hit upon one of the Visual Basic Editor's most dramatic shortcomings: the inability to copy or move a macro quickly from one project (a template or document) to another. But Word itself can take care of this task: choose Tools → Macro → Macros, click the Organizer button in the Macros dialog box, and then click the Macro Project Items tab. See which projects are open in the two "Macro Project Items available in" boxes; if necessary, click the Close File button to close one of the open projects, and then use the resulting Open File button to open the relevant project. With the projects open, select the item you want to copy, and click the Copy button. To move an item, copy it to the new location and then click the Delete button to delete it from the source project.

When you've finished copying or moving items, click the Close button to close the Organizer dialog box, and save the documents or templates with which you've been working.

Find Out Why Word Won't Run a Macro

The Annoyance: When I open the template that one of my colleagues has developed, Word says that the macros are disabled and tells me to check the host application's online help or documentation. Help! What's a host application, what's the problem, and—most of all—how do I fix it?

The Fix: Visual Basic for Applications is what's called a *hosted* programming language: instead of running on its own, as Visual Basic itself does, VBA requires a host application to provide it with an environment in which to work. Word is the host application here; the other Office applications, and many other applications, also host VBA.

The problem is that Word's security settings are set to protect you from potentially dangerous code. Because VBA can take a wide variety of actions on your computer without your intervention, it's a security threat. Consequently, Microsoft has bundled up Word (and the other Office applications) increasingly tightly against malefaction. When you open a VBA project that might be dangerous, Word disables its macros (see Figure 8-5).

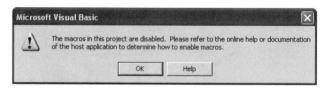

Figure 8-5. If Word automatically disables macros that you need to run, you may need to change your security settings.

To change the security settings so that you can run the macros (assuming that you trust the template's creator not to use them to wreak havoc on your machine), choose Tools → Macro → Security and select the appropriate option on the Security Level tab (see Figure 8-6). Word 2003 offers Very High, High, Medium, and Low levels; Word XP and Word 2000 do not offer the Very High level. Here's what you need to know about the details:

Trusted locations

By default, Word trusts macros in templates and add-ins (for example, global templates) installed on your computer. So, even if you set the security level to Very High or High, you can still run any macros that you create yourself. To prevent Word from trusting installed templates and add-ins, uncheck the "Trust all installed add-ins and templates" box on the Trusted Publishers tab (Trusted Sources tab in Word XP and Word 2000).

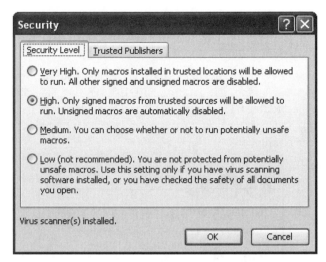

Figure 8-6. The Security Level tab lets you control whether Word will run macros that are not signed with digital signatures or installed in trusted locations.

Trusted publishers/trusted sources

Trusted publishers (in Word 2003), also known as trusted sources (in Word XP or Word 2000), are people or entities for whom a digital certificate is installed on your computer and who are designated as trustworthy. You can view the list on the Trusted Publishers tab or Trusted Sources tab. If you administer your computer, you will probably be able to add trusted publishers or sources; if so, Word will prompt you when you open a document, template, or add-in that has been signed by a digital certificate that's not yet trusted. In a corporate network, network administrators usually manage trusted sources.

> A *digital certificate* is encrypted code that uniquely identifies its holder. Digital certificates are available from *certification authorities* (CAs) such as VeriSign (*http://www.verisign.com*), Thawte (*http://www.thawte.com*; a VeriSign company), and GlobalSign NV (*http://www.globalsign.com*). Some companies also issue digital certificates to their own staff from in-house CAs.

Signed and unsigned macros

A signed macro is one that has been digitally signed by the holder of a digital certificate. Being signed doesn't mean that the macro is necessary benevolent or trustworthy, just that it has some form of audit trail attached to it. Similarly, being unsigned doesn't necessarily mean that a macro is malicious.

> If you distribute your macros to other people, you will need to sign them to ensure that they are trusted. Once you've installed a digital certificate on your PC, you can sign a macro project (for example, a template) in the Visual Basic Editor: click the project in the Project Explorer, choose Tools → Digital Signature, click the Choose button, pick the certificate in the Select Certificate dialog box, and click the OK button to close each dialog box.

Create an Add-in

The Annoyance: I've been putting AutoText entries, keyboard shortcuts, and custom toolbars and menus in *Normal.dot* so that they're available to all my documents. But I've had to delete and rebuild *Normal.dot* twice in the last couple of months, which was a huge waste of time.

The Fix: When *Normal.dot* gets cranky, Word's foundations start to quiver.

Your first line of defense is to back up *Normal.dot* often, so that even if it does get corrupted, you can recover quickly using an older version. But if *Normal.dot* is starting to corrupt frequently, you're probably keeping too much information in it, so you should transfer as much as possible of that information into other locations.

Create a new template (as discussed in Chapter 2) and save it. With the template still open, choose Tools → Macro → Macros, and click the Organizer button. Use the controls on the Organizer dialog box's four tabs to move the AutoText entries, keyboard shortcuts, and custom toolbars and menus to the new template. Save the template and close it.

Still in Word, choose Tools → Templates and Add-Ins, click the Add button, navigate to and select the template, and then click the OK button to load it as a global template. Back up this global template frequently as well, in case it too sustains corruption.

You can load the global template automatically, if you prefer, by placing it in your Word *Startup* folder. Choose Start → Run, type `%userprofile%\Application Data\Microsoft\Word\Startup`, and press Enter to open a Windows Explorer window to your Word *Startup* folder.

OLE, Mail Merge, and Office Applications

By this point, you should have wrestled Word more or less into submission—unless you're performing mail merges or using Word together with other Office applications (in which case, read this chapter), or you're using Word on the Mac (in which case, see Chapter 10).

This chapter starts by nailing the key object linking and embedding (OLE) annoyances: how to choose between linking and embedding, and how to deal with broken links after one of your colleagues has made the wrong choice. The chapter then shows you how to deal with the grievances typically aired about mail merging, from using filtering and fields to create a smarter mail merge to convincing Word that a document really isn't a merge document anymore.

The second half of the chapter deals with annoyances you may experience when using Word with Excel, PowerPoint, and Access. The topics covered range from keeping an Excel chart updated in a Word document to converting a Word table into an Access database.

OBJECT LINKING AND EMBEDDING

Choose Between Linking and Embedding Objects

The Annoyance: I need to put part of a spreadsheet into a Word document so that it all prints together. I've gotten as far as the Paste Special dialog box—but should I use the "Paste" option or the "Paste link" option? What is the "link" bit, and what's it for?

The Fix: As you're seeing, the Office applications provide two main ways of including information created in one application (here, the cells from the spreadsheet) in a document created in another application (here, your Word document). In either case, you want to use the Edit → Paste Special command and select the object with the application's name—for example, Microsoft Office Excel Worksheet Object—in the As list.

Embedding, or using the "Paste" command here, places the source information in the destination document in a format that you can edit (provided that your computer has the relevant application). For example, say you put those cells in your document and send it to your boss on another continent. As long as your boss has Excel on his computer, he can double-click the cells in the Word document to make Word load the relevant parts of Excel in the background so that he can edit the cells (see Figure 9-1). There's no link between the document and the spreadsheet from which the cells came. If your boss doesn't have Excel, he'll see the cells, but he won't be able to edit them.

Linking (using the "Paste link" command here) places the Excel cells in the document but also creates a link back to the source spreadsheet. That means that you can update the link to show the latest information in the spreadsheet—provided that it is available on the same path as it was on the computer that created it, if you're opening the document on a different machine. When you double-click the cells in the

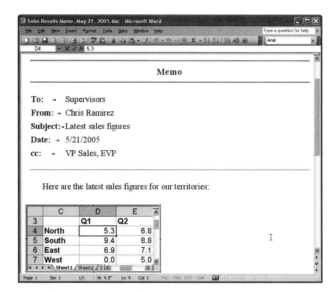

Figure 9-1. Embedding lets you put an editable section of a file created in another application—for example, some cells from an Excel spreadsheet—in a Word document.

Word document, Word activates Excel (again, assuming it is available on the computer) and takes you to those cells in the spreadsheet so that you can work on them directly. Linking breaks down if the application or the file isn't where the object in the Word document expects it to be.

If you're the only one who will be using your document, and you want to be able to print it out showing the latest information, link the cells rather than embedding them. If you want to be able to send the document to someone who doesn't have access to the spreadsheet, embed the cells.

> **Embedding creates a larger file size than linking, because Word needs to store more data in the Word document. However, file size typically becomes an issue only when you embed large graphical items—for example, if you embed a dozen complex PowerPoint slides in a Word document—and then need to squeeze the document onto a floppy disk or attach it to an email message.**

Update, Edit, and Break Links

The Annoyance: Right now, linking doesn't seem like such a good idea. Word says it can't even find the linked file with which I'm trying to update the document that my colleague in Finance sent me.

The Fix: Relax, the file is probably just on a different path for your computer. What you need to do is find out where the file actually is, and then update the link so that Word looks in the right place. Proceed as follows:

1. In the Word document, choose Edit → Links to display the Links dialog box (see Figure 9-2). Click the link that's not working (the Update column will probably say "N/A" to indicate that the link is not available), and then check the "Source file" readout in the "Source information for selected link" box. If the readout is too short for you to make out the file's path and name, click the Change Source button and use the "Look in" drop-down list to see the full path.

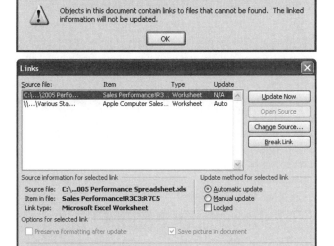

Figure 9-2. If Word tells you that it can't find the linked file, you may need to use the Links dialog box to edit the link to match the file's new location.

2. Open a Windows Explorer window to the folder that's supposed to contain the file and try to locate it. Most likely, either the folder is on a different path for your

computer, or someone has moved or renamed the file. If you're out of luck, someone has deleted the file.

3. Once you know where the file is, click the Change Source button and use the Change Source dialog box to tell Word where the file is.

4. In the Links dialog box, click the Update Now button to update the link.

> In the Links dialog box, you can also break a link so that it no longer works. It's a good idea to break a link before sending a document to someone for whom the link will not work. Update the link before breaking it, and the document will contain the latest data available.

MAIL MERGES

Perform a Basic Mail Merge

The Annoyance: I know that Word has a mass-mailing feature somewhere. Where is it, and how does it work?

The Fix: The feature you're looking for is called "mail merge" and is located on the Tools menu. Exactly where it is and what it's called depends on your version of Word. In Word 2003, choose Tools → Letters and Mailings → Mail Merge to open the Mail Merge task pane (Figure 9-3, left); in Word XP, choose Tools → Letters and Mailings → Mail Merge Wizard to open the wizard, which looks the same as the Mail Merge task pane. The task pane or wizard then walks you through the six steps of specifying the document type, choosing the starting document, selecting recipients or creating a new list of recipients, laying out the document, previewing the document, and then completing the merge.

In Word 2000, choose Tools → Mail Merge to display the Mail Merge Helper dialog box (shown in Figure 9-3, right, with most of a merge set up). The Mail Merge Helper organizes the steps differently than the task pane or wizard; the sequence of actions is essentially the same, but they are accomplished in only three steps.

> The name "mail merge" suggests that this feature is useful primarily for letters, email messages, or faxes, but it's also great for other items that use text drawn from some form of database and entered into a rigid format—for example, catalogs and mailing labels.

The main document and the data source

For each mail merge, you need a main document and a data source. The *main document* is the template according to which the merged documents are laid out, so if you're creating a form letter, the main document is a letter containing placeholders (called *fields*) for the information that will be merged in. The *data source* is the file that contains the data that will be merged into the fields in the main document to create the merge documents. The main document is always a Word document (or template), but the data source can be a Word document containing a table, an Excel spreadsheet, an Access database, your address book, or another file that contains data records.

Creating or designating the data source

The way in which Word presents the mail merge suggests that you should create the main document before you designate the data source, but this is putting the cart before the horse: you can't finish creating the main document until you know the names of the fields in the data source. First, tell Word whether to use the current document as the main document or open another document. Next, designate the data source to use (or create a new data source) and place the fields in the main document.

Word offers you the choice of using an existing data source or creating a new data source. You should almost always use an existing data source, because creating a new data source usually involves replicating data stored elsewhere. It's far better to spend a couple of hours sorting out your Windows Address Book, your Outlook Address Book, or your customer list in Excel or Access so that you can use it effectively for mail merges in the future than it is to spend an hour updating a custom list each time you need to perform a mail merge. This theory holds no matter what type of data you're working with: customer names, telephone numbers, parts listed in a catalog, or product details for a special offer.

Figure 9-3. Mail merge has a different face in Word 2003 (left) and Word XP than in Word 2000 (right), but the steps are largely the same—as are the results.

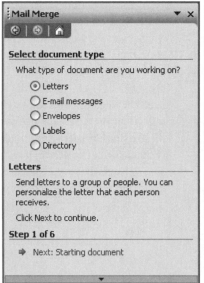

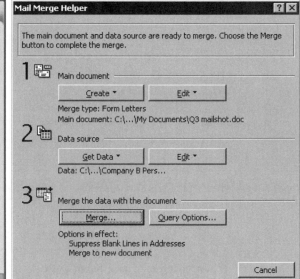

Sometimes, however, you will need to create a new data source for a merge. To do so, select the "Type a new list" option in Word 2003 or Word XP, and then click the Create link. In the New Address List dialog box, click the Customize button to display the Customize Address List dialog box (see Figure 9-4). Add, delete, and rename fields so that you have the list you need, and then use the Move Up and Move Down buttons to shuffle the fields into a suitable order.

Click the OK button to close the Customize Address List dialog box, and enter the details of the first record in the New Address List dialog box (see Figure 9-5).

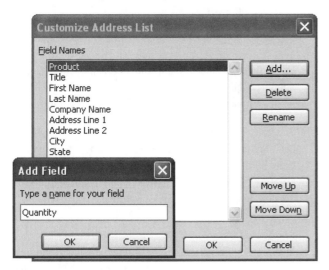

Figure 9-4. When creating a new database for a mail merge, first customize the "address list" so that it includes all the fields you need.

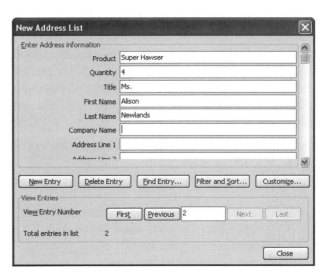

Figure 9-5. After setting up the fields, use the New Address List dialog box to create the records for the database.

THE MAIL MERGE HELPER

What's confusing about the Mail Merge Helper is that, because the dialog box is modal (and thus prevents you from working in a document while it is displayed), Word has to hide it so that you can edit the merge document. You then have to redisplay the dialog box manually (by choosing **Tools** → **Mail Merge** again or clicking the Mail Merge Helper button on the Mail Merge toolbar) so that you can switch to another action (such as editing the data source) or perform the merge. By contrast, the Mail Merge task pane and wizard remain open throughout the merge process, making it easier to see what's happening. The task pane and wizard also include other time-saving features, such as the ability to insert an entire standard address block of fields at once rather than having to insert them one at a time.

When you've entered all the records, click the Close button and save the database when Word prompts you to do so. Word then displays the Mail Merge Recipients dialog box (see Figure 9-6) so that you can select which people (or items) to include in the mail merge. Click the OK button after you've made your choices, and you'll be ready to create the main document.

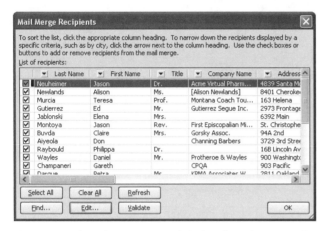

Figure 9-6. In the Mail Merge Recipients dialog box, choose the recipients for the mail merge. You can also perform quick filtering by clicking the drop-down arrows in the heading row.

In Word 2000, click the Get Data button and choose Create Data Source from the pop-up menu, and then work in the Create Data Source dialog box (see Figure 9-7). Add a field by typing its name in the "Field name" box and clicking the Add Field Name button; click the Remove Field Name button to remove the selected field name, and use the two Move buttons to rearrange the list into the right order. Click the OK button to close the Create Data Source dialog box, and then save your data source when Word prompts you to do so. Click the Edit Data Source button in the dialog box that Word displays to tell you that the data source contains no records. Word then displays the Data Form dialog box, in which you can add the details of each record in turn. Click the OK button when you've finished entering the records.

Creating the main document

The main document is the template for all the merge documents you're creating. The basic process is pretty simple: create the nonvariable parts of the document, and then insert a merge field wherever variable information is to be drawn in from the data source. Keep the following points in mind:

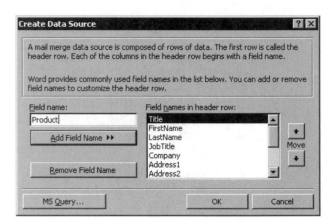

Figure 9-7. Word 2000 uses a different interface for creating a data source, but the process is similar.

- You can base the main document on any template or any existing document. For example, you might use your company's letterhead for a mail-merge letter.

- Include all the spaces and punctuation needed among your merge fields so that the resulting text will be correctly laid out. It's easy to miss the spaces and punctuation when looking at the field codes, but the results will look shoddy. If you normally work without formatting marks displayed, you may find it helpful to display them while laying out your merge. (Click the Show/Hide ¶ button on the Standard toolbar to toggle the display of formatting marks.)

- Use If fields (as discussed in the next Annoyance "Create a Smart Mail Merge with Sorting, Filtering, and If Fields," next) to make decisions where necessary in a merge.

- You can filter the records in your database so that you get only the ones that match your criteria, and then sort them so that they're in the right order (for example, state by state). Again, see "Create a Smart Mail Merge with Sorting, Filtering, and If Fields," next.

To insert a merge field:

- In Word 2003 or Word XP, click one of the links ("Address block," "Greeting line," "Electronic postage," "Postal bar code," or "More items") and use the resulting dialog box to enter the merge fields.

- In Word 2000, click the Insert Merge Field button on the Mail Merge toolbar and choose from the pop-up menu.

Create a Smart Mail Merge with Sorting, Filtering, and If Fields

The Annoyance: The way we've got mail merge set up at the moment, I have to go through the letters in the merge document to check them for blank lines in awkward places, fill in any missing information ("Dear [blank] Smith" doesn't cut it), and make sure we're not sending any letters to Delaware (don't ask). As you can imagine, this takes almost as much time as the merge itself saves.

The Fix: It sounds as though you could smarten up the mail merge a lot by using sorting, filtering, and If fields.

Use filtering and sorting

Unless you create a data source specifically for your mail merge and it's manageably small, chances are that your data source for the mail merge will be imperfect, with some fields blank and others containing the wrong type of information. Word's filtering capabilities and its fields can help you avoid consequences from the imperfections in your data source. Sorting can help put the merged documents in the best order for whatever you're going to do with them.

To use filtering on your mail merge, in Word 2003 or Word XP, click one of the "Edit recipient list" links in the Mail Merge task pane or wizard, click the Edit button in the Mail Merge Recipients dialog box, and then click the "Filter and Sort" button to display the Filter and Sort dialog box (see Figure 9-8). In Word 2000, click the Query Options button in the Mail Merge Helper dialog box to display the Query Options dialog box, which is the Filter and Sort dialog box by its earlier name.

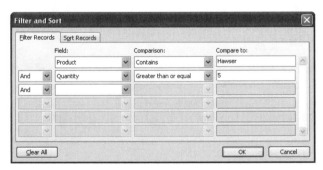

Figure 9-8. Filtering enables you to narrow down the records in your database to match only specific criteria—in this case, customers who bought five or more hawsers.

The Sort Records tab lets you sort the records in your database by one, two, or three fields; for example, you might sort records by city, then by last name, and then by first name. For each sort field, you can choose between ascending order (A to Z, low numbers to high) and descending order (the reverse).

Use If fields

Word's If fields enable you to enter specific text if a condition is true, and other text if it is not. The If fields give you great flexibility in your merges.

To use an If field, click the Insert Word Field button on the Mail Merge toolbar and choose "If... Then... Else..." from the pop-up menu. Set up the condition in the Insert Word Field: IF dialog box (see Figure 9-9): select the field name, the comparison type ("Equal to," "Not equal to," "Less than," "Greater than," "Less than or equal," "Greater than or equal," "Is blank," or "Is not blank"), and the text for the comparison (for any comparison except "Is blank" or "Is not blank"). Then type the text strings in the "Insert this text" and "Otherwise insert this text" boxes. Word displays the "Insert this text" string in the document until you perform the merge.

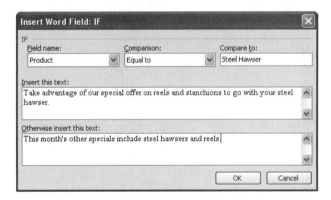

Figure 9-9. If fields let you customize the text of your mail merge documents depending on a condition.

If fields tend to be the most widely useful, but Word offers eight other field types (on the Insert Word Field drop-down list) that you should investigate if you need to perform complex merges. The next most useful field is probably the "Skip Record If" field, which lets you skip the current record if the comparison is true. Ask fields and Fill-in fields, which let you prompt the user for information as the merge runs, are also sometimes useful.

Insert Data Source Fields into a Merge Document

The Annoyance: When inserting data source fields into the main document in Word 2003 or Word XP, you must insert each field individually and then close the Insert Merge Field dialog box before inserting another. It's all a bit cumbersome.

The Fix: This is pretty much as you say, unless you need to place several fields right next to each other—or unless you want to put all the fields in at once and then drag (or move) them into place.

If you've upgraded from Word 2000 to Word 2003 or Word XP, you're probably longing for the Insert Merge Field button on the Mail Merge toolbar (see Figure 9-10), which allowed you to choose the fields in the data source from a drop-down list. Good news—you can add this button to the toolbar by clicking the Toolbar Options arrow and choosing Add or Remove Buttons → Mail Merge → Insert Merge Field.

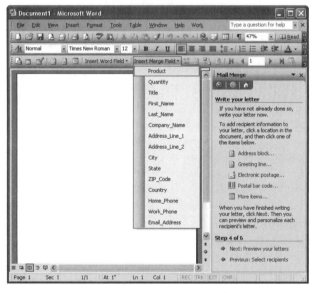

Figure 9-10. Many people find the Insert Merge Field drop-down list a faster way to insert merge fields than the links in the Mail Merge task pane and the dialog boxes they display.

Edit a Data Source Document

The Annoyance: In Word 2003 (and even Word XP), the data source documents are saved in Access format. If you want to do much editing, you need to know Access.

The Fix: As you say, whereas Word 2000 and earlier versions used a Word table to store a custom data source that you created in Word, later versions use the Access database format. You can edit a Word table easily enough by dragging rows and columns to different positions (or simply deleting them), but to edit an Access database directly you need to open Access—which is a can of worms that we won't go into here.

Fortunately, you don't actually need to edit the database directly. Just click one of the "Edit recipient list" links in the Mail Merge task pane or wizard to display the Mail Merge Recipients dialog box, and then click the Edit button to display the data-source dialog box (which is named according to the data-source file). Click the Customize button, and use the Customize Address List dialog box (see Figure 9-11) to add new fields to the database or to delete, rename, or reorder the existing fields.

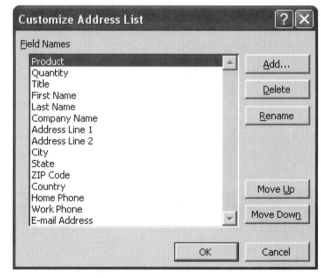

Figure 9-11. The Customize Address List dialog box puts a friendly (if clumsy) frontend on customizing a data source that's saved as an Access database.

Filter Using a Numerical Field

The Annoyance: I'm not having much luck with filtering using a numerical field. If I filter for all records with amounts under 50, for example, Word reads 100 from the left and includes those records, too.

The Fix: This problem most often occurs with street addresses (for example, 88 Acacia Blvd.), but it also occurs with other fields that mix numbers with text (e.g., 42 boxes). Word identifies such fields as alphanumerical rather than numerical, and the filtering is handled differently. In your case, it will include all records with amounts ranging from 0–49, 100–499, 1,000–4,999, and so on. To get around this, you'll need to split the non-numerical data from the numerical data in the field.

To apply filtering to a field, click the Edit button in the Mail Merge Recipients dialog box, click the "Filter and Sort" button to display the Filter and Sort dialog box, and then click the Filter Records tab. Choose the appropriate field, and enter the comparisons and values for it. The example in Figure 9-12 matches quantities from 1 up to and including 100, excluding records for which the quantity is blank (which typically implies a value of 0).

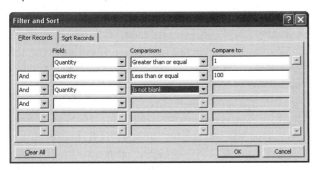

Figure 9-12. Use the Filter Records tab of the Filter and Sort dialog box to implement filtering on a numerical field.

Restore a Mail Merge Document to a Normal Word Document

The Annoyance: I bailed out of the mail merge process somewhere before the end—right at the point where I got really confused and decided I could paste the addresses into a dozen letters with less grief and gnashing of teeth. But

Word still thinks that the letter is a mail-merge document, so now it displays the Mail Merge toolbar every time I open the letter, and it sometimes gives me messages about the data source being missing.

The Fix: You need to tell Word that the document isn't part of a mail merge any more.

In Word 2003 or Word XP, click the Main Document Setup button (the leftmost button) on the Mail Merge toolbar to display the Main Document Type dialog box (see Figure 9-13). Select the "Normal Word document" option, click the OK button, and save the document. You may still need to close the Mail Merge toolbar manually, but it shouldn't return the next time you open the document.

Figure 9-13. If you terminate a merge, you may need to tell Word that the document isn't a merge document anymore.

In Word 2000, choose Tools → Mail Merge Helper to display the Mail Merge Helper dialog box, click the Create button, and choose Restore to Normal Word Document from the pop-up menu. Click the Yes button in the confirmation message box, click the Close button in the Mail Merge Helper dialog box, and save the document.

WORD AND EXCEL

Keep an Excel Chart Updated in a Word Document

The Annoyance: My department keeps its production data in an Excel spreadsheet with a chart that gives a quick idea of how things are going. I need to put that chart in our Monday-and-Thursday report for a visual update. So far, I've been copying the chart and pasting it into the Word document. This works fine, but it means that to make sure it's up to date, I need to paste in the chart about five seconds before I print the document—which feels more than a little tense.

The Fix: It sounds as though you'd do better to link the chart to your report template. Each time you create a new report based on the template, it'll pull in the latest version of the chart. Follow these general steps:

1. Create the chart as usual in Excel. Right-click the chart and choose Copy from the shortcut menu.

2. Switch to Word (or start Word), open the report template, and position the insertion point where you want the chart. Choose Edit → Paste Special, click the item called Microsoft Office Excel Chart Object (Microsoft Excel Chart Object in Word XP or Word 2000), select the "Paste link" option rather than the "Paste" option, and click the OK button.

3. In Word, format the chart as necessary: right-click it, choose Format Object from the shortcut menu, and use the options in the Format Object dialog box. For example, you might change the layout of the chart by wrapping the text of your report around it.

4. Save the template and close it.

When you create a new document based on the template, Word warns you that the document contains links that may refer to other files (see Figure 9-14). Click the No button: you don't want to change the chart in the template itself, only in the document that you create based on the template.

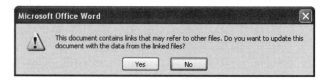

Figure 9-14. Link a chart to a template to make the chart appear in each document you base on the template. When you start a new document based on the template, choose not to update the chart in the template.

You'll still need to update the chart in the report before you print it, but you can have Word do this for you. Choose Tools → Options, click the Print tab, and check the "Update links" box. Word then updates the document automatically before printing it.

If automatic updating will cause problems with other links that you don't want to have updated, update the chart manually: right-click it and choose Update Link from the shortcut menu.

Transfer Data from Word to Excel

The Annoyance: Every now and then, I receive data in a Word table that I need to paste into an Excel spreadsheet. Each time I do this, I seem to get different results: sometimes the text just snaps into the spreadsheet cells perfectly; other times, I get Word's table borders and font formatting in my spreadsheet, and—worse—some table cells are spread across multiple rows. If I undo this unsuccessful paste and repeat it, I get different results again. If it makes any difference, this is Word 2003 I'm using.

The Fix: Word is trying to be helpful, but it's not quite managing what you want. Word 2003 tends to behave as you describe; Word XP and Word 2000 behave a little differently (and Word 2000 doesn't have the Paste Options Smart Tag).

Here's what's probably happening:

- If the table you copy has only one paragraph to each cell, when you paste, the data snaps into place with one Word table cell to one Excel cell. This is probably the result you want.

- If the table contains cells that have two or more paragraphs in them, Word pastes in the table as a Word object by default. That means the that table keeps its Word formatting, so you get the text formatting and borders, and multiparagraph cells end up occupying multiple rows (one row per paragraph). You can fix this quickly: click the Smart Tag button and choose Match Destination Formatting to redo the paste operation as plain text. The multiparagraph cells will still occupy one row per paragraph, so you'll need to fix them manually, but Word's formatting will be gone.

- If you undo the paste operation and then repeat it, Word may say to itself (in binary) "Oh, she didn't like what I did; I'll do it the other way this time" and paste in plain text instead of the Word object. This will give you the effect described in the previous paragraph, but it doesn't happen consistently (and you're not allowed to ask me why).

If this degree of uncertainty annoys you, use Paste Special instead: right-click the upper-left destination cell, choose Paste Special from the shortcut menu, choose the Unicode Text option in the As list, and click the OK button.

WORD AND POWERPOINT

Create a Document from a Presentation

The Annoyance: My boss brought back this wonderful presentation from *his* boss—our master plan for the next week, month, decade, or something. More to the point, he wants me to create a memo of the presentation so that we can issue copies to everyone in the office. I've heard of cut and paste, but this is going to work my fingers raw.

The Fix: If you need just the text of the presentation, you can simply select it in the Outline pane in PowerPoint, copy it, and paste it into a Word document. Word carries over the PowerPoint heading levels and font formatting, so the document will be laid out with Heading styles. If the size of the font has been adjusted in PowerPoint (for example, to make more text fit on a slide), restore the regular size in Word by selecting the entire document (choose Edit → Select All) and pressing Ctrl+Spacebar.

If you want the graphics on the slides as well as the text, use PowerPoint's built-in tool for sending the document to Word. Choose File → Send To → Microsoft Office Word (or File → Send To → Microsoft Word for Word XP and Word 2000), choose the appropriate options in the Send To Microsoft Office Word dialog box (see Figure 9-15) or the Send To Microsoft Word dialog box, and click the OK button.

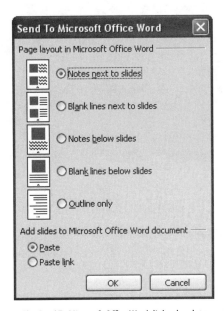

Figure 9-15. The Send To Microsoft Office Word dialog box lets you put an entire presentation, or just its outline, into a new Word document in seconds.

The layouts are self-explanatory, so the main decision is whether to paste the slides or paste-link them. Pasting the slides makes the Word document far bigger than linking them, but it enables you to send the document to people who won't have access to the PowerPoint presentation and who otherwise wouldn't be able to see the slides.

If you need only the text from the presentation, select the "Outline only" option in the Send To Microsoft Office Word (or Send To Microsoft Word) dialog box. You won't need to worry about pasting or linking, and you'll get the same result as you would by selecting the text in the Outline pane, copying it, and pasting it into Word.

Create a Presentation from a Document

The Annoyance: I get sales reports from our reps once a week (well, that's the theory) so I can create a department-wide memo. Now the VP has decided that she needs a presentation made from this material.

The Fix: You can paste bits and pieces into PowerPoint as needed, as you'd expect, but your best bet here is probably to use Word's feature for exporting a document outline directly to PowerPoint as the skeleton for a presentation.

Set up the document as a standard outline using Heading styles (Heading 1, Heading 2, and so on) or equivalent styles with the appropriate heading levels set (in the "Outline level" drop-down list in the Paragraph dialog box). The easiest way to arrange the outline is to choose View → Outline and work in Outline view (see "Views" in Chapter 3). Each Heading 1 paragraph starts a new slide, each Heading 2 paragraph is a first-level bullet point, and each Heading 3 paragraph is a second-level bullet point; any further levels of heading will induce eyestrain or narcolepsy in your audience.

When the outline is ready, choose File → Send To → Microsoft Office PowerPoint (or File → Send To → Microsoft PowerPoint in Office XP and Office 2000). Word starts PowerPoint if it's not already running, creates a new presentation, and enters the text on the slides. Save the presentation immediately, apply a slide design (Format → Slide Design), change the slide layout if you want (Format → Slide Layout), and add any graphics, videos, sounds, and other finishing touches you deem necessary.

Put a Word Table on a PowerPoint Slide

The Annoyance: I'm trying to copy a fully formatted table from a Word document to a PowerPoint slide. But when I paste, all I get is the text of the table, without formatting, in a new placeholder.

The Fix: In Word, position your cursor in the table, choose Table → Select → Table, and press Ctrl+C to copy the table. Switch to PowerPoint, choose Edit → Paste Special, select the Microsoft Office Word Document Object item (Microsoft Word Document Object in Office XP or Office 2000) in the As list, and click the OK button.

When pasting a table directly onto a PowerPoint slide, you may need to adjust the table dimensions or the font size to get the table to appear at a suitable size and readability on the slide. You can edit the embedded table in PowerPoint by double-clicking it, but for major repairs, it's usually easier to return to Word, adjust the table, and then copy and paste it again.

Another approach you may want to try is pasting a Word table into a PowerPoint table. Create the table in Word, and copy it to the Clipboard. In PowerPoint, choose Insert → Table, create a table with the same number of columns and rows, select the table, and paste in the Word table.

WORD AND ACCESS

Convert a Word Table to an Access Database

The Annoyance: The genius who flew this desk before me created our sales database in a Word table. It's huge, it's ugly, and it doesn't exactly run like a gazelle. I'm not an Access expert, but I kinda suspect that using a database program might be a better choice than using a word processor. Unfortunately, that means it's up to me to shunt the Word table into Access.

The Fix: Unless the table is *really* ugly, you can probably transfer its contents to Access without too many hairs going gray. Follow these general steps:

1. Delete from the document any text that isn't in the table. (If this means major changes, use File → Save As to save a copy of the document under a different name, and then work on the copy.)

2. Make sure the table has a heading row that identifies the fields. If not, add a heading row: click in the first row, choose Table → Insert → Rows Above, format the new row differently from the other rows (for example, make the text bold and larger), and type the field names in it.

3. Check that no cell in the table contains two or more paragraphs. If any does, rearrange the table to eliminate the extra paragraphs. (For example, if an address cell contains two lines, you might split it into two separate cells.) The easiest way to check is to select the table (choose Table → Select → Table), press Ctrl+F, and search for ^p (the code for a paragraph mark).

4. Click in the table, choose Table → Convert → Table to Text, select the Tabs option, and click the OK button.

5. Choose File → Save As, select Text Only in the "Save as type" drop-down list, and save the document as a text file.

6. Launch Access (or switch to it), open the database (or create a new database), right-click an empty space in the Tables list, and choose Import from the shortcut menu.

7. Select Text Files in the "Files of type" drop-down list.

8. Select the Word document you saved as a text file, click the OK button, and follow the steps in the Import Text Wizard.

Move Data from an Access Table to a Word Document

The Annoyance: I need to use some data from an Access table in a Word document. I've tried selecting rows and then copying and pasting the data, but I don't usually want full rows, and Word seems to give me different formatting each time I paste data from Access, anyway.

The Fix: For more consistent results, export the entire table in a format that Word can read easily, open the resulting file in Word, and copy the parts you need to your document.

To export from Access, open the table, choose File → Export and select the appropriate format in the "Save as type" drop-down list: Rich Text Format if you want all the formatting in the Access table, or Microsoft Word Merge if you want only the text without any formatting. The former creates an actual table in the document, while the latter creates tab-delimited text that you can easily convert back into a table using Word's Table → Convert → Text to Table command.

In Word, choose File → Open, select Rich Text Format or Text Files in the "Files of type" drop-down list, and then open the file you saved. Copy the appropriate parts of the table or text, and paste them into the Word document that needs them.

Mac Word Annoyances

You can get almost any regular Mac user to tell you dozens of ways in which Mac OS X is superior to Windows, from its more "intuitive" interface to its BSD-based resistance to most of the less sophisticated forms of attack that can cripple even Windows XP systems updated with the latest patches.

But get that same Mac user talking about Word for the Mac, and you're more likely to hear a litany of annoyances than a paean of praise. Word for the Mac shares many of the features that have made Word for Windows a prerequisite of the modern business world, but not all of them. Even when Word for the Mac leapfrogs Word for Windows with a version—as Word 2004 leapfrogged Word 2003—and adds new features (for example, note recording), it still lags behind Word for Windows in many areas that are important to many users. Not surprisingly, Word for the Mac also has bugs—plenty of them. And even where it doesn't have bugs, much of its behavior is, well, hinky.

This is a chapter, not a whole book, so it concentrates on the Word annoyances that are most likely to crop up for Mac users. The chapter starts with severe annoyances that might make you want to encourage your Mac to fly—for example, Word starting incredibly slowly, quitting unexpectedly when running, or refusing to save a document to a server (or even to your home folder). The chapter then goes on to show you how to deal with lesser annoyances, such as markup balloons not printing, page numbering going haywire, version comments mysteriously disappearing, and the Word Count feature hamstringing your Mac so that it can only hobble along miserably instead of running like the tiger, panther, or jaguar that it usually resembles.

CRASHES AND PERFORMANCE

Speed Up Startup

The Annoyance: Word for the Mac takes forever and a day to start up.

The Fix: Check that you haven't got two copies of the application on your Mac. One possibility is that you've installed Word or Office twice, but what's more likely is that you've tried to create an alias to Word by ⌘+Option-dragging and the Option key wasn't pressed far enough to register, so the Word executable has been copied instead.

If you have two copies of Word, delete one of them. Word should then start at normal speed. If your Mac is old, or sick, that normal speed may still be glacial, but at least you won't be contributing to the problem.

> You can save yourself a lot of time and grief by keeping Mac OS X and Word (or Office) updated to the latest versions available. Run Software Update (Apple → Software Update) regularly to check for Mac OS X patches and updates. To check for updates to Word 2004, choose Help → Check for Updates and use Microsoft AutoUpdate. In Word X, choose Help → Downloads and Updates and use the browser-based update mechanism.

Replace Your CarbonLib File

The Annoyance: When I start Word X, I get the error message "Shared library error (CarbonLib)." I tried installing the evaluation version of Word 2004 to see if that'd make the error message go away, but it didn't.

The Fix: The intriguingly named CarbonLib is a Mac OS X system file that's needed for running some applications. This message means that CarbonLib is damaged, which can pre-

vent you from running Word. Download the latest version from the Apple web site (*http://www.apple.com/support/*), install it, and then run Word again.

Look to Your Font Files When Word X Quits on Startup

The Annoyance: When I try to start Word X, it gets as far as the splash screen and then dies. The splash screen I could do without; Word itself I can't.

The Fix: If you've been trying to guess what's causing this problem, stop now. Chances are, you haven't come up with a font file—but that's most likely what it is. A corrupted font file, a duplicate font file, or both together can cause Word to crash on startup.

Tackling this problem can be a little tricky, because the guilty font can be located either in one of the Mac OS X fonts folders or in the Classic *Fonts* folder (*/System Folder/Fonts*) if you have System 9 installed. Proceed as follows:

1. If there's an update to Word X that you haven't installed, install it immediately. See if that cures the problem. If not, carry on with the steps in this list.

2. Switch to the Finder. Open a window to the Classic *Fonts* folder (in the */System Folder/Fonts* folder on your hard disk). Next, open one window to the OS X shared fonts folder, *~/Library/Fonts*, and another window to your fonts folder, *~/Users/<your_user_name>/Library/Fonts*. Line up the three windows so that you can see the contents of each, and delete any duplicate font files. Once you're confident you've deleted all the ringers, restart Mac OS X and try launching Word. If Word starts, all is well. If not, go to Step 3.

3. Still with me? That's a pity. Next, you must find out whether your Mac has a corrupted font menu cache. If your Mac has System 9 installed on it, restart in System 9, either by using Startup Disk (choose Apple → System Preferences, click Startup Disk, choose the System 9 startup disk, click the Restart button, and confirm your choice) or by starting from the System 9 CD. In the Finder, open the */System Folder/Fonts* folder and see if it contains any fonts. If it does, rename the folder *OldFonts* or another distinctive name. Reboot, and then try starting

Word. If it starts okay, create a replacement *Fonts* folder, drag all the fonts from the *OldFonts* folder into it, and delete the *OldFonts* folder. Reboot again, and try starting Word. If Word crashes again, go to Step 4; otherwise, you're off the hook.

4. Still in System 9, create a folder called *TempFonts* on your Desktop. Open the */System Folder/Fonts* folder and drag all its contents to the *TempFonts* folder. Reboot into Mac OS X and try to start Word. If Word starts, one of your Classic fonts is causing the crash. To find the guilty party you'll need to restore the fonts from the *TempFonts* folder to the *Fonts* folder one by one, rebooting and testing Word after each one. When you find it, delete it and then restore the remainder of the fonts. If Word *doesn't* start, repeat this step first for the *~/Library/Fonts* folder and then, if necessary, for the *~/Users/<your_user_name>/Library/Fonts* folder, until you have eliminated the offending font.

Repair Your Disk Permissions

The Annoyance: Word starts okay and lets me work for a while—but then it crashes without so much as an "¡Hasta la vista, Baby!"

The Fix: What's probably wrong is that your disk permissions have become damaged, preventing Word from writing to some of the files or folders that it needs to be able to use. Start by repairing your disk permissions:

1. Quit Word if it hasn't already quit itself.

2. Click the Desktop to activate the Finder, open the *Utilities* folder (choose Go → Utilities, or choose Go → Applications and then double-click the *Utilities* folder), and then double-click Disk Utility to open it.

3. Click the entry for your hard disk, click the First Aid tab, and then click the Repair Disk Permissions button.

4. When the repair is complete, restart Mac OS X.

5. If repairing your disk permissions doesn't resolve this problem, try the steps in the next Annoyance. You can also try updating your copy of Word (or Office) with the latest update available.

Repair Your Preferences or Settings Files

The Annoyance: Sometimes I'm working away happily enough (I'd rather be surfing—who wouldn't?) and Word 2004 just decides to up and quit on me. I was going to say that Word crashes unexpectedly, but every crash is unexpected, isn't it? On a Mac, anyway....

The Fix: These crashes could be caused by various problems, but one possibility that should appear fairly high on your list is damaged preferences or settings files. Here's how to fix them:

1. Open a Finder window to your *~/Library/Preferences/Microsoft* folder and check out the following files, depending on whether you're using Word 2004 or Word X:

   Word 2004

   > *com.microsoft.Word.prefs.plist* and *com.microsoft.Office.prefs.plist*

   Word X

   > *Word Settings (10)*, *Microsoft Component Preferences*, *Microsoft Office Settings (10)*, and *Carbon Registration Database*

2. Quit Word, and then drag the *com.microsoft.Word.prefs.plist* file or the *Word Settings (10)* file from the *~/Library/Preferences/Microsoft* folder to the Desktop. Relaunch Word (which makes it automatically create a replacement for the missing file) and see if the problem has disappeared. If it has, you'll need to reset some of your preferences and restore your custom AutoCorrect entries; if not, drag the new file from the *~/Library/Preferences/Microsoft* folder to the Trash, drag the old file back from the Desktop to the *~/Library/Preferences/Microsoft* folder, and proceed with the next step.

3. Quit Word (if it hasn't crashed) and any other Office applications you're running, and repeat the drag-to-the-Desktop process with each of the other files in turn, checking Word at each stage.

Speed Up Word's Performance When Scrolling

The Annoyance: When I start to scroll, Word X goes all glacial on me. Any ideas?

The Fix: This sounds like the notorious problem of Live Word Count consuming every spare processor cycle. Try turning off this feature: choose Word → Preferences, click the View tab, uncheck the Live Word Count box, and click the OK button.

If that doesn't help, choose Word → Preferences again, click the General tab, uncheck the "WYSIWYG font and style menus" box, and click the OK button. This makes Word display the Font menu and the Style menu using system fonts rather than the actual fonts. It doesn't sound like much, but if your Mac has a ton of fonts installed, it can make a noticeable performance difference.

Still no good? Choose Word → Preferences a third time, click the Spelling and Grammar tab, and clear both the "Check spelling as you type" box and the "Check grammar as you type" box. Both of these options chew up more processor cycles than they deserve.

Reinstall Updaters When Necessary

The Annoyance: I'm a good citizen, and I've been keeping Office updated. But Word keeps asking me to reapply the Office updaters I've already applied.

The Fix: Relax, this is normal. You'll need to reapply updaters if you install or reinstall any Office component or if you install options from the Value Pack. Use the Help → Check for Updates command to keep Word updated with minimal effort on your part.

Recover from a Corrupted Normal Template

The Annoyance: Word starts more or less okay, but then it begins to misbehave: I get either long periods of nonresponse between intervals of normal behavior, or an unexpected quit—sometimes with an error message, sometimes without. I'm really not enjoying this.

The Fix: Your Normal template might well have become corrupted. Quit Word if it's running, navigate to the ~/Documents/Microsoft User Data folder (for Word 2004) or the /Applications/Microsoft Office X/Templates folder (for Word X), rename *Normal* to another name (for example, *BadNormal*), and then start Word again. If Word runs stably and responsively, you've nailed the problem.

If your old Normal template contains code or customizations that you want to keep, choose Tools → Macro → Macros, click the Organizer button, and use the four tabs of the Organizer dialog box to copy the styles, AutoText entries, toolbars, and macro project items from your old Normal template (*BadNormal*) to the new Normal template. After you close the Organizer dialog box, Shift-click the File menu and choose Save All, and then save your Normal template if Word prompts you to do so.

Beware When Page Numbering Goes Haywire

The Annoyance: The page numbering in my document has gone nuts. Help!

The Fix: Red flag! This usually means that the document has become corrupted. Recover it immediately as follows:

1. Choose File → Save As and save a copy of the document under a new name (rather than overwriting the current version with any outstanding unsaved changes). This is your primary backup of the document, but you should also save the document in other formats (as described in the rest of this list) in case this document turns out to be too corrupted to use.

2. Choose File → Save as Web Page, make sure the "Save entire file into HTML" option is selected (rather than the "Save only display information into HTML" option, which dispenses with non-display items such as headers and footnotes), and then click the Save button. This HTML version of the document contains almost all the contents of the Word document and is saved in a stable format.

3. With the document still open, choose Edit → Select All, hold down Shift, and press ← to deselect the last paragraph mark in the document. (The last paragraph mark is the default section break, which contains the master

formatting table for the document.) Press ⌘+C to copy the selection, and then press ⌘+N to create a new blank document. Press ⌘+V to paste in what you copied, press ⌘+S to save the document as a backup, and then press ⌘+W to close the document.

Now reopen the document you saved in Step 1 and see if it is usable. If not, use the document you saved in Step 3 instead. If this document too proves corrupted, use the HTML document you saved in Step 2 as the last resort for re-creating the document.

> OpenOffice.org (free from *http://www.openoffice.org*) is very good at opening corrupt Word documents and recovering their contents.

OPENING AND SAVING

Wrest Back Control from Word 2004 Test Drive

The Annoyance: I downloaded the Office 2004 Test Drive, installed it, test-drove it, and removed it. Now when I double-click a document to open it in Word X, the Finder tells me "The operation could not be completed." Arrgh! I'm asking to have a file opened, not my heart transplanted.

The Fix: This error (see Figure 10-1) occurs because the Test Drive has grabbed your file associations and forgotten to give them back. Open a Finder window to a folder containing any Word document, right-click the document, choose Open With, and select the entry for Word X from the menu. Doing so restores the file association.

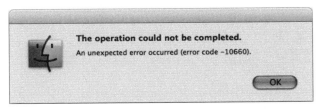

Figure 10-1. This inscrutable error message means that you need to restore Word X's association with Word documents.

Field the "Permission Currently Restricted" Error

The Annoyance: I tried to open a document created in Word for Windows, but it displayed the message "Permission for this document is currently restricted."

The Fix: Okay, you really are stuck this time. This message means that the document is protected with Windows-only information rights management.

The only fix is to have a Windows user unprotect the document for you by opening the document in Word 2003 and choosing File → Permission → Unrestricted Access. You can't unprotect it in Word for the Mac.

Avoid the "Unable to Save" Message When Saving to a Server

The Annoyance: My Mac connects to a Windows server so that I can share files with my coworkers. I can open a file on the server, make changes, and save it a few times, but after a while, I get an "Unable to save: Disk full or too many files are open" message. This is my only open file in Word, no other application is running except Mail, and the server has about as much free space as Alaska. Someone is lying to me!

The Fix: This is a communications issue between early versions of Panther (or Jaguar, if you're still using it) and Windows and Mac servers. If possible, upgrade to Mac OS X 10.3.3 or a later version. Failing that, choose Word → Preferences, click the Save tab, uncheck the "Allow fast saves" box, and check the "Always make backup copy" box. Doing so will usually let you save 50 times or more. To stay safe, close and reopen the document periodically, rather than leaving it open for long stretches.

Work Around the Erroneous "Disk Full" Error

The Annoyance: Word X claims my Mac's disk is full when I know there's enough free space to hold half the Library of Congress. Why can't I save my file?

The Fix: The brief answer is that Word has opened more temporary files than it can handle. These temporary files are mostly used for storing Undo information. The longer you spend editing a particular document without closing it, the more temporary files build up.

There's no easy fix, but there are two easy workarounds. First, if the document contains page numbers in the header and footer, edit in Normal view rather than Page Layout view. (Each recalculation of page numbers is added to the Undo list, making Word reach the OS's open-file limit sooner.) Second, close and reopen the document periodically to force Word to get rid of the temporary files.

If neither of these workarounds appeals to you, quit Word and steer your web browser to *http://word.mvps.org/Downloads/FixDiskFullIssue.sit*. When the file downloads automatically, let StuffIt unstuff it, and then drag the *FixDiskFullIssue.dot* template to your */Applications/Microsoft Office X/Office/Startup/Word* folder. Restart Word and see if there's now a "Disk is Full error?" command on the File menu. If so, wait for the error to occur, choose this command, and click the OK button in the resulting dialog box (see Figure 10-2) to remove the temporary files.

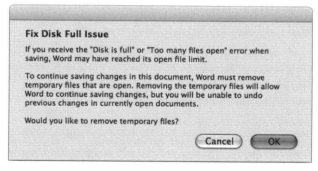

Figure 10-2. The "Fix Disk Full Issue" command lets you remove excess temporary files that are burdening Word X.

If the "Disk is Full error?" command doesn't appear on the File menu, choose Tools → Templates and Add-Ins, click the Add button, navigate to and select *DiskIsFullIssue.dot*, click the Open button, and then click the OK button. Check the File menu again to make sure the command is there.

Help Word Rediscover How to Write to Folders

The Annoyance: Now I'm totally stuck. Word can't even create files in my user folder!

The Fix: This problem most likely means that you need to repair your disk permissions and then restart Mac OS X. See "Repair Your Disk Permissions," earlier in this chapter, for instructions.

DOCUMENTS AND EDITING

Insert Text at the End of a Document

The Annoyance: I've got a minor peeve (probably because things work differently in most other programs, including Entourage): if I want to add more text below the last line in a document, I can't just click in the white area beneath the line; instead, I have to click at the *end* of the last line and hit Return.

The Fix: You should be able to do this the way you want—at least, if you're double-clicking rather than single-clicking, and you're using Page Layout view or Online Layout view. Choose Word → Preferences, click the Edit item, and check the "Enable click and type" box. You'll then be able to double-click however far after the end of the document you want, and Word will automatically add the necessary blank paragraphs and spaces to get you there.

That said, if you don't want Word inserting extra paragraphs and tabs to bring the insertion point to the exact space where you clicked, you may prefer to click at the end of the last paragraph and create another paragraph manually.

Turn Off Auto-Capping in Tables

The Annoyance: Brilliant! Word 2004's AutoCorrect feature doesn't include a "Capitalize first letter of table cells" checkbox—so you can't tell Word not to capitalize the first word inside a table cell. At least AutoCorrect in Word X didn't mess with table contents.

The Fix: It's hard to see how Microsoft could claim that this omission of a user interface control is a feature rather than a fault—but fortunately, there's a fix. Insert a table, type a word starting with a lowercase letter in one of the cells, and press the spacebar to trigger the AutoCorrect action. Click the AutoCorrect Smart Tag, and choose "Stop Auto-capitalizing First Letter of Table Cells" from the menu (see Figure 10-3). A quick warning, though: once you turn off this option, you can never turn it back on.

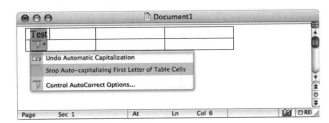

Figure 10-3. Use the AutoCorrect Options Smart Tag to turn off auto-capitalization in tables.

Recover Missing Graphics

The Annoyance: All the graphics in my Word document appear as red Xs. I support the Red Cross, but this is ridiculous.

The Fix: This problem usually means that one of the global templates or add-ins you've loaded is causing a conflict with Word. Choose Tools → Templates and Add-Ins, remove the first global template listed in the "Global templates and add-ins" area, restart Word, and see if your graphics reappear. (Removing a template only removes it from the list that Word loads, not from your computer.) If your graphics don't reappear, try the next global template, and keep working through them until you identify the culprit. Reload those that weren't guilty if you still need their functionality.

Avoid Mixing Orientations if You Want to Print Markup Balloons

The Annoyance: I can't print the markup balloons from Word 2004. Usually it works, but not in this document.

The Fix: No fix, just a workaround: print all revisions without using balloons. Choose Word → Preferences, click the Track Changes item, uncheck the "Use balloons to display changes" box, and click the OK button. Then press ⌘+P to display the Print dialog box, select Microsoft Word in the Options list, select "Document showing markup" in the Print What drop-down list, and click the Print button.

This problem happens only when the document containing the markup balloons has sections that use different orientations (i.e., portrait and landscape). If you desperately want to be able to print the balloons, you'll need to avoid mixing the orientations.

Save Your Document When You Paste in an OLE Object

The Annoyance: I pasted an equation from my working document into my thesis. Word 2004 flatlined, and I had to force-quit it. What gives?

The Fix: Most likely, you closed the working document before you saved your thesis. This shouldn't cause problems, but it sometimes does. Always save the destination document before closing the source document of the OLE object.

Save Graphics in PNG Format, Not PICT

The Annoyance: I used the "Save As Picture" command in Word 2004 to save a graphic as a PICT. That seemed to work, but when I opened the graphic in Photoshop, it looked weird.

The Fix: This happens sometimes with the PICT format, whose support in Word 2004 is a little undernourished. Try using the PNG (Portable Network Graphics) format instead, and you should get good results.

Restore Page Setup to Your Preferred Settings

The Annoyance: I created a landscape document a while ago and somehow set landscape as the default orientation. I've tried choosing File → Page Setup, but I don't see a way to change it back.

The Fix: Choose Format → Document; choose the margins, layout, and any other settings that you want as defaults for your documents; click the Default button; and then click the Yes button in the confirmation dialog box (see Figure 10-4).

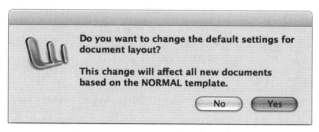

Figure 10-4. Word double-checks when you try to change the default orientation of your documents.

WORD X

Avoid Versioning When Switching Between Word 2004 and Word X

The Annoyance: I saved several versions of a document using Word 2004 on my PowerMac, but when I open the document in Word X on my iMac, I can't see any versions. Where are they?

The Fix: They're hiding. Word X has trouble identifying versions created by Word 2004. If it's any consolation, if you now save a new version or two using Word X, Word 2004 will be able to read them just fine (and when you open the document again in Word 2004, your original versions will still be there).

It's best not to use versions at all. See "Keep Separate Versions of the Same Document" in Chapter 2 for details of their disadvantages.

Do Away with the "Unknown Author"

The Annoyance: When I'm editing with Track Changes on, Word suddenly starts identifying the text I insert as being by "Unknown Author" instead of me. Then it switches back to me. And then back to Unknown Author again. This is driving me up the wall!

The Fix: This problem is usually triggered by an AutoCorrect change, so one workaround—a poor one—is to disable Auto-Correct while Track Changes is on. A marginally better work-around is to open a new Word document, enter the full text of each change (and allow any AutoCorrect changes to be made), and then select the text and paste it into the document in which you're tracking changes.

The only long-term solution is to upgrade to Word 2004, which not only fixes this problem but also offers change balloons (as do Word 2003 and Word XP for Windows).

Move Your Word X Normal Template to Safety

The Annoyance: Word X was acting up persistently, so I reinstalled Office. Everything's fine, except—and it's a big "except"—Word has wiped out all the changes I'd made in the Normal template and issued me a completely vanilla one.

The Fix: Bad luck. When you reinstall Word X, your Normal template gets overwritten if it is in its default location. However, if you've checked the "Always create backup copy" box in the Save tab of the Preferences dialog box (Word → Preferences), there should be a backup copy of the last time you saved the Normal template. Quit Word, navigate to the */Applications/Microsoft Office X/Templates* folder, and look for a file named *Backup of Normal*. Rename this to *Normal*, and restart Word.

To avoid losing customizations you've made to your Normal template from now on, move it to a different folder. Here's what to do:

1. Quit Word. If it prompts you to save changes to the Normal template, save them.

2. In the Finder, create a folder to hold your templates. For example, you might create a *Microsoft User Data* folder in the *~/Documents* folder, which is what Word 2004 uses. Move the Normal template to this folder.

3. Restart Word, choose Word → Preferences, click the File Locations tab, click the "User templates" item, and click the Modify button. Select the new folder, click the Choose button, and then click the OK button to close the Preferences dialog box.

Index

Colophon

Our look is the result of reader comments, our own experimentation, and feedback from distribution channels. Distinctive covers complement our distinctive approach to technical topics, breathing personality and life into potentially dry subjects.

Sanders Kleinfeld was the production editor and proofreader for *Word Annoyances.* Rachel Wheeler was the copyeditor. Sanders Kleinfeld did the typesetting and page makeup. Genevieve d'Entremont and Claire Cloutier provided quality control. Julie Hawks wrote the index.

Ellie Volckhausen designed the cover of this book using Adobe Illustrator and produced the cover layout with Adobe InDesign CS using Gravur Condensed, Glypha, and Adobe Sabon fonts. The cover is based on a series design by Volume Design, Inc.

Patti Capaldi designed the interior layout using Adobe InDesign CS. The text and heading fonts are Rotis Sans Serif, Lineto Gravur Condensed, and Myriad Pro; the code font is TheSans Mono Condensed. Joe Wizda converted the text to Adobe InDesign CS. The screenshots and technical illustrations that appear in the book were produced by Robert Romano, Jessamyn Read, and Lesley Borash using Macromedia FreeHand MX and Adobe Photoshop 7. The cartoon illustrations used on the cover and in the interior of this book are copyright © 2004 and 2005 Hal Mayforth.